REIGNING CATS & DOGS

Edited by
Lois L. Kaufman

With Illustrations by
Martha Holland Bartsch

PETER PAUPER PRESS, INC.
WHITE PLAINS • NEW YORK

What's worse than raining cats and dogs?

☞ *Hailing taxis.*

Table of Contents

Every dog has his day.

Cervantes

Quotes

Dogs come when they're called; cats take a
message and get back to you.

Mary Bly

Cat: a pygmy lion who loves mice, hates
dogs and patronizes human beings.

Oliver Herford

A country man between two lawyers is like
a Fish between two Cats.

Benjamin Franklin

He that lieth down with Dogs shall rise up
with Fleas.

Benjamin Franklin

If a man could be crossed with a cat, it
would improve man, but it would deteriorate
the cat.

Mark Twain

5

The cat and the love you give away come back to you.

I call my kittens *Shall* and *Will* because no one can tell them apart.

Christopher Morley

When a man's dog turns against him, it is time for a wife to pack her trunk and go home to mama.

Mark Twain

There are three faithful Friends—an old Wife, an old Dog, and ready Money.

Benjamin Franklin

A dog knows its master, a cat does not.

Talmud

When I play with my cat, who knows if I am not a pastime to her more than she is to me?

Michel E. de Montaigne

I like a bit of a mongrel myself, whether it's
a man or a dog; they're the best for every
day.

George Bernard Shaw

The great pleasure of a dog is that you
make a fool of yourself with him and not
only will he not scold you, but he will make
a fool of himself too.

Samuel Butler

What's virtue in man can't be vice in a cat.

Gail Hamilton

No man is so poor that he can't afford to
keep one dog, and I've seen them so poor
they could afford to keep three.

Henry Wheeler Shaw ("Josh Billings")

If you pick up a starving dog and make
him prosperous, he will not bite you. This
is the principal difference between a dog
and a man.

Mark Twain

They say a reasonable amount o' fleas is good fer a dog—keeps him from broodin' over bein' a dog, mebbe.

Edward Noyes Westcott

... What counts is not necessarily the size of the dog in the fight—it's the size of the fight in the dog.

Dwight D. Eisenhower

Our German forefathers had a very kind religion. They believed that, after death, they would meet again all the good dogs that had been their companions in life. I wish I could believe that, too.

Otto von Bismarck

Cats know how to obtain food without labor, shelter without confinement, and love without penalties.

W. L. George

There are more ways of killing a cat than choking her with cream.

Charles Kingsley

It is a very inconvenient habit of kittens
(Alice had once made the remark) that
whatever you say to them, they *always* purr.
Lewis Carroll

We tie bright ribbons around their necks,
and occasionally little tinkling bells, and
we affect to think that they are as sweet and
vapid as the coy name "kitty" by which we
call them would imply. It is a curious
illusion. For, purring beside our fireplaces
and pattering along our back fences, we
have got a wild beast as uncowed and
uncorrupted as any under heaven.
Alan Devoe

He cannot be a gentleman which loveth
not a dog.
John Northbrooke

Confront a child, a puppy, and a kitten
with a sudden danger; the child will turn
instinctively for assistance, the puppy will
grovel in abject submission, the kitten will
brace its tiny body for a frantic resistance.
H. H. Munro ("Saki")

If dogs could talk, perhaps we'd find it just as hard to get along with them as we do with people.

Karel Capek

Things that upset a terrier may pass virtually unnoticed by the Great Dane.

Dr. Smiley Blanton

No favor can win gratitude from a cat.

La Fontaine

It has been the providence of nature to give this creature [the cat] nine lives instead of one.

Pilpay

A dog teaches a boy fidelity, perseverance, and to turn around three times before lying down.

Robert Benchley

The cat in gloves catches no mice.

Benjamin Franklin

Keep running after the dog, and he will never bite you.

Rabelais

The way to keep a cat is to try to chase it away.

Ed Howe

Bark: This is a sound made by dogs when excited. Dogs bark at milkmen, postmen, yourself, visitors to the house and other dogs; some of them bark at nothing. For some reason dogs tend not to bark at burglars, bailiffs and income tax collectors, at whom they wag their tails in the most friendly manner.

Geoffrey Williams

Histories are more full of examples of the fidelity of dogs than of friends.

Alexander Pope

A kitten does not discover that her tail belongs to her until you tread upon it.

Henry David Thoreau

There is no doubt that every healthy, normal boy (if there is such a thing in these days of Child Study) should own a dog at some time in his life, preferably between the ages of 45 and 50.

Robert Benchley

The possession of a dog today is a different thing from the possession of a dog at the turn of the century, when one's dog was fed on mashed potato and brown gravy and lived in a doghouse with an arched portal. Today a dog is fed on scraped beef and Vitamin B1, and lives in bed with you.

E. B. White

Cowardly dogs bark loudest.

John Webster

Now a cat will not take an excursion merely because a man wants a walking companion. Walking is a human habit into which dogs readily fall but it is a distasteful form of exercise to a cat unless he has a purpose in view.

Carl Van Vechten

**Cats and monkeys, monkeys and cats—
all human life is there.**

Henry James

A man who was loved by 300 women
singled me out to live with him. Why? I was
the only one without a cat.

Elayne Boosler

Dog, *n.* A kind of additional or subsidiary
Deity designed to catch the overflow and
surplus of the world's worship. This Divine
Being in some of his smaller and silkier
incarnations takes, in the affection of
Woman, the place to which there is no
human male aspirant. The Dog is a
survival—an anachronism. He toils not,
neither does he spin, yet Solomon in all his
glory never lay upon a door-mat all day
long, sun-soaked and fly-fed and fat, while
his master worked for the means wherewith
to purchase an idle wag of the Solomonic
tail, seasoned with a look of tolerant
recognition.

Ambrose Bierce

Cat, *n.* A soft, indestructible automaton
provided by nature to be kicked when
things go wrong in the domestic circle.

Ambrose Bierce

REFLECTIONS ON PARTING
WITH HIS DOGS

*When threatened with the loss of his
Abbotsford estate, Scott wrote, in part, in his
diary, on December 18, 1825:*

How live a poor indebted man when I was
once the wealthy, the honored? My
children are provided; thank God for that. I
was to have gone there on Saturday in joy
and prosperity to receive my friends. My
dogs will wait for me in vain. It is foolish—
but the thoughts of parting from these
dumb creatures have moved me more than
any of the painful reflections I have put
down. Poor things, I must get them kind
masters; there may be yet those who loving
me may love my dog because it has been
mine. I must end this or I shall lose the
tone of mind with which men should meet
distress.

I find my dogs' feet on my knees. I hear
them whining and seeking me everywhere—
this is nonsense, but it is what they would
do could they know how things are.

Sir Walter Scott

Men are generally more careful of the breed of their horses and dogs than of their children.

William Penn

We should be careful to get out of an experience only the wisdom that is in it—and stay there, lest we be like the cat that sits down on a hot stove-lid. She will never sit down on a hot stove-lid again—and that is well; but also she will never sit down on a cold one any more.

Mark Twain

In the whole history of the world there is but one thing that money cannot buy—the wag of a dog's tail.

Henry Wheeler Shaw ("Josh Billings")

Barking dogs don't bite, but they themselves don't know it.

Sholom Aleichem

A living dog is better than a dead lion.

Ecclesiastes 9:4

A cat can be trusted to purr when she is pleased, which is more than can be said for human beings.

William Ralph Inge

The more I see of the representatives of the people, the more I admire my dogs.

Alphonse de Lamartine

A dog starved at his master's gate
Predicts the ruin of the state.

William Blake

No man has ever dared to manifest his boredom so insolently as does a Siamese tomcat, when he yawns in the face of his amorously importunate wife. No man has ever dared to proclaim his illicit amours so frankly as this same tom caterwauling on the tiles.

Aldous Huxley

Success has the character of a cat. It won't come when coaxed.

Franz Werfel

I saw the most beautiful cat today. It was sitting by the side of the road, its two front feet neatly and graciously together. Then it gravely swished around its tail to completely and snugly encircle itself. It was so *fit* and beautifully neat, that gesture, and so self-satisfied—so complacent.

Anne Morrow Lindbergh

Were my Maker to grant me but one single glance through these sightless eyes of mine . . . I would without question or recall choose to see first a child, then a dog.

Helen Keller

The censure of a dog is something no man can stand.

Christopher Morley

Newfoundland dogs are good to save children from drowning, but you must have a pond of water handy and a child, or else there will be no profit in boarding a Newfoundland.

Henry Wheeler Shaw ("Josh Billings")

Dachshunds are ideal dogs for small children, as they are already stretched and pulled to such a length that the child cannot do much harm one way or the other.

Robert Benchley

"Not like cats!" cried the Mouse in a shrill, passionate voice. "Would *you* like cats if you were me?"

Lewis Carroll

Ignorant people think it's the noise which fighting cats make that is so aggravating, but it ain't so; it's the sickening grammar they use.

Ambrose Bierce

No matter how much cats fight, there always seem to be plenty of kittens.

Abraham Lincoln

To his dog, every man is Napoleon; hence the constant popularity of dogs.

Aldous Huxley

The nose of the bulldog has been slanted backwards so that he can breathe without letting go.

Winston Churchill

Anyone who hates children and dogs can't be all bad.

W. C. Fields

The dog was created especially for children. He is the god of frolic.

Henry Ward Beecher

It is easy to understand why the rabble dislike cats. A cat is beautiful; it suggests ideas of luxury, cleanliness, voluptuous pleasures . . . etc.

Charles Baudelaire

A home without a cat—and a well-fed, well-petted and properly revered cat—may be a perfect home, perhaps, but how can it prove title?

Mark Twain

The dog is a Yes-animal, very popular
with people who can't afford to keep a
Yes-man.

When you command a dog to "sit up," the
poor idiot thinks he has to do it. The
average cat throws off, pretends to be
stupid and not to understand what you
want. He really understands you too well,
but he sees "nothing in it" for him. Why
sit up?

William Lyon Phelps

I am his Highness' dog at Kew;
Pray tell me, sir, whose dog are you?
*Alexander Pope (on collar of dog
given by him to Prince of Wales)*

Think of cats, for instance. They are
neither Chinese or Tartars. They do not go
to school, nor read the Testament . . . What
sort of philosophers are we, who know
absolutely nothing of the origin and
destiny of cats?

Henry David Thoreau

Tho' the Mastiff be gentle, yet bite him not by the Lip.

Benjamin Franklin

When a dog barks at the moon, then it is religion; but when he barks at strangers, it is patriotism.

David Starr Jordan

Cats are smarter than dogs. You can't get eight cats to pull a sled through snow.

Jeff Valdez

Those who'll play with cats must expect to be scratched.

Cervantes

I have been studying the traits and dispositions of the "lower animals" (so called) and contrasting them with the traits and dispositions of man. I find the result humiliating to me.

Mark Twain

A dog, I will maintain, is a very tolerable judge of beauty, as appears from the fact that any liberally educated dog does, in a general way, prefer a woman to a man.

Francis Thompson

It often happens that a man is more humanely related to a cat or dog than to any human being.

Henry David Thoreau

Who loves me will love my dog also.

St. Bernard of Clairvaux

The dog has seldom been successful in pulling man up to its level of sagacity, but man has frequently dragged the dog down to his.

James Thurber

Animals are such agreeable friends—they ask no questions, they pass no criticisms.

George Eliot

When is it socially correct to serve milk in a saucer?

☞ *When you're feeding the cat.*

Riddles and Jokes

What do you call a young dog who earns $50,000 a year, drives a Mercedes and lives in a condo?

☞ *A yuppie puppy.*

What do you call a dog in the middle of a muddy road?

☞ *A mutt in a rut.*

Why is your puppy shivering?

☞ *He's a chili dog.*

Little girl: "How much are those puppies, sir?"
Pet store owner: "$10 apiece."
Little girl: "How much does a whole one cost?"

What is the difference between an
ambassador and a hot dog?

☞ *An ambassador wears full dress, a hot dog
just pants.*

Ten cats sat on a fence. One jumped off.
How many were left?

☞ *None—the others were copycats.*

That dog doesn't look at all like a police
dog.

☞ *That's because he's in the secret service.*

Why does that dog have a cauliflower ear?

☞ *Because he's a boxer.*

What does a cat put on his French fries?

☞ *Catsup.*

Does your dog have a license?

☞ No, he's not old enough to drive.

Why is a cat longer at night than in the morning?

☞ Because he is taken in in the morning, and let out at night.

How can you find your lost dog in the woods?

☞ By putting an ear to a tree and listening to the bark.

Why is that watchdog running around in circles?

☞ Because he's all wound up.

What does a running dog wear on his feet?

☞ Reebarks.

How come you're teacher's pet?

☞ *She can't afford a dog.*

My dog is a genius. I asked him what is 100 minus 100 and he said nothing.

Why should every boy with a dog have a mother?

☞ *So the dog will be fed regularly.*

Why is a dog biting his tail like a good manager?

☞ *Because he makes both ends meet.*

Suppose there was a cat in each corner of the room; a cat sitting opposite each cat; a cat looking at each cat; and a cat sitting on each cat's tail. How many cats would there be?

☞ *Four. Each cat was sitting on its own tail.*

What is a cat's favorite flower?

☞ *Pussywillow.*

My dog is a terrible bloodhound. I cut my hand once and he fainted.

"Mother," said the boy, "will you help me with some words? Is it correct to say you 'water a horse' when he's thirsty?"
"Yes, quite correct."
"Then," said the boy, picking up a saucer, "I'm going to milk the cat."

Dachshund: a dog and a half long and half a dog high.

If you pat a dachshund's head on Monday, he'll wag his tail on Tuesday.

How can you tell a dogwood tree?

☞ *By its bark.*

Letting the cat out of the bag is much easier than putting it back.

What's a small dog suffering from chills?

☞ *A pupsickle.*

The bachelor-girl hooted when anyone suggested that it was too bad she lacked a husband.

"I have a dog that growls, a parrot that swears, a fireplace that smokes, and a cat that stays out all night. Why should I want a husband?"

Uncle: Does your puppy have a pedigree?
Nephew: Sure.
Uncle: Do you have papers for it?
Nephew: All over the house.

Lady (in a pet shop)—"I like this dog, but his legs are too short."
Salesman—"Too short! Why, madam, all four touch the floor."

Did you hear what happened to the flea circus?

☞ *A dog came along and stole the show.*

What does a cat wear to a formal?

☞ *Cat O' Nine Tails.*

Why did the cat eat the cheese?

☞ *So he could hunt mice with baited breath.*

"Johnny, the kitten has disappeared."
"That's funny. It was there just now when I tried to clean it with the vacuum cleaner."

Patient: Doctor, please help me.
Psychiatrist: What's the matter?
Patient: I think I'm a dog.
Psychiatrist: Come and lie down on my couch.
Patient: But I'm not allowed on the furniture.

What happened to the boy who threw a lighted firecracker?

☞ *He got a big bang out of it when his retriever brought it back to him.*

My dog loves garlic. His bark is *really* worse than his bite!

What is the difference between a cat and a document?

☞ *One has claws at the end of its paws, and the other has pauses at the end of its clauses.*

Teacher: What is an octopus?
Pupil: An eight-sided cat.

Does your dog have fleas?

☞ *Of course not. Dogs don't have fleas—they have puppies!*

A cat also has nine wives.

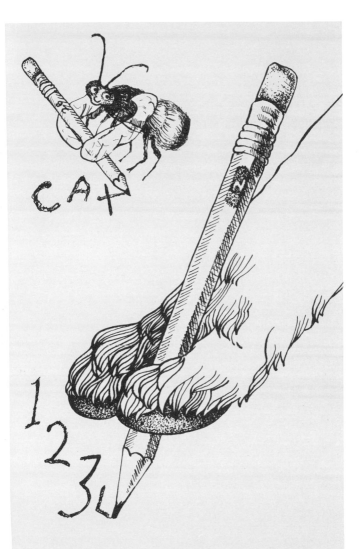

What is more wonderful than a counting dog?

☞ *A spelling bee.*

The only two who can live as cheaply as one are a dog and a flea.

Why is poker a cat's favorite game?

☞ *Because he might get to take the kitty home.*

When the Rev. Spooner dropped his cat on the floor he would always remark, "See how she pops on her drawers."

Why did the cat have a long puss?

☞ *Because it was run over by a steamroller.*

What is a cat's favorite room?

☞ *The kit-chen.*

Why is a dog's tail like the heart of a tree?

☞ *Because it is farthest from the bark.*

What do you call a cat with 100 feet?

☞ *A caterpillar.*

What kind of a dog has ticks?

☞ *A watchdog.*

**I'm a lean dog, a keen dog,
a wild dog, and lone . . .**
Irene Rutherford McLeod

Poetry

LONE DOG

I'm a lean dog, a keen dog, a wild dog, and
    lone;
I'm a rough dog, a tough dog, hunting on my
    own;
I'm a bad dog, a mad dog, teasing silly sheep;
I love to sit and bay the moon, to keep fat
    souls from sleep.

I'll never be a lap dog, licking dirty feet,
A sleek dog, a meek dog, cringing for my
    meat,
Not for me the fireside, the well-filled plate,
But shut door, and sharp stone, and cuff, and
    kick and hate.

Not for me the other dogs, running by my
    side,
Some have run a short while, but none of
    them would bide.
O mine is still the lone trail, the hard trail, the
    best,
Wide wind, and wild stars, and hunger of the
    quest!

Irene Rutherford McLeod

I wish she would not ask me if I love the
    Kitten more than her.
Of course I love her. But I love the Kitten too:
    and It has fur.

Josephine Preston Peabody

Of a sudden the great prima donna
Cried "Gawd, my voice is a goner!"
    But a cat in the wings
    Said, "I know how she sings,"
And finished the solo with honor.

Why so lean, my lady cat?
    Is it fasting causes that?
        Say, or is it love?

Matsuo Basho

The cat, if you but singe her tabby skin,
The chimney keeps, and sits content within:
But once grown sleek, will from the corner
    run,
Sport with her tail and wanton in the sun:
She licks her fair round face, and frisks
    abroad
To show her fur, and to be catterwaw'd.

Alexander Pope

Observe the Cat upon this page.
Philosophers in every age,
The very *wisest* of the wise
Have tried her mind to analyze
In vain, for nothing can they learn.
She baffles them at every turn
Like Mister Hamlet in the play.
She leads their reasoning astray;
She feigns an interest in string
Or yarn or any rolling thing.
Unlike the Dog, she does not care
With common Man her thoughts to share.
She teaches us that in life's walk
'Tis better to let others talk,
And listen while *they* say instead
The foolish things *we* might have said.

Oliver Herford

A cat in despondency sighed,
And resolved to commit suicide;
   She passed under the wheels
   Of eight automobiles,
And after the ninth one she died.

I've got a little cat,
And I'm very fond of that,
But I'd rather have a bowwow, wow.

Joseph Tabrar

39

THE SPHINX

In a dim corner of my room for longer than
    my fancy thinks,
A beautiful and silent Sphinx has watched me
    through the shifting gloom.

Inviolate and immobile she does not rise, she
    does not stir
For silver moons are naught to her and
    naught to her the suns that reel.

Red follows grey across the air, the waves of
    moonlight ebb and flow,
But with the Dawn she does not go and in the
    night-time she is there.

Dawn follows Dawn and Nights grow old and
    all the while this curious cat
Lies crouching on the Chinese mat with eyes
    of satin rimmed with gold.

Upon the mat she lies and leers and on the
    tawny throat of her
Flutters the soft and silky fur or ripples to
    her pointed ears.

Come forth, my lovely langorous Sphinx! and
    so statuesque!

Come forth, you exquisite grotesque! half
  woman and half animal!

Come forth, my lovely langorous Sphinx! and
  put your head upon my knee!
And let me stroke your throat and see your
  body spotted like the Lynx!

And let me touch those curving claws of
  yellow ivory, and grasp
The tail that like a monstrous Asp coils round
  your heavy velvet paws!

Oscar Wilde

Hey diddle diddle
The cat and the fiddle
The cow jumped over the moon;
The little dog laughed
To see such sport,
And the dish ran away with the spoon.

Nursery Rhyme

Cruel, but composed and bland,
Dumb, inscrutable and grand,
So Tiberius might have sat,
Had Tiberius been a cat.

Matthew Arnold

41

THE OWL AND THE PUSSY-CAT

The Owl and the Pussy-Cat went to sea
    In a beautiful pea-green boat:
They took some honey, and plenty of money
    Wrapped up in a five-pound note.
The Owl looked up to the stars above,
    And sang to a small guitar,
"O lovely Pussy, O Pussy, my love,
    What a beautiful Pussy you are,
        You are,
        You are!
    What a beautiful Pussy you are!"

Pussy said to the Owl, "You elegant fowl,
    How charmingly sweet you sing!
O! let us be married; too long we have tarried;
    But what shall we do for a ring?"
They sailèd away, for a year and a day,
    To the land where the bong-tree grows;
And there in a wood a Piggy-wig stood,
    With a ring at the end of his nose,
        His nose,
        His nose,
    With a ring at the end of his nose.

"Dear Pig, are you willing to sell for
one shilling
    Your ring?" Said the Piggy, "I will."

So they took it away, and were married
next day
   By the Turkey who lives on the hill.
They dinèd on mince and slices of quince,
   Which they ate with a runcible spoon;
And hand in hand, on the edge of the sand,
   They danced by the light of the moon,
      The moon,
      The moon,
   They danced by the light of the moon.
                              Edward Lear

NINE LIVES

My kitty cat has nine lives.
Yes, nine long lives has she.
Three to spend in eating,
Three to spend in sleeping
And three to spend up the chestnut tree.

There once were two cats of Kilkenny
Each thought there was one cat too many.
      So they fought and they fit,
      And they scratched and they bit,
Till instead of two cats there weren't any.

43

AN ELEGY ON THE DEATH OF
A MAD DOG

Good people all, of every sort,
 Give ear unto my song;
And if you find it wondrous short,
 It cannot hold you long.

In Islington there was a man
 Of whom the world might say,
That still a godly race he ran,
 Whene'er he went to pray.

A kind and gentle heart he had,
 To comfort friends and foes:
The naked every day he clad,
 When he put on his clothes.

And in that town a dog was found,
 As many dogs there be,
Both mongrel, puppy, whelp, and hound,
 And curs of low degree.

This dog and man at first were friends;
 But when a pique began
The dog, to gain some private ends,
 Went mad, and bit the man.

Around from all the neighboring streets
  The wondering neighbors ran,
And swore the dog had lost his wits,
  To bite so good a man.

The wound it seemed both sore and sad
  To every Christian eye:
And while they swore the dog was mad,
  They swore the man would die.

But soon a wonder came to light
  That showed the rogues they lied:
The man recovered of the bite.
  The dog it was that died.

                              Oliver Goldsmith

There was a young man from the city,
Who saw what he thought was a kitty.
    To make sure of that
    He gave it a pat.
They buried his clothes—what a pity!

Crossed in love, the tom-cat gazes
  Sadly at the sky
    And sings mournfully!

                              Makai Kyorai

45

TO A CAT

Nellie, methinks, twixt thee and me
There is a kind of sympathy;
And could we interchange our nature,—
If I were cat, thou human creature,—
I should, like thee, be no great mouser,
And thou, like me, no great composer;
For, like thy plaintive mews, my muse
With villainous whine doth fate abuse,
Because it hath not made me sleek
As golden down on Cupid's cheek;
And yet thou canst upon the rug lie,
Stretched out like snail, or curled up snugly,
As if thou wert not lean or ugly;
And I, who in poetic flights
Sometimes complain of sleepless nights,
Regardless of the sun in heaven,
Am apt to doze till past eleven—
The world would just the same go round
If I were hanged and thou wert drowned;
There is one difference, 'tis true,—
Thou dost not know it, and I do.

Hartley Coleridge

Weary now of love's defeat,
  The tom-cat steals a bit of meat . . .
    O faithful love!

Kagami Shiko

46

I dream of my love; her eyes like thine,
Profound and cold, sweet cat of mine,
My Soul dart-wounds fret.

A subtle air, a deadly sweet
Breathes round her, and from head to feet
Envelopes my brunette.

Charles Baudelaire

Down in the silent hallway
   Scampers the dog about,
And whines, and barks, and scratches,
   In order to get out.

Once in the glittering starlight,
   He straightway doth begin
To set up a doleful howling
   In order to get in.

Richard Kendall Munkittrick

I have a dog of Blenheim birth,
With fine long ears and full of mirth;
And sometimes, running o'er the plain,
   He tumbles on his nose:
But quickly jumping up again
   Like lightning on he goes!

John Ruskin

THE KITTEN AND THE FALLING LEAVES

See the kitten on the wall,
Sporting with the leaves that fall,
Withered leaves—one, two and three—
From the lofty elder-tree!
Through the calm and frosty air
Of this morning bright and fair,
Eddying round and round they sink
Softly, slowly: one might think,
From the motions that are made,
Every little leaf conveyed
Sylph or Faery hither tending,
To this lower world descending,
Each invisible and mute,
In his wavering parachute.

But—the Kitten, how she starts,
Crouches, stretches paws, and darts!
First at one, and then its fellow
Just as light and just as yellow.
There are many now—now one—
Now they stop and there are none.

What intenseness of desire
In her upward eye of fire!
With a tiger-leap half way
Now she meets the coming prey,
Lets it go as fast, and then

Has it in her power again:
Now she works with three or four,
Like an Indian conjurer;
Quick as he in feats of art,
Far beyond in joy of heart.
Were her antics played in the eye
Of a thousand standers-by,
Clapping hands with shout and stare,
What would little Tabby care
For the plaudits of the crowd?

William Wordsworth

Man loves the Dog because he'll stay
And listen to his talk all day,
And wag his tail and show delight
At all his jokes, however trite.
His bark is far worse than his bite,
So people say. They may be right;
Yet if to make a choice I had,
I'd choose his bark, however bad.

Oliver Herford

There was an old spinster from Fife,
Who had never been kissed in her life;
   Along came a cat,
   And she said "I'll kiss that!"
But the cat meowed: "Not on your life!"

THE DUEL

The gingham dog and the calico cat
Side by side on the table sat;
'Twas half-past twelve, and (what do you
   think!)
Nor one nor t'other had slept a wink!
   The old Dutch clock and the Chinese plate
   Appeared to know as sure as fate
There was going to be a terrible spat.
   (I wasn't there; I simply state
    What was told to me by the Chinese
    plate!)

The gingham dog went "bow-wow-bow!"
And the calico cat replied "mee-ow!"
The air was littered, an hour or so,
With bits of gingham and calico,
   While the old Dutch clock in the chimney-
    place
   Up with its hands before its face,
For it always dreaded a family row!
   (Never mind: I'm only telling you
    What the old Dutch clock declares is
    true!)

The Chinese plate looked very blue,
And wailed, "Oh, dear! what shall we do!"
But the gingham dog and calico cat

Wallowed this way and tumbled that,
   Employing every tooth and claw
   In the awfullest way you ever saw—
And, oh! how the gingham and calico flew!
   (Don't fancy I exaggerate—
   I got my news from the Chinese plate!)

Next morning where the two had sat
They found no trace of dog or cat;
And some folks think unto this day
That burglars stole that pair away!
   But the truth about the cat and pup
   Is this: they ate each other up!
Now what do you really think of that!
   (The old Dutch clock it told me so,
   And that is how I came to know.)
                              Eugene Field

He prayeth well who loveth well
Both man and bird and beast.
He prayeth best, who loveth best
   All things both great and small;
For the dear God who loveth us,
   He made and loveth all.
                    Samuel Taylor Coleridge

**When the mouse laughs
at the cat, there is a hole nearby.**
African Proverb

Proverbs, Fables & Epitaphs

Don't show a beaten dog the stick.

Yiddish Proverb

An old dog does not bark for nothing.

Proverb

When the cat's away the mice will play.

English Proverb

A dog is wiser than a woman; it does not bark at its master.

Russian Proverb

An old cat laps as much as a young kitten.

Proverb

Dogs and children know who likes them.

Proverb

Don't send a dog to the butcher's for meat.

Yiddish Proverb

Do not keep a dog and bark yourself.

Proverb

Throw a cat over a house and it will land on its feet.

English Proverb

A white dog does not bite another white dog.

African Proverb

A lean dog gets nothing but fleas.

Spanish Proverb

Beware of a silent dog and still water.

Latin Proverb

Show a dog a finger and he wants the whole hand.

Yiddish Proverb

The cat shuts its eyes when stealing the cream.

Proverb

Every dog is a lion at home.

Italian Proverb

Cut off the dog's tail; he remains a dog.

Italian Proverb

Don't kick a sleeping dog.

African Proverb

A kitchen dog was never good for the chase.

Italian Proverb

When the dog is awake the shepherd may sleep.

German Proverb

A house without either a dog or a cat is the house of a scoundrel.

Portuguese Proverb

A borrowed cat catches no mice.

Japanese Proverb

The more I see of men, the more I admire dogs.

French Proverb

The slowest barker is the surest biter.

Proverb

A snappish cur never wants a sore ear.

French Proverb

It is a hard winter when dog eats dog.

Proverb

If you wish the dog to follow you, feed him.

Proverb

Do not call to a dog with a whip in your hand.

African Proverb

Killing the dog does not cure the bite.

Proverb

The dog's bark is not might, but fright.

African Proverb

If you do not step on the dog's tail, he will not bite you.

African Proverb

A cat may go to a monastery, but she still remains a cat!

African Proverb

Every dog is entitled to one bite.

English Proverb

No dog is so sad that he cannot wag his tail.

Proverb

It is hard to teach an old dog new tricks.

Proverb

THE HARE & THE HOUND

A Hound having put up a Hare from a bush, chased her for some distance, but the Hare had the best of it, and got off. A Goatherd who was coming by jeered at the Hound, saying that Puss was the better runner of the two. You forget, replied the Hound, ☞ *It is one thing to be running for your dinner, and another for your life.*

Aesop

THE OLD HOUND

An old Hound, who had been a fine hunter in his youth, one day was out with his master in the forest. They saw a wild Boar, and the Hound ran after him. He caught the Boar, but the Boar was young and strong, and after a struggle got away. Then the Hound's master came up, and was about to beat him. But the Hound said: Master, remember what I was in the old days, and do not beat me for my weakness now. ☞ *The old should be pitied, not punished, for their weakness.*

Aesop

THE THIEF & THE DOG

A Thief came one night to rob a Farmer's house; but the Dog saw him, and started to bark. There, there! Good doggie! said the Thief, and threw the Dog a fine piece of meat. At this the faithful Dog barked louder than ever, for, said he to the Thief: I was suspicious of you at first, but now I know you are up to no good whatsoever! ☞ *Honeyed words and a bribe in hand always precede some villainy.*

Aesop

THE DOG & HIS REFLECTION

A Dog had snatched a piece of meat from a Butcher's shop, and was taking it home. As he trotted over a low bridge, he looked over the edge, and saw his own reflection in the water below. He thought it was another dog, also with a piece of meat. He snapped at the other dog, thinking to chase him away and so get the second piece of meat also; but no sooner did he open his mouth than his own meat dropped into the water, and he lost both what he had and what he hoped to get. ☞ *Never let go a real good to reach for an illusion.*

Aesop

THE DONKEY & THE LAP-DOG

There once was a Donkey and a Lap-dog belonging to the same master. The Lap-dog was a great favorite with all the family. He often would run through the house, gambol, play and bark, and climb into people's laps and lick their hands. The Donkey was well-fed and well cared-for too, but all day long he had to work hard carrying wood and turning the mill, and he envied the Lap-dog. One day, thinking that if he acted like the Lap-dog he would be treated as the Dog was, the Donkey broke from his halter, and rushed into the house. He trotted into the living-room, and gamboled about. He stood up on his hind legs and brayed.

Swishing his tail and imitating the dog's tricks, he crashed into the dining-room table and smashed all the dishes. Then he tried to get into the Master's lap and lick his face. But by this time the farmhands had come after the Donkey. They believed he had gone crazy, so instead of catching him, they beat him with clubs until he died.

☞ *A clumsy joke spoils good humor.*

Aesop

THE CAT & THE MICE

A wily old Cat, who had been having
trouble catching Mice because she was now
a little slow, and the Mice were getting too
smart, thought up a scheme for fooling
them. She hung herself up by the hind legs
from a beam in the barn, and expected that
the Mice would take her for a bag or an old
coat. In came the Mice, as soon as all was
dark; but at the first glance the leader said:
Hm! Many a bag have I seen in my day but
never a one with a Cat's head! And all the
other Mice, even the baby Mice, laughed
and laughed at the Cat until she could stay
still no longer, but angrily started to untie
herself. Then all of the Mice scampered
safely away. ☞ *If a Mouse can smell cheese,
he can also smell trouble.*

Aesop

THE BLACKSMITH & HIS DOG

A Blacksmith once took in a Dog, who
asked if he could have a home and make
himself useful. While the Blacksmith
hammered away at his metal, the Dog
slept; but when he sat down to dinner, the

Dog woke up and wagged his tail. Sluggard cur! said the disgusted Blacksmith, throwing him a bone, You sleep through all the noise of the anvil, but wake up at the first clatter of dishes. ☞ *If you avoid your friend at work, do not join him at meals.*

Aesop

EPITAPH TO A DOG

His friends he loved. He fellest earthly foes—
   Cats—I believe he did but feign to hate.
My hand will miss the insinuated nose,
   Mine eyes the tail that wagged contempt
      at fate.

William Watson

EPITAPH

BATHSHEBA: —
To whom none ever said scat.
No worthier cat
Ever sat on a mat
Or caught a rat: —
   Requies-cat.

John Greenleaf Whittier

EPITAPH FOR HIS DOG
BURIED AT NEWSTEAD ABBEY, 1808:

Near this spot
Are deposited the remains of one
Who possessed beauty without vanity,
Strength without insolence,
Courage without ferocity,
And all the virtues of man without his vices.
This praise, which would be unmeaning
flattery
If inscribed over human ashes,
Is but a just tribute to the memory of
Boatswain, a dog.

Lord Byron

EPITAPH ON A DOG'S GRAVE
IN MARYLAND

Major
Born a dog
Died a gentleman

EVERYMAN, I will go with thee,

and be thy guide,

In thy most need to go by thy side

PLATO

Born at Athens, 428–427 B.C. After the death
of Socrates (399) he travelled in Greece,
Egypt and Italy. About 387 he returned to
Athens and founded the Academy, over
which he presided for the remainder of
his life, except for two visits to Sicily on
political business (367 and 361). He died
in 348–347 B.C.

PLATO

Symposium
and other Dialogues

INTRODUCTION BY
JOHN WARRINGTON

DENT: LONDON
EVERYMAN'S LIBRARY
DUTTON: NEW YORK

Symposium, Ion and Meno
first included in Everyman's Library 1910
This translation of Symposium first included 1938
This translation of Ion first published in Everyman's Library 1952
These translations of Meno, Laches and Euthydemus
first published in Everyman's Library 1964

NO. *418*

INTRODUCTION

THIS new volume takes the place of an earlier title in Everyman's Library,[1] which included *The Symposium* (translated by Michael Joyce), *Ion* (translated by Michael Oakley), *Meno*,[2] *Phaedrus* and *Phaedo*. The first two are reprinted here. *Phaedo*, in a new translation by myself, now forms part of *The Trial and Death of Socrates* (E.M.L. No. 457). The publishers decided to omit *Phaedrus*, and at their request I have translated *Laches* and *Euthydemus* as substitutes.

The Symposium professes to record the speeches in honour of Eros by a number of famous Athenians at a dinner-party held to celebrate Agathon's first victory at the Lenæa in 416 B.C. Its immediate purpose is threefold: (1) to show that the most lofty manifestation of the 'Love' which controls the world consists in the mystical longing for union with the eternal and transcendent Beauty; (2) to represent Socrates as the type of one who has achieved that union; (3) to contrast with him the handsome, able and wealthy (but shallow) personality of Alcibiades, who has dedicated himself to earthly pleasures and ambitions.

The philosophical interest of this sublime dialogue centres upon the speech delivered by Socrates, which he claims to have learned at about the age of thirty from the priestess Diotima of Mantinea. Eros, that is to say, appetitive love in whatever form, is a reaching out of the soul towards a good for which it craves but upon which it has not yet laid hold. This appetitive love is roused first by Beauty, which is eternal. Its crudest form is love for a beautiful person; but this is in fact a longing to beget off-spring by that person and thus to attain the nearest substitute for immortality—perpetuation of one's stock—which is all that lives within the body's power. A more exalted form of the longing for eternity is man's aspiration to achieve undying renown by

---

[1] *Five Dialogues*, No. 456. This number, now entitled *Parmenides and Other Dialogues*, contains *Parmenides*, *Theaetetus*, *The Sophist* and *The Statesman*.

[2] *For the solution of the problem on page 103, with its diagram, I am indebted to Mr E. F. Bozman.*

uniting himself with a kindred soul to produce wise institutions and sound rules of life. Higher still is the striving, along with an intellectual *élite*, to enrich philosophy and science.

But the final objective lies far beyond these stages. Having travelled by way of all three, a man suddenly espies a Supreme Beauty, the ultimate source and the cause of the beauty he has previously recognized in material or spiritual things. Union with this alone can give him true immortality. This 'beatific vision', to which the philosopher has at long last attained, has as its object 'Beauty sole and eternal', and this can only mean what Plato himself calls in *The Republic* the 'Good' or 'Form of Good'.

Ion is a mere occasional piece, though not without charm and a certain literary interest. It will be remembered that in the *Apology* (22 A–C) Socrates declared that he found the poets, who were reckoned by the ordinary of mankind as 'wise', quite incapable of explaining how they arrived at their noblest utterances or what those utterances really meant. Here, in *Ion*, Plato develops this view into the theory that neither the poet himself, nor the *rhapsode* who recites his work, obtains his effect 'by science', that is, by conscious artistry; the effect in each case is the fruit of non-rational inspiration—of something we today call 'natural genius'. This theory is of significance because it rules out any appeal to the poets as competent authorities on the conduct of life, an appeal which is forbidden with greater emphasis in *The Republic*.

Meno, a work of considerable importance, is concerned fundamentally with the question of what virtue is and whether it can be taught. Our answer to the second part of this question will depend upon that given to the first. The dialogue leads to a point at which virtue appears as the 'ability to secure good things by honest means'; but here we find ourselves in a vicious circle, for honesty itself is a 'good thing'. There is the further dilemma that all such inquiries appear futile, since it is a waste of time to inquire into what we know, and futile to inquire into what we don't know (since we could not recognize an unknown even if we met it). The only way of surmounting this difficulty is to show that the soul is immortal and has learned all truth in a previous existence, needing now only to be 'reminded' by sense-perception of truths it once knew but has forgotten. This is the famous doctrine of *anamnesis* (recollection), one of the twin pillars of the Ideal Theory, and Socrates proceeds to justify it by a famous experiment. He demonstrates that a boy who has never studied geometry can be led to recognize mathematical truths by merely showing him a diagram drawn on the ground and asking him a number of simple questions about it.

So if virtue is knowledge it can certainly be taught. But *is* it knowledge? If it is, one might safely assume that there are professional teachers of it, as the sophists claim to be. At this point the democratic politician Anytus comes upon the scene. He was the principal author of the prosecution of Socrates, and there is reason to think that the brief episode of his appearance is used by Plato to suggest that the real grounds of the prosecution was Socrates's criticism of the leading figures of Athenian democracy. Anytus angrily rejects the claim of the sophists, whom he denounces as worthless impostors, and assures Socrates that any Athenian gentleman is qualified to teach virtue. This is refuted by Socrates, who cites Themistocles, Pericles and others as having failed to teach it to their own sons. Those great men, therefore, can have had no genuine knowledge of truth; whatever success they enjoyed was the result, not of knowledge, but only of 'correct opinions'. Yet while correct opinions are as good as knowledge for all practical purposes, they have this disadvantage, that one cannot rely upon them as permanent unless they can be firmly based on reasons, in which case they become knowledge.

The conclusion is that *if* a man arose who was capable of teaching statesmanship to others, he would be one who really knew what good is; and his virtue would be to that of other men as substance is to shadow.

Laches belongs to a group of short dialogues in which some critical problem is brought forward, several tentative answers are examined and are all found inadequate, so that, although we learn nothing from the conversation, we are made painfully aware of our basic ignorance of those things which we have most need to know. These so-called dialogues of search perpetuate Socrates's method; and their search for definition, for the unity behind plurality, was of course an initial step towards the Ideal Theory. *Laches* itself is concerned with courage, the military virtue *par excellence*, and we have a delightful picture of two elderly generals under cross-examination. The gradual collapse of their self-assurance is altogether delightful, and the whole little dialogue has an air of exquisite courtesy. Courage, it seems at first, may be defined as knowledge of what is and what is not really to be dreaded. But Socrates shows that this is equivalent to saying that virtue is true knowledge of good and evil, which leads to the definition of courage as 'knowledge of good'; and this in turn identifies courage with the whole 'goodness of man' —an impossible definition unless we can refute the popular objection to Socrates's theory that 'virtue is one'.

This question of courage and the unity of virtue is raised again in *Protagoras*. There the great sophist, after some hesitation, is prepared to identify all the virtues with wisdom or sound judgment; all, that is to say, except one—courage, which popular opinion regards as outstandingly non-rational. Socrates, however, argues against this exception. Popular opinion, he urges, despite its firm belief in the non-rational character of courage, would have no objection to identifying the good and the pleasant, or to allowing that the goodness of courage means that by confronting pain and danger one avoids worse pain and danger. On its own admission, therefore, courage and all the rest of virtue amounts simply to the prudent estimate of pleasures and pains.

The final dialogue, *Euthydemus*, is a masterpiece of satire on the eristics, those extreme sophists led by Eucleides of Megara, whose aim was rather to win an argument than to discover truth. Their method consisted in getting a man to make some definite assertion, and then misusing the logic of Zeno for the purpose of ensnaring him in fallacies [1] due to linguistic ambiguity. But over and above this brilliant satire, with its verbal acrobatics and boisterously amusing climax, the dialogue has a deeper purpose. Contrasting the ridiculous contradiction-mongering of Euthydemus and Dionysodorus with the protreptic of Socrates, it reads like a manifesto for the type of education offered by the Academy in place of the sophistic system, which Plato held to be vitiating public and private life at every level. Young Cleinias is simply confused by the questions hurled at him by the two itinerant professors, while those put by Socrates are planned to convince him that the happiness for which all men crave is not guaranteed by mere possession of those things which the world reckons as

[1] Arostotle draws freely on this dialogue in *De Sophisticis Elenchis*.

good, but depends upon our making *right use* of them. If a man is to achieve happiness, he must comply with the ruling principle of Socrates's teaching, namely that the supreme business of life is to 'tend the soul'. He must acquire the 'royal' science, the *knowledge* of good and evil, which alone will enable him to make right use of all the gifts of mind, body and external fortune.

JOHN WARRINGTON.

1964.

SELECT BIBLIOGRAPHY

EDITIONS. Complete Works: A. P. Manutius and M. Musurus (Aldine Ed.), Venice, 1513; H. Stephanus and J. Serranus, Paris, 1578; G. Stalbaum, 1850; C. F. Hermann, 1851–3; I. Bekker, 10 vols. (Greek and Latin), 1816–1823; J. G. Baiter, J. C. Orelli and A. G. Winckelmann, 21 vols., 1839–41; R. B. Hirschig and C. E. C. Schneider, 1856–73; M. Schanz, 12 vols., 1875–1879; J. Burnet, 5 vols., 1899–1907.

TRANSLATIONS. F. Sydenham, 1759, 1776; T. Taylor and F. Sydenham, 1804; H. Cary and H. Davis, 1848–52, 1900; W. Whewell (Dialogues), 3 vols., 1859–61; B. Jowett (Dialogues), 3rd ed., 1892; H. N. Fowler, W. R. Lamb, R. G. Bury and P. Shorey, 12 vols. (Loeb Library), with text, 1919–1937.

GENUINE WORKS. *Hippias Major, Hippias Minor, Ion, Menexenus, Charmides, Laches, Lysis, Cratylus, Euthydemus, Gorgias, Meno, Protagoras, Euthyphro, Apology, Crito, Phaedo, Symposium, Phaedrus, Republic, Parmenides, Theaetetus, Sophistes, Politicus, Philebus, Timaeus, Critias, Laws.* Separate editions and translations of the foregoing dialogues are numerous. Opinion is divided as to the authenticity of *Epinomis*. It is safe to admit the *Epistles* as genuine, with the exception of I and XII which are undoubtedly spurious. Plato's will (Diogenes Laertius III. 41–3) is certainly authentic; but the great majority, if not all, of the 32 epigrams attributed to him in the *Greek Anthology* are by other hands.

CRITICAL. F. Zeller, *History of Greek Philosophy*, 1881; W. Pater, *Plato and Platonism*, 1893; E. Barker, *Greek Political Theory : Plato and his Predecessors*, 1918; P. E. More, *The Religion of Plato*, 1921; A. E. Taylor, *Platonism and its Influence*, 1925; *Plato, the Man and his Work*, 1926; R. C. Lodge, *Plato's Theory of Logic*, 1928; C. Ritter, *The Essence of Plato's Philosophy* (trans. E. Alles), 1933; F. H. Anderson, *The Argument of Plato*, 1935; R. L. Nettleship, *The Theory of Education in Plato's Republic*, 1935; R. Demos, *The Philosophy of Plato*, 1939; *Plato's Academy : the Birth of the Idea and its Rediscovery*, 1939; J. Wild, *Plato's Theory of Man*, 1946; G. C. Field, *The Philosophy of Plato*, 1949; N. R. Murphy, *The Interpretation of Plato's Republic*, 1951; Sir W. D. Ross, *Plato's Theory of Ideas*, 1951; R. Robinson, *Plato's Earlier Dialectic*, 1953; R. C. Lodge, *Plato's Theory of Art*, 1953; R. B. Levinson, *In Defence of Plato*, 1954; J. Gould, *The Development of Plato's Ethics*, 1955; R. C. Lodge, *The Philosophy of Plato*, 1956; A. Wedberg, *Plato's Philosophy of Mathematics*, 1956; A. D. Winspear, *The Genesis of Plato's Thought*, 1956; P. Friedlander, *Plato*, 1958; R. H. S. Crossman, *Plato Today*, 1959; R. G. Bury, *The Symposium of Plato*, 1962.

CONTENTS

SYMPOSIUM, OR THE DRINKING PARTY

ST. III. 172–223

PERSONS OF THE DIALOGUE:

Apollodorus and his Friends

APOLLODORUS. Oh, if that's what you want to know, it isn't long since I had occasion to refresh my memory. Only the day before yesterday, as I was coming up to the city from my place at Phalerum, a friend of mine caught sight of me from behind; and while I was still a long way ahead he shouted after me: 'Here, I say, Apollodorus! Can't you wait for me?' So I stopped and waited for him.

'Apollodorus,' he said as he came up, 'you're the very man I'm looking for. I want to ask you about this party at Agathon's, when Socrates and Alcibiades and the rest of them were at dinner there. What were all these speeches they were making about Love? I've heard something about them from a man who'd been talking to Phoenix, but his information was rather sketchy and he said I'd better come to you. So you'll have to tell me the whole story; for you know we always count on you, Apollodorus, to report your beloved Socrates. But before you begin, tell me, were you there yourself?'

'Well,' said I, 'whoever was your informant I can well believe he wasn't very clear about it if you gathered it was such a recent party that I could have been there!'

'That was my impression,' said he.

'My dear Glaucon,' I protested, 'how could it have been? Have you forgotten how long Agathon's been away from Athens? And don't you know it's only two or three years since I started spending so much of my time with Socrates, and making it my business to follow everything he says and does from day to day? Because, you know, before that I used

I

to go dashing about all over the place, firmly convinced that I was leading a full and interesting life, when I was really as wretched as could be—much the same as you, for instance; for I know philosophy's the last thing *you*'d spend your time on.'

'Now don't start girding at me,' said Glaucon, 'but tell me: when was this party, then?'

'It was given', I told him, 'when you and I were in the nursery, the day after Agathon's celebrations with the players when he'd won the prize with his first tragedy.'

'Yes,' he admitted; 'that must have been a good many years ago. But who told you about it—Socrates himself?'

'No, no,' I said. 'I had it from the same source as Phoenix: Aristodemus of Cydathenaeum, a little fellow who used to go about barefoot. He was there himself; indeed I fancy he was one of Socrates' most impassioned admirers at the time. As a matter of fact I did ask Socrates about one or two points later on, and he confirmed what Aristodemus had told me.'

'Very well,' said Glaucon; 'then you must tell me all about it before we reach the city. I'm sure it'll pass the time most agreeably.'

Well, I told him all about it as we went along; and so, as I was saying, I've got the story pretty pat; and if you want to hear it too I suppose I may as well begin. For that matter I don't know anything that gives me greater pleasure, or profit either, than talking or listening to philosophy. But when it comes to ordinary conversation, such as the stuff you talk about financiers and the money market, well, I find it pretty tiresome personally, and I feel sorry that my friends should think they're being very busy when they're really doing absolutely nothing. Of course, I know your idea of me: you think I'm just a poor unfortunate, and I shouldn't wonder if you're right. But then, I don't *think* that *you*'re unfortunate— I *know* you are.

A FRIEND. There you go again, Apollodorus! Always running down yourself and everybody else! You seem to have some extravagant idea that the whole world, with the sole exception of Socrates, is in a state of utter misery—beginning with yourself. You're always the same—perhaps that's why people think you're mad: always girding at yourself and all the rest of us—except Socrates of course.

APOLL. My dear man, of course I am! And of course I shouldn't *dream* of thinking such things about myself or about my friends if I weren't completely crazy.

THE FRIEND. Oh, come now, Apollodorus! We needn't go into that. For heaven's sake, man, don't fly off at a tangent, but simply answer our question: What were these speeches about Love?

APOLL. Well then, they were something like this—but perhaps I'd better begin at the beginning and tell you in Aristodemus' own words.

'I met Socrates', he told me, 'looking very spruce after his bath, with a nice pair of shoes on although, as you know, he generally goes about barefoot. So I asked him where he was going to, cutting such a dash. "I'm going to dinner with Agathon," he said. "I kept away from the public celebrations yesterday because I was afraid there'd be a crush; but I promised I'd go along this evening. And I've got myself up like this because I don't want to disgrace such a distinguished host. But what about you?" he went on. "How would you like to join the party uninvited?"

'"Just as you think," I replied.

'"Then come along with me," he said, "and we'll adapt the proverb, 'Unbidden do the good frequent the tables of the good.' Though, if it comes to that, Homer himself has not so much adapted that very proverb as exploded it; for after making Agamemnon extremely stout and warlike, and Menelaus a most indifferent spearman, he shows Agamemnon making merry after the sacrifice and Menelaus coming to his table uninvited—that is, the lesser man coming to supper with the greater."

'"I'm afraid", said I, "that Homer's version is the apter so far as I'm concerned—an uninvited ignoramus going to dinner with a man of letters. So you'd better be preparing your excuses on the way; for you needn't think I'll apologize for coming without an invitation—I shall plead that you invited me."

'"Two heads are better than one", he said, "when it comes to excuses. Well, anyway, let's be off."

'Having settled this point,' continued Aristodemus, 'we started out; and as we went along Socrates fell into a fit of abstraction and began to lag behind, but when I was going to wait for him he told me to go on ahead. So when I arrived at Agathon's, where the door was standing wide open, I found myself in rather a curious position; for a servant immediately showed me in and announced me to the assembled company, who were already at table and just about to begin. However, the moment Agathon saw me he cried: "Ah! Here's Aristodemus—just in time for dinner; and if you've come on business it'll have to wait, that's flat. I was going to invite you yesterday, only I couldn't get hold of you. But I say, where's Socrates? Haven't you brought him with you?"

'I looked round, supposing that Socrates was bringing up the rear, but he was nowhere to be seen; so I explained that we'd been coming along together, and that I'd come at his invitation.

'"Very nice of you," said Agathon; "but what on earth can have happened to the man?"

'"He was coming in just behind me; I can't think where he can be."

'"Here," said Agathon to one of the servants, "run along and see if you can find Socrates, and show him in. And now, my dear Aristodemus, may I put you next to Eryximachus?"

'And so', Aristodemus went on, 'I made my toilet and sat down, the servant meanwhile returning with the news that our friend Socrates had retreated into the next-door neighbour's porch. And there he stood, said the man: and when he asked him in he wouldn't come.

'"This is very odd," said Agathon. "You must speak to him again, and insist."

'But here I broke in. "I shouldn't do that," I said; "you'd much better leave him to himself. It's quite a habit of his, you know; off he goes and there he stands, no matter where it is. I've no doubt he'll be with us before long, so I really don't think you'd better worry him."

'"Oh, very well," said Agathon; "I expect you know best. We won't wait then," he said, turning to the servants. "Now you understand, you fellows are to serve whatever kind of dinner you think fit; I'm leaving it entirely to you. I know it's a new idea; but you'll simply have to imagine that we've all come here as your guests. Now go ahead and show us what you can do."

'Well, we started dinner, and still there was no sign of Socrates; Agathon still wanted to send for him, but I wouldn't let him. And when at last he did turn up, we weren't more than half way through dinner, which was pretty good for him. As he came in, Agathon, who was sitting by himself at the far end of the table, called out:

'"Here you are, Socrates; come and sit next to me; I want to share this great thought that's just struck you in the porch next door. I'm sure you must have mastered it, or you'd still be standing there."

'"My dear Agathon," Socrates replied as he took his seat beside him, "I only wish that wisdom *were* the kind of thing one could share by sitting next to someone: if it flowed, for instance, from the one that was full to the one that was empty, like the water in two cups finding its level through a piece of worsted. If that were how it worked, I'm sure I'd congratulate myself on sitting next to you, for you'd soon have me brimming over with the most exquisite kind of wisdom. My own understanding is a shadowy thing at best, as equivocal as a dream; but yours, Agathon, glitters and dilates—as which of us can forget that saw you the other day, resplendent in your youth, visibly kindled before the eyes of more than thirty thousand of your fellow Greeks."

'"Now, Socrates," said Agathon, "I know you're making fun of me; however, I shall take up this question of wisdom with you later on, and let Bacchus judge between us. In the meantime you must really show a little interest in your food."

'So Socrates drew up and had his dinner with the rest of them; and then, after the libation and the usual hymn and so forth, they began to turn their attention to the wine. It was Pausanias, so far as Aristodemus could remember, who opened the conversation. "Well, gentlemen," he began, "what do you say? What sort of a night shall we make of it? Speaking for myself, I'm not quite up to form; I'm still a bit the worse for what I had last night; and I don't suppose you're most of you much better—we were all in the same boat. Anyhow, what do you say? How does everybody feel about the drink?"

'"That's a most sensible question of yours, Pausanias," said Aristophanes; "we don't want to make a burden of it—I speak as one who was pretty well soaked last night."

'"I quite agree," observed Eryximachus; "and there is just one question I should like to add: what about Agathon? Has he sufficiently recovered to feel like drinking?"

'"Not I," said Agathon. "You can count me out."

'"So much the better for me, then," said Eryximachus; "and so much the better for Aristodemus and Phaedrus and one or two more I could mention; we never could keep up with heavy drinkers like the rest of you. I say nothing of Socrates; for we know he's equal to any occasion, drunk or sober. And now, gentlemen, since nobody seems very anxious to get drunk tonight, I may perhaps be pardoned if I take this opportunity of saying a few words on the true nature of inebriation. My own experience in medicine has entirely satisfied me that vinous excess is detrimental to the human frame. And therefore I can never be a willing party to heavy drinking, as regards either myself or my friends—especially when one is only partially recovered from the excesses of the previous night."

'But here Phaedrus broke in. "My dear Eryximachus," he said, "I always do what you tell me to, specially when it really is a case of 'doctor's orders'; and I think the others would be well advised to do the same." Whereupon it was unanimously agreed that this was not to be a drunken party, and that the wine was to be served merely by way of refreshment.

'"Very well, then," said Eryximachus, "since it is agreed that we need none of us drink more than we think is good for us, I also propose that we dispense with the services of the flute-girl who has just come in, and let her go and play to herself or to the women inside there, whichever she prefers, while we spend our evening in discussion of a subject which, if you think fit, I am prepared to name."

'It was generally agreed that he should go on with his proposal, so he continued: "If I may preface my remarks by a tag from Euripides, 'the tale is not my own,' as Melanippe says, that I am going to tell, but properly belongs to my friend Phaedrus here, who is continually coming to me with the following complaint: Is it not, he asks me, an extraordinary thing, that, for all the hymns and anthems that have been addressed to the other deities, not one single poet has ever sung a song in praise of so ancient and so powerful a god as Love? Take such distinguished men of letters as Prodicus, for instance, with their eulogies in prose of Heracles and all the rest of them—not that *they*'re so much out of the way either, but do you know, I once came across a book which enumerated the uses of common salt and sang its praises in the most extravagant terms, and not only salt but all kinds of everyday commodities. Now isn't it, as I say, an extraordinary thing, Eryximachus, that while all these screeds have been written on such trivial subjects, the god of Love has found no man bold enough to sing his praises as they should be sung. Is it not, in short, amazing that there should be so little reverence shown to such a god!

'"This, gentlemen, is Phaedrus' complaint; and I must say I think it is justified. And, moreover, not only am I willing to oblige him with a contribution on my own account, but also I suggest that this is a most suitable occasion for each one of us to pay homage to the god. If, therefore, gentlemen, this meets with your approval, I venture to think we may spend a very pleasant evening in discussion. I suppose the best way would be for each in turn from left to right to address the company and speak to the best of his ability in praise of Love. Phaedrus, I think, should open the debate; for, besides being head of the table, he is the real author of our discussion."

'"The motion is carried, Eryximachus," said Socrates, "unanimously, I should think. Speaking for myself, I couldn't very well dissent when I claim that Love is the one thing in the world I understand; nor could Agathon and Pausanias; neither could Aristophanes, whose whole life is devoted to Dionysus and Aphrodite; no more could any of our friends who are here with us tonight. Of course, your procedure will come very hard on us who are sitting at the bottom of the table; but if the earlier speeches are fine enough, I promise you we shan't complain. So let Phaedrus go ahead with his eulogy of Love—and good luck to him."'

Then all the rest of them agreed, and told Phaedrus to begin—but before I go on I must make it quite clear that

Aristodemus did not pretend to reproduce the various speeches verbatim, any more than I could repeat them word for word as I had them from him. I shall simply recount such passages as the speaker or the thought itself made, so far as I could judge, especially memorable. As I was saying, then, Phaedrus opened with some such arguments as these: That Love was a great god, wonderful alike to the gods and to mankind: and that of all the proofs of this the greatest was his birth. 'The worship of this god,' he said, 'is of the oldest; for Love is unbegotten, nor is there mention of his parentage to be found anywhere in either prose or verse; while Hesiod tells us expressly that chaos first appeared, and then

> From chaos rose broad-bosomed earth, the sure
> And everlasting seat of all that is;
> And after, Love . . .

Acusilaus agrees with Hesiod, for he holds that after chaos were brought forth these twain, earth and Love; and Parmenides writes of the creative principle:

> And Love she framed the first of all the gods.

'Thus we find that the antiquity of Love is universally admitted, and in very truth he is the ancient source of all our highest good. For I, at any rate, could hardly name a greater blessing to the man that is to be, than a generous lover; or to the lover, than the beloved youth. For neither family, nor privilege, nor wealth, nor anything but Love can light that beacon which a man must steer by when he sets out to live the better life. How shall I describe it—as that contempt for the vile, and emulation of the good, without which neither cities nor citizens are capable of any great or noble work. And I will say this of the lover, that, should he be discovered in some inglorious act, or in abject submission to ill-usage, he could better bear that anyone—father, friends, or who you will—should witness it than his beloved. And the same holds good of the beloved: that his confusion would be more than ever painful if he were seen by his lovers in an unworthy light.

'If only, then, a city or an army could be composed of none but lover and beloved, how could they deserve better of their country than by shunning all that is base, in mutual emulation;

and men like these fighting shoulder to shoulder, few as they were, might conquer—I had almost said—the whole world in arms. For the lover would rather anyone than his beloved should see him leave the ranks or throw away his arms in flight—nay, he would sooner die a thousand deaths. Nor is there any lover so faint of heart that he could desert his beloved or fail to help him in the hour of peril; for the very presence of Love kindles the same flame of valour in the faintest heart that burns in those whose courage is innate. And so, when Homer writes that some god "breathed might" into one of the heroes, we may take it that this is what the power of Love effects in the heart of the lover.

'And again, nothing but Love will make a man offer his life for another's—and not only man but woman; of which last we Greeks can ask no better witness than Alcestis; for she alone was ready to lay down her life for her husband, for all he had a father and a mother, whose love fell so far short of hers in charity that they seemed to be alien to their own son, and bound to him by nothing but a name. But hers was accounted so great a sacrifice, not only by mankind but by the gods, that in recognition of her magnanimity it was granted—and among the many doers of many noble deeds there is only the merest handful to whom such grace has been given—that her soul should rise again from the Stygian depths.

'Thus heaven itself has a peculiar regard for ardour and resolution in the cause of Love. And yet the gods sent Orpheus away from Hades empty-handed, and showed him the mere shadow of the woman he had come to seek: Eurydice herself they would not let him take, because he seemed, like the mere minstrel that he was, to be a lukewarm lover, lacking the courage to die as Alcestis died for love, and choosing rather to scheme his way, living, into Hades. And it was for this that the gods doomed him, and doomed him justly, to meet his death at the hands of women.

'How different was the fate of Achilles, Thetis' son, whom they sent with honours to the Islands of the Blessed, because, after learning from his mother that if he slew Hector he should die, while if he spared him he should end his days at home in the fullness of his years, he made the braver choice and went to rescue his lover Patroclus, avenged his death, and so died, not only *for* his friend, but to be with his friend in death. And it was because his lover had been so precious to him that he was honoured so signally by the gods.

'I may say that Aeschylus has reversed the relation between them by referring to Patroclus as Achilles' darling; whereas Achilles, we know, was much handsomer than Patroclus or any of the heroes, and was besides still beardless and, as Homer says, by far the younger of the two. I make a point of this because, while in any case the gods display especial admiration for the valour that springs from Love, they are even more amazed, delighted, and beneficent when the beloved shows such devotion to his lover, than when the lover does the same for his beloved. For the lover, by virtue of Love's inspiration, is always nearer than his beloved to the gods. And this, I say, is why they paid more honour to Achilles than to Alcestis, and sent him to the Islands of the Blessed.

'In short, this, gentlemen, is my theme: that Love is the oldest and most glorious of the gods; the great giver of all goodness and happiness to men, alike to the living and to the dead.'

This, to the best of Aristodemus' recollection, was Phaedrus' speech. It was followed by several more which had almost, if not quite, escaped him; so he went straight on to Pausanias, who spoke as follows:

'I am afraid, my dear Phaedrus, that our arrangement won't work very well if it means that we are simply to pronounce a eulogy of Love. It would be all very well if there were only one kind of Love; but unfortunately this is not the case, and we should therefore have begun by stipulating which kind in particular was to receive our homage. In the circumstances I will try to set the matter right by first defining the Love whom we are to honour, and then singing his praises in terms not unworthy, I hope, of his divinity.

'Now you will all agree, gentlemen, that without Love there could be no such goddess as Aphrodite. If, then, there were only one goddess of that name, we might suppose that there was only one kind of Love; but since in fact there are two such goddesses there must also be two kinds of Love. No one, I think, will deny that there are two goddesses of that name: one, the elder, sprung from no mother's womb but from the heavens themselves, we call the Uranian, the heavenly Aphrodite; while the younger, daughter of Zeus and Dione, we call Pandemus, the earthly Aphrodite. It follows, then, that Love should be known as earthly or as heavenly according to the goddess in whose company his work is done. And our business, gentlemen—I need hardly say that every god must command our homage—our business at the moment is to define the attributes peculiar to each of these two.

'Now it may be said of any kind of action that the action itself, as such, is neither good nor bad. Take, for example, what we are doing now: neither drinking nor singing nor talking have any virtue in themselves, for the outcome of each action depends upon how it is performed. If it is done rightly and finely, the action will be good: if it is done basely, bad. And this holds good of loving, for Love is not of himself either admirable or noble, but only when he moves us to love nobly.

'Well then, gentlemen, the earthly Aphrodite's Love is a very earthly Love indeed, and does his work entirely at random. It is he that governs the passions of the vulgar; for, first, they are as much attracted by women as by boys; next, whoever they may love, their desires are of the body rather than of the soul; and, finally, they make a point of courting the shallowest people they can find, looking forward to the mere act of fruition and careless whether it be a worthy or unworthy consummation. And hence they take their pleasures where they find them, good and bad alike; for this is the Love of the younger Aphrodite, whose nature partakes of both male and female.

'But the heavenly Love springs from a goddess whose attributes have nothing of the female, but are altogether male; and who is also the elder of the two, and innocent of any hint of lewdness. And so those who are inspired by this other Love turn rather to the male, preferring the more vigorous and intellectual bent. One can always tell—even among the lovers of boys—the man who is wholly governed by this elder Love; for no boy can please him until he has shown the first signs of dawning intelligence, signs which generally appear with the first growth of beard. And it seems to me that the

man who falls in love with a youth of such an age will be prepared to spend all his time with him, to share his whole life
with him, in fact; nor will he be likely to take advantage of the
lad's youth and credulity by seducing him and then turning
with a laugh to some newer love.

'But I cannot help thinking, gentlemen, that there should
be a law to forbid the loving of mere boys, a law to prevent so
much time and trouble being wasted upon an unknown
quantity—for what else, after all, is the future of any boy, and
who knows whether he will follow the paths of virtue or of
vice, in body and in soul? Of course, your man of principle is
a law unto himself; but these followers of the earthly Love
should be legally compelled to observe a similar restraint—
just as we prevent them, as far as possible, from making love
to our own wives and daughters—for it is their behaviour that
has brought the name of Love into such disrepute that one has
even heard it held to be degrading to yield to a lover's solicitation. Anyone who can hold such a view must surely have in
mind these earthly lovers, with their offensive importunities;
for there can be nothing derogatory in any conduct which is
sanctioned both by decency and custom.

'Then again, gentlemen, may I point out that, while in all
the other States of Hellas the laws that deal with Love are so
simple and well defined that they are easy enough to master,
our own code is most involved. In Elis and Boeotia, for
instance, and wherever else the people are naturally inarticu-
late, it has been definitely ruled that it is right for the lover to
have his way; nor does any one, old or young, presume to say
that it is wrong; the idea being, I suppose, to save themselves
from having to plead with the young men for their favours—
which is rather difficult for lovers who are practically dumb.

'On the other hand, in Ionia and many other countries
under oriental rule, the very same thing is held to be disgrace-
ful. Indeed, the Oriental thinks ill not only of Love but also of
both philosophy and sport, on account of the despotism under
which he lives; for I suppose it does not suit the rulers for
their subjects to indulge in high thinking, or in staunch friendship and fellowship, which Love more than anything is likely
to beget. And those who seized the power here in Athens
learnt the same lesson from bitter experience, for it was the

might of Aristogeiton's love and Harmodius' friendship that brought their reign to an end. Thus, wherever the law enacts that it is wrong to yield to the lover, you may be sure that the fault lies with the legislators; that is to say, it is due to the oppression of the rulers and the servility of their subjects. On the other hand, wherever you find the same thing expressly sanctioned, you may blame the legislators' mental inertia.

'But in Athens, gentlemen, we have a far more admirable code—a code which, as I was saying, is not nearly so easy to understand. Take for instance our maxim that it is better to love openly than in secret, especially when the object of one's passion is eminent in nobility and virtue, and even if his personal appearance should lack the same distinction; and think how we all love to cheer the lover on, without the least idea that he is doing anything unworthy, and how we see honour in his success and shame in his defeat. And remember, gentlemen, what latitude the law offers to the lover in the prosecution of his suit, and how he may be actually applauded for conduct which, in any other circumstances or in any other cause, would call down upon him the severest censure.

'Imagine what would happen to a man who wanted to get money out of someone, or a post, or powers of some kind, and who therefore thought fit to behave as the lover behaves to his beloved—urging his need with prayers and entreaties, and vowing vows, and sleeping upon doorsteps; subjecting himself, in short, to a slavery which no slave would ever endure—why, gentlemen, not only his friends, but his very enemies, would do their best to stop him; for his enemies would accuse him of the most abject servility, while his friends would take him to task because they felt ashamed of him.

'But when it is a lover who does this kind of thing people only think the more of him; and the law expressly sanctions his conduct as the means to an honourable end. And, what is the most extraordinary thing of all, it is popularly supposed that the lover is the one man whom the gods will pardon for breaking his vows: for lovers' promises, they say, are made to be forsworn. And so, gentlemen, we see what complete indulgence, not only human but divine, is accorded to the lover by our Athenian code.

'In view of this, one would have thought that, here if anywhere, loving and being kind to one's lover would have been
positively applauded. Yet we find in practice that if a father
discovers that someone has fallen in love with his son, he puts
the boy in charge of an attendant, with strict injunctions not to
let him have anything to do with his lover; and if the boy's
little friends and playmates see anything of that kind going on,
you may be sure they'll call him names; while their elders will
neither stop their being rude nor tell them they are talking
nonsense. So if there were no more to it than that, anyone
would think that we Athenians were really shocked at the idea
of yielding to a lover.

'But I fancy we can account for the apparent contradiction
if we remember that the moral value of the act is not what one
might call a constant. We agreed that Love itself, as such, was
neither good nor bad, but only in so far as it led to good or bad
behaviour. It is base to indulge a vicious lover viciously, but
noble to gratify a virtuous lover virtuously. Now the vicious
lover is the follower of the earthly Love who desires the body
rather than the soul; his heart is set on what is mutable and
must be inconstant. And as soon as the body he loves begins to
pass the first flower of its beauty, he "spreads his wings and
flies away", giving the lie to all his pretty speeches and dis-
honouring vows: whereas the lover whose heart is touched by
moral beauties is constant all his life, for he has become one
with what will never fade.

'Now it is the object of the Athenian law to make a firm
distinction between the lover who should be encouraged and
the lover who should be shunned. And so it enjoins pursuit in
certain cases, and flight in others; and applies various touch-
stones and criteria to discriminate between the two classes of
lover and beloved. And this is why it is immoral, according to
our code, to yield too promptly to solicitation; there should
first be a certain lapse of time, which is generally considered to
be the most effective test. Secondly, it is immoral when the
surrender is due to financial or political considerations, or to
unmanly fear of ill-treatment; it is immoral, in short, if the
youth fails to show the contempt he should for any advantage
he may gain in pocket or position. For in motives such as these
we can find nothing fixed or permanent, except, perhaps, the

certainty that they have never been the cause of any noble friendship.

'There remains, therefore, only one course open to the beloved if he is to yield to his lover without offending our ideas of decency: it is held that, just as the lover's willing and complete subjection to his beloved is neither abject nor culpable, so there is one other form of voluntary submission that shall be blameless—a submission which is made for the sake of virtue. And so, gentlemen, if anyone is prepared to devote himself to the service of another in the belief that through him he will find increase of wisdom or of any other virtue, we hold that such willing servitude is neither base nor abject.

'We must therefore combine these two laws—the one that deals with the love of boys and the one that deals with the pursuit of wisdom and the other virtues—before we can agree that the youth is justified in yielding to his lover. For it is only when lover and beloved come together, each governed by his own especial law—the former lawfully enslaving himself to the youth he loves, in return for his compliance: the latter lawfully devoting his services to the friend who is helping him to become wise and good; the one sharing his wealth of wisdom and virtue, and the other drawing, in his poverty, upon his friend for a liberal education—it is then, I say, and only then, when the observance of the two laws coincides, that it is right for the lover to have his way.

'There is no shame in being disappointed of such hopes as these; but any other kind of hope, whether it comes true or not, is shameful in itself. Take the case of a youth who gratifies his lover in the belief that he is wealthy and in the hope of making money: such hopes will be none the less discreditable if he finds in the event that he has been the prey of a penniless seducer; for he will have shown himself for what he is, the kind of person, namely, who will do anything for money—which is nothing to be proud of. But suppose that he had yielded because he believed in his lover's virtue, and hoped to be improved by such an association: then, even if he discovered in the end that he had been duped by an unholy blackguard, there would still have been something noble in his mistake; for he, too, would have shown himself for what he was—the kind of person who will do anything for anybody for the sake of progress in the ways of virtue; and what, gentlemen, could be more admirable than that? I conclude, therefore, that it is right to let the lover have his way in the interests of virtue.

'Such, then, is the Love of the heavenly Aphrodite, heavenly in himself and precious alike to cities and to men, for he constrains both lover and beloved to pay the most earnest heed to their moral welfare; but all the rest are followers of the other, the earthly Aphrodite. And this, Phaedrus, is all I have to say, extempore, on the subject of Love.'

When Pausanias had paused—you see the kind of tricks we catch from our philologists, with their punning derivations—the next speaker, so Aristodemus went on to tell me, should have been Aristophanes; only as it happened—whether he'd been overeating I don't know—he had got the hiccups so badly that he really wasn't fit to make a speech. So he said to the doctor, Eryximachus, who was sitting next below him:

'Eryximachus, you'll either have to cure my hiccups or take my turn and go on speaking till they've stopped.'

'I'm prepared to do both,' said Eryximachus; 'I'll take your turn to speak, and then when you've recovered you can take mine. Meanwhile, you'd better try holding your breath, or if that won't stop your hiccups try gargling with a little water; or if it's particularly stubborn you'll have to get something that you can tickle your nostrils with, and sneeze; and by the time you've done that two or three times you'll find that it will stop, however bad it is.'

'Go ahead, then,' said Aristophanes; 'you make your speech; and I'll be doing as you say.'

Whereupon Eryximachus spoke as follows: 'Well, gentlemen, since Pausanias broke off, after an excellent beginning, without having really finished, I must try to wind up his argument myself. I admit that in defining the two kinds of Love he has drawn a very useful distinction; but the science of medicine seems to me to prove that, besides attracting the souls of men to human beauty, Love has many other objects and many other subjects; and that his influence may be traced both in the brute and the vegetable creations, and, I think I may say, in every form of existence—so great, so wonderful, and so all-embracing is the power of Love in every activity, whether sacred or profane.

'I propose, in deference to my own profession, to begin with the medical aspect. I would have you know that the body comprehends in its very nature the dichotomy of Love; for, as we all agree, bodily health and sickness are both distinct and dissimilar; and unlike clings to unlike. And so the desires of health are one thing, while the desires of sickness are quite another. I confirm what Pausanias has observed, that it is right to yield to the virtuous and wrong to yield to the vicious lover; and similarly, in the case of the body, it is both right and necessary to gratify such desires as are sound and healthy in each particular case; and this is what we call the art of medicine. But it is utterly wrong to indulge such desires as are bad and morbid, nor must anyone who hopes to become expert in this profession lend his countenance to such indulgence. For medicine may be described as the science of what the body loves, or desires, as regards repletion and evacuation; and the man who can distinguish between what is harmful and what is beneficial in these desires may claim to be a physician in the fullest sense of the word. And if he can replace one desire with another, and produce the requisite desire when it is absent, or, if necessary, remove it when it is present, then we shall regard him as an expert practitioner.

'Yes, gentlemen, he must be able to reconcile the jarring elements of the body, and force them, as it were, to fall in love with one another. Now, we know that the most hostile elements are the opposites; hot and cold, sweet and sour, wet and dry, and so on; and if, as I do myself, we are to believe these poets of ours, it was his skill in imposing love and concord upon these opposites that enabled our illustrious progenitor Asclepius to found the science of medicine.

'And so, gentlemen, I maintain that medicine is under the sole direction of the god of Love; as are also the gymnastic and the agronomic arts. And it must be obvious to the most casual observer that the same holds good of music—which is, perhaps what Heracleitus meant us to understand by that rather cryptic pronouncement: "The one in conflict with itself is held together, like the harmony of the bow and of the lyre." Of course it is absurd to speak of harmony as being in conflict, or as arising out of elements which are still conflicting; but perhaps he meant that the art of music was to create harmony by resolving the discord between the treble and the bass. There can certainly be no harmony of treble and bass while they are still in conflict, for harmony is concord, and concord is a kind of sympathy; and sympathy between things which are in conflict is impossible so long as that conflict lasts. There is, on the other hand, a kind of discord which it is not impossible to resolve, and here we may effect a harmony—as, for instance, we produce rhythm by resolving the difference between fast and slow. And just as we saw that the concord of the body was brought about by the art of medicine, so this other harmony is due to the art of music, as the creator of mutual love and sympathy. And so we may describe music, too, as a science of love, or of desire—in this case in relation to harmony and rhythm.

'It is easy enough to distinguish the principle of Love in this rhythmic and harmonic union; nor is there so far any question of Love's dichotomy. But when we come to the application of rhythm and harmony to human activities—as for instance the composition of a song, or the instruction of others in the correct performance of airs and measures which have already been composed—then, gentlemen, we meet with difficulties which call for expert handling. And this brings us back to our previous conclusion, that we are justified in yielding to the desires of the temperate—and of the intemperate in so far as such compliance will tend to sober them; and to this Love, gentlemen, we must hold fast, for he is the fair and heavenly one, born of Urania, the muse of heaven. But as for that other, the earthly Love, he is sprung from Polymnia, the muse of many songs; and whatever we have to do with him we must be very careful not to add the evils of excess to the enjoyment of the pleasures he affords—just as, in my own profession, it is an important part of our duties to regulate the pleasures of the table so that we may enjoy our meals without being the worse for them. And so in music, in medicine, and in every activity, whether sacred or profane, we must do our utmost to distinguish the two kinds of Love, for you may be sure that they will both be there.

'And again, we find these two elements in the seasons of

the year; for when the regulating principle of Love brings together those opposites of which I spoke—hot and cold, wet and dry—and compounds them in an ordered harmony, the result is health and plenty for mankind, and for the animal and vegetable kingdoms; and all goes as it should. But when the seasons are under the influence of that other Love, all is mischief and destruction; for now plague and disease of every kind attack both herds and crops; and not only these, but frost and hail and blight—and all of them are due to the uncontrolled and the acquisitive in that great system of Love which the astronomer observes when he investigates the movements of the stars and the seasons of the year.

'And further, the sole concern of every rite of sacrifice and divination—that is to say, the means of communion between god and man—is either the preservation or the repair of Love. For most of our impiety springs from our refusal to gratify the more temperate Love, and to respect and defer to him in everything we do; and from our following that other Love in our attitude towards our parents, whether alive or dead, and towards the gods. It is the diviner's office to be the guide and healer of these Loves, and his art of divination, with its power to distinguish those principles of human love that tend to decency and reverence, is, in fact, the source of concord between god and man.

'And so, gentlemen, the power of Love in its entirety is various and mighty, nay, all-embracing; but the mightiest power of all is wielded by that Love whose just and temperate consummation, whether in heaven or on earth, tends towards the good. It is he that bestows our every joy upon us, and it is through him that we are capable of the pleasures of society, aye, and friendship even, with the gods our masters.

'And now, gentlemen, if, as is not unlikely, there are many points I have omitted in my praise of Love, let me assure you that such omissions have been unintentional. It is for you, Aristophanes, to make good my deficiencies; that is unless you're thinking of some other kind of eulogy. But in any case, let us hear what you have to say—now you've recovered from your hiccups.'

To which, Aristodemus went on to tell me, Aristophanes replied:

'Yes, I'm better now, thank you; but not before I'd had recourse to sneezing—which made me wonder, Eryximachus, how your orderly principle of the body could possibly have called for such an appalling union of noise and irritation: yet there's no denying that the hiccups stopped immediately I sneezed.'

'Now, Aristophanes, take care,' retorted Eryximachus, 'and don't try to raise a laugh before you've even started. You'll only have yourself to thank if I'm waiting to pounce on your silly jokes, instead of giving your speech a proper hearing.'

Aristophanes laughed. 'You're quite right, Eryximachus,' he said. 'I take it all back. But don't be too hard on me. Not that I mind if what I'm going to say is funny—all the better if it is; besides, a comic poet is supposed to be amusing. I'm only afraid of being utterly absurd.'

'Now, Aristophanes,' said Eryximachus, 'I know the way you loose your shafts of ridicule and run away. But don't forget that anything you say may be used against you—and yet, who knows?—perhaps I shall decide to let you go with a caution.'

'Well then, Eryximachus,' Aristophanes began, 'I propose, as you suggested, to take quite a different line from you and Pausanias. I am convinced that mankind has never had any conception of the power of Love; for if we had known him as he really is, surely we should have raised the mightiest temples and altars, and offered the most splendid sacrifices, in his honour, and not—as in fact we do—have utterly neglected him. Yet he of all the gods has the best title to our service, for he, more than all the rest, is the friend of man: he is our great ally, and it is he that cures us of those ills whose relief opens the way to man's highest happiness. And so, gentlemen, I will do my best to acquaint you with the power of Love; and you in your turn shall pass the lesson on.

'First of all I must explain the real nature of man, and the change which it has undergone—for in the beginning we were nothing like we are now. For one thing, the race was divided into three; that is to say, besides the two sexes, male and female, which we have at present, there was a third which partook of the nature of both, and for which we still have a name, though the creature itself is forgotten. For though "hermaphrodite" is used nowadays only as a term of contempt, there really was a man-woman in those days, a being which was half male and half female.

'And secondly, gentlemen, each of these beings was globular in shape, with rounded back and sides, four arms and four legs, and two faces, both the same, on a cylindrical neck; and one head, with one face one side and one the other, and four ears, and two lots of privates, and all the other parts to match. They walked erect, as we do ourselves, backwards or forwards, whichever they pleased; but when they broke into a run they simply stuck their legs straight out and went whirling round and round like a clown turning cartwheels. And since they had eight legs, if you count their arms as well, you can imagine that they went bowling along at a pretty good speed.

'The three sexes, I may say, arose as follows: the males were descended from the sun, the females from the earth, and the hermaphrodites from the moon, which partakes of either sex; and they were round and they *went* round, because they took after their parents. And such, gentlemen, was their strength and energy, and such their arrogance, that they actually tried—like Ephialtes and Otus in Homer—to scale the heights of heaven and set upon the gods.

'At this Zeus took counsel with the other gods as to what was to be done. They found themselves in rather an awkward position; they didn't want to blast them out of existence with thunderbolts as they did the giants, because that would be saying goodbye to all their offerings and devotions; but at the same time they couldn't let them get altogether out of hand. At last, however, after racking his brains, Zeus offered a solution.

'"I think I can see my way", he said, "to put an end to this disturbance by weakening these people without destroying them. What I propose to do is to cut them all in half, thus killing two birds with one stone; for each one will be only half as strong, and there'll be twice as many of them, which will suit us very nicely. They can walk about, upright, on their two legs; and if ", said Zeus, "I have any more trouble with them, I shall split them up again, and they'll have to hop about on one".

'So saying, he cut them all in half just as you or I might chop up sorb-apples for pickling, or slice an egg with a hair. And as each half was ready he told Apollo to turn its face, with the half-neck that was left, towards the side that was cut away —thinking that the sight of such a gash might frighten it into keeping quiet—and then to heal the whole thing up. So Apollo turned their faces back to front, and, pulling in the skin all the way round, he stretched it over what we now call the belly—like those bags you pull together with a string— and tied up the one remaining opening so as to form what we call the navel. As for the creases that were left, he smoothed most of them away, finishing off the chest with the sort of tool a cobbler uses to smooth down the leather on the last; but he left a few puckers round about the belly and the navel, to remind us of what we suffered long ago.

'Now, when the work of bisection was complete it left each half with a desperate yearning for the other; and they ran together and flung their arms around each other's necks, and asked for nothing better than to be rolled into one. So much so, that they began to die of hunger and general inertia, for neither would do anything without the other. And whenever one half was left alone by the death of its mate, it wandered about questing and clasping in the hope of finding a spare half-woman—or a whole woman, as we should call her nowadays —or half a man. And so the race was dying out.

'Fortunately, however, Zeus felt so sorry for them that he devised another scheme. He moved their privates round to the front; for of course they had originally been on the outside— which was now the back—and they had begotten and conceived not upon each other, but, like the grasshoppers, upon the earth. So now, as I say, he moved their members round to the front and made them propagate among themselves, the male begetting upon the female—the idea being that if, in all these clippings and claspings, a man should chance upon a woman, conception would take place and the race could be continued; while if man should conjugate with man, he might at least obtain such satisfaction as would allow him to turn his attention and his energies to the everyday affairs of life. So you see, gentlemen, how far back we can trace our innate love for one another; and how this love is always trying to redintegrate our former nature, to make two into one, and to bridge the gulf between one human being and another.

'And so, gentlemen, we are all like pieces of the coins that children break in half for keepsakes—making two out of one, like the flat-fish—and each of us is for ever seeking the half that will tally with himself. The man who is a slice of the hermaphrodite sex, as it was called, will naturally be attracted by women—the adulterer, for instance; and women who run after men are of similar descent—as, for instance, the unfaithful wife. But the woman who is a slice of the original female is attracted by women rather than by men—in fact she is a Lesbian: while men who are slices of the male are followers of the male, and show their masculinity throughout their boyhood by the way they make friends with men, and the delight they take in lying beside them and being taken in their arms. And these are the most hopeful of the nation's youth, for theirs is the most virile constitution.

'I know there are some people who call them shameless; but they are wrong. It is not immodesty that leads them to such pleasures, but daring, fortitude, and masculinity; the very virtues that they recognize and welcome in their lovers—which is proved by the fact that in after years they are the only men who show any real manliness in public life. And so, when they themselves have come to manhood, their love in turn is lavished upon boys: they have no natural inclination to marry and beget children. Indeed, they only do so in deference to the usage of society, for they would just as soon renounce marriage altogether and spend their lives with one another.

'Such a man, then, gentlemen, is of an amorous disposition, and gives his love to boys, always clinging to his like. And so, when this boy-lover—or any lover, for that matter—is fortunate enough to meet his other half, they are both so intoxicated with affection, with friendship, and with love, that they cannot bear to let each other out of sight for a single instant. It is such reunions as these that impel men to spend their lives together, although they may be hard put to it to say what they really want with one another; and indeed, the purely sexual pleasures of their friendship could hardly account for the huge delight they take in one another's company. The fact is that both their souls are longing for a something else—a something to which they can neither of them put a name, and of which they can only give an inkling in cryptic sayings and prophetic riddles.

'Now, supposing Hephaestus were to come and stand over them with his tool-bag as they lay there side by side; and suppose he were to ask:

'"Tell me, my dear creatures; what do you really want with one another?"

'And suppose they didn't know what to say, and he went on:

'"How would you like to be rolled into one, so that you could always be together, day and night, and never be parted again? Because if that's what you want, I can easily weld you together; and then you can live your two lives in one, and, when the time comes, you can die a common death and still be two-in-one in the lower world. Now, what do you say? Is that what you'd like me to do? And would you be happy if I did?"

'We may be sure, gentlemen, that no lover on earth would dream of refusing such an offer, for not one of them could imagine a happier fate. Indeed, they would be convinced that this was just what they'd been waiting for—to be merged, that is, into an utter one-ness with the beloved.

'And so all this to-do is a relic of that original state of ours, when we were whole; and now, when we are longing for and following after that primeval wholeness, we say we are in love. For there was a time, I repeat, when we were one; but now, for our sins, God has scattered us abroad, as the Spartans scattered the Arcadians. Moreover, gentlemen, there is every reason to fear that, if we neglect the worship of the gods, they will split us up again; and then we shall have to go about with our noses sawn asunder, part and counterpart, like the *basso-rilievos* on the tombstones. And therefore it is our duty one and all to inspire our friends with reverence and piety, for so we may ensure our safety and attain that blessed union by enlisting in the army of Love and marching beneath his banners.

'For Love must never be withstood—as we do, if we incur the displeasure of the gods. But if we cling to him in friendship and reconciliation, we shall be among the happy few to whom it is given in these latter days to meet their other halves.

Now, I don't want any coarse remarks from Eryximachus. I don't mean Pausanias and Agathon, though for all I know they may be among the lucky ones, and both be sections of the male. But what I am trying to say is this: that the happiness of the whole human race, women no less than men, is to be found in the consummation of our love, and in the healing of our dissevered nature by finding each his proper mate. And if this be a counsel of perfection, then we must do what, in our present circumstances, is next best, and bestow our love upon the natures most congenial to our own.

'And so I say that Love, the god who brings all this to pass, is worthy of our hymns; for his is the inestimable and present service of conducting us to our true affinities; and it is he that offers this great hope for the future: that, if we do not fail in reverence to the gods, he will one day heal us and restore us to our old estate, and establish us in joy and blessedness.

'Such, Eryximachus, is my discourse on Love—as different as could be from yours. And now I must ask you again: will you please refrain from making fun of it, and let us hear what all the others have to say—or rather, the other two, for I see there's no one left but Agathon and Socrates.'

'Well, you shall have your way,' said Eryximachus; 'and, joking apart, I enjoyed your speech immensely. Indeed, if I were not aware that Socrates and Agathon were both authorities on Love, I should be wondering what they could find to say after being treated to such a wealth and variety of eloquence. But, knowing what they are, I've no doubt we'll find them equal to the occasion.'

To which Socrates retorted: 'It's all very well for you to talk, Eryximachus, after your own magnificent display; but if you were in my shoes now—or rather when Agathon has finished speaking—you'd be just as nervous as I am.'

'Now, Socrates,' said Agathon; 'I suppose you're trying to upset me by insisting on the great things my public is expecting of me.'

'My dear Agathon,' said Socrates, 'do you think I don't remember your ease and dignity as you took the stage with the actors the other day; and how you looked that vast audience in the face, as cool as you please, and obviously prepared to show them what you were made of? And am I to suppose that the sight of two or three friends will put you out of countenance?'

'Ah, but, Socrates,' protested Agathon, 'you mustn't think I'm so infatuated with the theatre as to forget that a man of any judgment cares more for a handful of brains than an army of blockheads.'

'Oh, I should never make such a mistake', Socrates assured him, 'as to credit *you*, my dear Agathon, with ideas that smacked of the illiterate. I've no doubt that if you found yourself in what you really considered intellectual company, you'd be more impressed by their opinion than by the mob's. But we, alas, can't claim to be your intelligent minority; for we were there too, you know, helping to swell that very crowd. But tell me: if you were with some other set of people, whose judgment you respected, I suppose you'd feel uncomfortable if they saw you doing anything you thought beneath you. Am I right?'

'Perfectly,' said Agathon.

'And yet', Socrates went on, 'you wouldn't feel uncomfortable if the *mob* saw you doing something equally unworthy?'

But here Phaedrus stepped in. 'My dear Agathon,' he said, 'if you go on answering his questions he won't care twopence what becomes of our debate, so long as there's someone he can argue with—especially if it's somebody good-looking. Now, much as I enjoy listening to Socrates' arguments, it's my duty as chairman to insist that each man makes his speech. So I must ask you both to pay your tribute to the god, and then you can argue as much as you please.'

'Phaedrus is right,' said Agathon; 'I'm quite prepared to speak. After all, I can argue with Socrates any day.

'Now, before I begin my speech I want to explain what sort of a speech I think it ought to be. For to my way of thinking the speakers we have heard so far have been at such pains to congratulate mankind upon the blessings of Love that they have quite forgotten to extol the god himself, and have thrown no light at all upon the nature of our divine benefactor. Yet surely, if we are to praise anyone, no matter whom, no matter how, there is only one way to go about it, and that is to indicate the nature of him whose praises we are to sing, and of

the blessings whose author he is. And so, gentlemen, with
Love: our duty is first to praise him for what he is; and
secondly, for what he gives.

'And so I shall begin by maintaining that, while all the gods
are blessed, Love—be it said in all reverence—is the blessedest
of all, for he is the loveliest and the best. The loveliest, I say,
because first of all, Phaedrus, he is the youngest of the gods,
which is proved by his flight, aye, and his escape, from the
ravages of Time, who travels fast enough—too fast, at any
rate, for us poor mortals. But Love was born to be the enemy
of age, and shuns the very sight of senility, clinging always to
his like in the company of youth, because he is young himself.

'I agree with most of Phaedrus' speech, but not with his
suggestion that Love was older than even Kronos or Iapetus.
No, gentlemen; Love, in his imperishable youth, is, I repeat,
the youngest of them all. And as for those old stories of the
gods we have read in Hesiod and Parmenides, we may be sure
that any such proceedings were the work not of Love but of
Necessity—if, indeed, such tales are credible at all. For if Love
had been among them then, they would neither have fettered
nor gelded one another; they would have used no violence at
all, but lived together in peace and concord as they do today,
and as they have done since Love became their heavenly over-
lord.

'It is clear, then, that he is young, and not only young but
dainty, with a daintiness that only a Homer could describe.
For it is Homer, is it not, who writes of Ate as being both
divine and dainty—dainty of foot, that is.

'He says:

> How delicate her feet who shuns the ground,
> Stepping a-tiptoe on the heads of men.

Now, you will agree that to prefer what is soft to what is hard
is proof enough of being dainty; and the same argument will
demonstrate the daintiness of Love; for he never treads upon
the ground, nor even on our heads—which, after all, are not so
very soft—but lives and moves in the softest thing in the whole
of nature. He makes the dispositions and the hearts of gods
and men his dwelling-place; not, however, without dis-
crimination; for if the heart he lights upon be hard he flies

away to settle in a softer. And so, not only treading on but altogether clinging to the softest of the soft, he must indeed be exquisitely dainty.

'We see, then, that Love is for one thing the youngest, and for another the most delicate, thing in the world; and thirdly, gentlemen, we find that he is tender and supple. For if he were hampered by the least inflexibility, how could he wind us in such endless convolutions, and steal into all our hearts so secretly; aye, and leave them, too, when he pleases? And that elegance of his which all the world confesses bears witness to his suppleness and symmetry; for Love and unsightliness will never be at peace. Moreover, his life among the flowers argues in himself a loveliness of hue; for Love will never settle upon bodies, or souls, or anything at all where there is no bud to blossom, or where the bloom is faded; but where the ground is thick with flowers and the air with scent, there he will settle, gentlemen, and there he loves to linger.

'I shall say no more about Love's loveliness—though much remains to say—because we must now consider his moral excellence, and in particular the fact that he is never injured by, nor ever injures, either god or man; for, whatever Love may suffer, it cannot be by violence—which, indeed, cannot so much as touch him; nor does he need to go to work by force, for the world asks no compulsion, but is glad to serve him; and, as we know, a compact made in mutual goodwill is held to be just and binding by the sovereign power of the law.

'Added to his righteousness is his entire temperance. I may take it, I suppose, for granted that temperance is defined as the power to control our pleasures and our lusts, and that none of these is more powerful than Love. If, therefore, they are weaker, they will be overcome by Love, and he will be their master; so that Love, controlling, as I said, our lusts and pleasures, may be regarded as temperance itself.

'Then, as to valour—as the poet sings:

> But him not even Ares can withstand.

For, as the story goes, it was not Ares that captured Love, but Love that captured Ares—love, that is, of Aphrodite. Now, the captor is stronger than the captive; and therefore Love, by overcoming one who is mightier than all the rest, has shown himself the mightiest of all.

'So much, gentlemen, for the righteousness of Love, his temperance, and his valour; there remains his genius, to which I must do such scanty justice as I can. First of all, then—if, like Eryximachus, I may give pride of place to my own vocation—Love is himself so divine a poet that he can kindle in the souls of others the poetic fire; for, no matter what dull clay we seemed to be before, we are every one of us a poet when we are in love. We need ask no further proof than this that Love is a poet deeply versed in every branch of what I may define succinctly as creative art; for, just as no one can give away what he has not got, so no one can teach what he does not know.

'And who will deny that the creative power by which all living things are begotten and brought forth is the very genius of Love? Do we not, moreover, recognize that in every art and craft the artist and the craftsman who work under the direction of this same god achieve the brightest fame, while those that lack his influence grow old in the shadow of oblivion? It was longing and desire that led Apollo to found the arts of archery, healing, and divination—so he, too, was a scholar in the school of Love; it was thus that the fine arts were founded by the Muses, the smithy by Hephaestus, and the loom by Pallas; and thus it was that Zeus himself attained the "governance of gods and men". And hence the actions of the gods were governed by the birth of Love—love, that is, of beauty; for, as we know, he will have none of ugliness. We are told, as I have already said, that in the beginning there were many strange and terrible happenings among them, because Necessity was king; but ever since the birth of the younger god, Love—the love of what is lovely—has showered every kind of blessing upon gods and men.

'And so I say, Phaedrus, that Love, besides being in himself the loveliest and the best, is the author of those very virtues in all around him. And now I am stirred to speak in numbers, and to tell how it is he that brings

>Peace upon earth; the breathless calm
>   That lulls the long-tormented deep;
>Rest to the winds; and that sweet balm
>   And solace of our nature, sleep.

And it is he that banishes estrangement and ushers friendship in; it is he that unites us in such friendly gatherings as this, presiding at the table, at the dance, and at the altar; cultivating courtesy and weeding out brutality; lavish of kindliness and sparing of malevolence; affable and gracious; the wonder of the wise, the admiration of the gods; the despair of him that lacks, and the happiness of him that has; the father of delicacy, daintiness, elegance, and grace, of longing and desire; heedful of the good and heedless of the bad; in toil or terror, in drink or dialectic, our helmsman and helper, our pilot and preserver; the richest ornament of heaven and earth alike; and, to conclude, the noblest and the loveliest of leaders, whom every one of us must follow, raising our voices in harmony with the heavenly song of Love that charms both mortal and immortal hearts.

'And there, my dear Phaedrus,' he said, 'you have my speech; such is my offering to the god of Love. I have done my best to be at once amusing and instructive.'

Agathon took his seat, continued Aristodemus, amid a burst of applause, for everybody felt that his youthful eloquence did honour to himself as well as to the god. Then Socrates turned to Eryximachus and said: 'Well, Eryximachus, you laughed at my misgivings, but you see—they've been justified by the event. There's not much left for *me* to say after the wonderful speech we've just had from Agathon.'

'I admit', Eryximachus replied, 'that your prognosis was correct so far as Agathon's eloquence was concerned; but as to your own embarrassment, I'm not so sure.'

'My dear sir,' protested Socrates, 'what chance have I or anyone of knowing what to say, after listening to such a flood of eloquence as that? The opening, I admit, was nothing out of the way, but when he came to his peroration, why, he held us all spellbound with the sheer beauty of his diction; while I, personally, was so mortified when I compared it with the best that I could ever hope to do, that for two pins I'd have tried to sneak away. Besides, his speech reminded me so strongly of that master of rhetoric, Gorgias, that I couldn't help thinking of Odysseus, and his fear that Medusa would rise from the lower world among the ghosts; and I was afraid that when Agathon got near the end he would arm his speech against mine with the Gorgon's head of Gorgias' eloquence, and strike me as dumb as stone.

'And then I saw what a fool I'd been to agree to take part in this eulogy of yours; and, what was worse, to claim a special knowledge of the subject, when, as it turned out, I had not the least idea how this or any other eulogy should be conducted. I had imagined in my innocence that one began by stating the facts about the matter in hand, and then proceeded to pick out the most attractive points and display them to the best advantage. And I flattered myself that my speech would be a great success, because I knew the facts. But the truth, it seems, is the last thing the successful eulogist cares about; on the contrary, what he does is simply to run through all the attributes of power and virtue, however irrelevant they may be; and the whole thing may be a pack of lies, for all it seems to matter.

'I take it then that what we undertook was to flatter, rather than to praise, the god of Love; and that's why you're all prepared to say the first thing about him that comes into your heads, and to claim that he either is, or is the cause of, everything that is loveliest and best. And of course the uninitiated are impressed by the beauty and grandeur of your encomiums; yet those who know will not be taken in so easily. Well then, I repeat, the whole thing was a misunderstanding, and it was only in my ignorance that I agreed to take part at all. I protest, with Euripides' Hippolytus, it was my lips that promised, not my soul; and that, gentlemen, is that. I won't have anything to do with your eulogy; and what is more, I couldn't if I tried. But I don't mind telling you the truth about Love, if you're interested; only, if I do, I must tell it in my own way; for I'm not going to make a fool of myself, at my age, trying to imitate the grand manner that sits so well on the rest of you. Now, Phaedrus, it's for you to say: have you any use for a speaker who only cares whether his matter is correct and leaves his manner to take care of itself?'

Whereupon Phaedrus and the others told him to go ahead and make whatever kind of speech he liked.

'Very well,' said he; 'but there's just one other thing: has our chairman any objection to my asking Agathon a few simple questions? I want to make certain we're not at cross purposes before I begin my speech.'

'Ask what you like,' said Phaedrus; 'I don't mind.'

Whereupon Socrates began, so far as Aristodemus could trust his memory, as follows:

'I must say, my dear Agathon, that the remarks with which you prefaced your speech were very much to the point. You were quite right in saying that the first thing you had to do was to acquaint us with the nature of the god, and the second to tell us what he did. Yes, your introduction was admirable. But now that we've had the pleasure of hearing your magnificent description of Love, there's just one little point I'm not quite clear about. Tell me; do you think it is the nature of Love to be the love of somebody, or of nobody? I don't mean, is he a mother's or a father's love?—that would be a silly sort of question: but suppose I were to ask you whether a father, *as* a father, must be *somebody*'s father, or not; surely the only reasonable answer would be that a father must be the father of a son or a daughter; am I right?'

'Why, yes,' said Agathon.

'And could we say the same thing about a mother?'

'Yes.'

'Good; and now, if you don't mind answering just one or two more questions, I think you'll see what I'm driving at. Suppose I were to ask: what about a brother, *as* a brother? Must he be *somebody*'s brother, or not?'

'Of course he must.'

'You mean, he must be the brother of a brother or a sister.'

'Precisely,' said Agathon.

'Well, then,' Socrates went on, 'I want you to look at Love from the same point of view; is he the love of something, or of nothing?'

'Of something, naturally.'

'And now,' said Socrates, 'bearing in mind what Love is the love of, tell me this: does he long for what he is in love with, or not?'

'Of course he longs for it.'

'And does he long for whatever it is he longs for, and is he in love with it, when he's got it, or when he hasn't?'

'When he hasn't got it, probably.'

'Then isn't it probable,' said Socrates, 'or rather isn't it certain, that everything longs for what it lacks; and that nothing longs for what it doesn't lack? I can't help thinking, Agathon, that that's about as certain as anything could be. Don't you think so?'

'Yes, I suppose it is.'

'Good. Now, tell me: is it likely that a big man will want to be big; or a strong man to be strong?'

'Not if we were right just now.'

'Quite; for the simple reason that neither of them would be lacking in that particular respect.'

'Exactly.'

'For if', Socrates continued, 'the strong were to long for strength, and the swift for swiftness, and the healthy for health—for I suppose it *might* be suggested that, in such cases as these, people long for the very things they have, or are, already; and so I'm trying to imagine such a case, to make quite sure we're on the right track—people in their position, Agathon, if you stop to think about them, are bound here and now to have those very qualities, whether they want them or not; so why should they trouble to want them? And so, if we heard someone saying, "I'm healthy, and I want to be healthy; I'm rich, and I want to be rich; and in fact I want just what I've got," I think we should be justified in saying, "But, my dear sir, you've *got* wealth and health and strength already, and what you want is to go on having them, for at the moment you've got them whether you want them or not. Doesn't it look as if, when you say, 'I want these things here and now,' you really mean, 'What I've got now, I want to go on keeping'?" Don't you think, my dear Agathon, that he'd be bound to agree?'

'Why, of course he would,' said Agathon.

'Well, then,' continued Socrates, 'desiring to secure something to oneself for ever may be described as loving something which is not yet to hand.'

'Certainly.'

'And therefore, whoever feels a want is wanting something which is not yet to hand; and the object of his love and of his desire is whatever he isn't, or whatever he hasn't got—that is to say, whatever he is lacking in.'

'Absolutely.'

'And now,' said Socrates, 'are we agreed upon the following

conclusions?—One, that Love is always the love of something; and two, that that something is what he lacks.'

'Agreed,' said Agathon.

'So far, so good,' said Socrates; 'and now, do you remember what you said were the objects of Love, in your speech just now? Perhaps I'd better jog your memory. I fancy it was something like this: that the actions of the gods were governed by the love of beauty—for of course there was no such thing as the love of ugliness. Wasn't that pretty much what you said?'

'It was,' said Agathon.

'No doubt you were right, too,' said Socrates; 'and if that's so, doesn't it follow that Love is the love of beauty, and not of ugliness?'

'It does.'

'And haven't we agreed that Love is the love of something which he hasn't got, and consequently lacks?'

'Yes.'

'Then Love has no beauty, but is lacking in it?'

'Yes, that must follow.'

'Well then, would you suggest that something which lacked beauty and had no part in it was beautiful itself?'

'Certainly not.'

'And, that being so, can you still maintain that Love is beautiful?'

To which Agathon could only reply: 'I begin to be afraid, my dear Socrates, that I didn't know what I was talking about.'

'Never mind,' said Socrates, 'it was a lovely speech; but there's just one more point: I suppose you hold that the good is also beautiful?'

'I do.'

'Then, if Love is lacking in what is beautiful, and if the good and the beautiful are the same, he must also be lacking in what is good.'

'Just as you say, Socrates,' he replied; 'I'm afraid you're quite unanswerable.'

'No, no, dear Agathon: it's the truth you find unanswerable, not Socrates. And now I'm going to leave you in peace, because I want to talk about some lessons I was given, once upon a time, by a Mantinean woman called Diotima; a woman who was deeply versed in this and many other fields of knowledge. It was she who brought about a ten years' postponement of the great plague of Athens on the occasion of a certain sacrifice; and it was she who taught me the philosophy of Love. And now I am going to try to connect her teaching—as well as I can without her help—with the conclusions that Agathon and I have just arrived at. Like him, I shall begin by stating who and what Love is, and go on to describe his functions; and I think the easiest way will be to adopt Diotima's own method of inquiry by question and answer. I'd been telling her pretty much what Agathon has just been telling me—how Love was a great god, and how he was the love of what is beautiful; and she used the same arguments on me that I've just brought to bear on Agathon to prove that, on my own showing, Love was neither beautiful nor good.

'Whereupon: "My dear Diotima," I asked, "are you trying to make me believe that Love is bad and ugly?"

'"Heaven forbid," she said; "but do you really think that if a thing isn't beautiful it's therefore bound to be ugly?"

'"Why, naturally."

'"And that what isn't learned must be ignorant? Have you never heard of something which comes between the two?"

'"And what's that?"

'"Don't you know," she asked, "that holding an opinion which is in fact correct, without being able to give a reason for it, is neither true knowledge—how can it be knowledge without a reason?—nor ignorance—for how can we call it ignorance when it happens to be true? So may we not say that a correct opinion comes midway between knowledge and ignorance?"

'"Yes," I admitted, "that's perfectly true."

'"Very well, then," she went on, "why must you insist that what isn't beautiful is ugly, and that what isn't good is bad? Now, coming back to Love: you've been forced to agree that he is neither good nor beautiful; but that's no reason for thinking that he must be bad and ugly. The fact is that he's between the two."

'"And yet", I said, "it's generally agreed that he's a great god."

'"It all depends", she said, "on what you mean by 'generally'; do you mean simply people that don't know anything about it; or do you include the people that do?"

'"I mean everybody."

'At which she laughed, and said: "Then can you tell me, my dear Socrates, how people can agree that he's a great god when they deny that he's a god at all?"

'"What people do you mean?" I asked her.

'"You for one, and I for another."

'"What on earth do you mean by that?"

'"Oh, it's simple enough," she answered. "Tell me: wouldn't you say that all the gods were happy and beautiful? Or would you suggest that any of them were neither?"

'"Good heavens, no!" said I.

'"And don't you call people happy when they possess the beautiful and the good?"

'"Why, of course."

'"And yet you agreed just now that Love lacks, and consequently longs for, those very qualities?"

'"Yes, so I did."

'"Then, if he has no part in either goodness or beauty, how can he be a god?"

'"I suppose he can't be," I admitted.

'"And now," she said, "haven't I proved that you're one of the people who don't believe in the divinity of Love?"

'"Yes, but what can he be, then," I asked her, "—a mortal?"

'"Not by any means."

'"Well, what then?"

'"What I told you before—half way between mortal and immortal."

'"And what do you mean by that, Diotima?"

'"A very powerful spirit, Socrates; and spirits, you know, are half way between god and man."

'"What powers have they, then?" I asked.

'"They are the envoys and interpreters that ply between heaven and earth, flying upwards with our worship and our prayers, and descending with the heavenly answers and commandments; and since they are between the two estates they weld both sides together and merge them into one great whole. They form the medium of the prophetic arts, of the priestly rites of sacrifice, initiation, and incantation, of divination and of sorcery; for the divine will not mingle directly with the human, and it is only through the mediation of the spirit world that man can have any intercourse, whether waking or sleeping, with the gods. And the man who is versed in such matters is said to have spiritual powers, as opposed to the mechanical powers of the man who is expert in the more mundane arts. There are many spirits, and many kinds of spirits, too; and Love is one of them."

"'Then who were his parents?" I asked.

"'I'll tell you,' she said, "though it's rather a long story. On the day of Aphrodite's birth the gods were making merry, and among them was Resource, the son of Craft; and when they had supped, Need came begging at the door because there was good cheer inside. Now, it happened that Resource, having drunk deeply of the heavenly nectar—for this was before the days of wine—wandered out into the garden of Zeus and sank into a heavy sleep; and Need, thinking that to get a child by Resource would mitigate her penury, lay down beside him and in time was brought to bed of Love. So Love became the follower and servant of Aphrodite because he was begotten on the same day that she was born; and further, he was born to love the beautiful, since Aphrodite is beautiful herself.

"'Then again, as the son of Resource and Need, it has been his fate to be always needy; nor is he delicate and lovely as most of us believe, but harsh and arid, barefoot and homeless, sleeping on the naked earth, in doorways, or in the very streets beneath the stars of heaven, and always partaking of his mother's poverty. But, secondly, he brings his father's resourcefulness to his designs upon the beautiful and the good; for he is gallant, impetuous, and energetic, a mighty hunter, and a master of device and artifice; at once desirous and full of wisdom, a lifelong seeker after truth, an adept in sorcery, enchantment, and seduction.

"'He is neither mortal nor immortal; for in the space of a day he will be now, when all goes well with him, alive and blooming, and now dying, to be born again by virtue of his father's nature, while what he gains will always ebb away as fast. So Love is never altogether in or out of need; and stands,

D 418

moreover, midway between ignorance and wisdom. You must understand that none of the gods are seekers after truth; they do not long for wisdom, because they are wise—and why should the wise be seeking the wisdom that is already theirs? Nor, for that matter, do the ignorant seek the truth or crave to be made wise; and indeed, what makes their case so hopeless is that, having neither beauty, nor goodness, nor intelligence, they are satisfied with what they are, and do not long for the virtues they have never missed."

"'Then tell me, Diotima,' I said, "who are these seekers after truth, if they are neither the wise nor the ignorant?"

"'Why,' she replied, "a schoolboy could have told you that, after what I've just been saying; they are those that come between the two, and one of them is Love. For wisdom is concerned with the loveliest of things; and Love is the love of what is lovely; and so it follows that Love is a lover of wisdom; and, being such, he is placed between wisdom and ignorance —for which his parentage also is responsible, in that his father is full of wisdom and resource, while his mother is devoid of either.

"'Such, my dear Socrates, is the spirit of Love, and yet I'm not altogether surprised at your idea of him, which was, judging by what you said, that Love was the beloved rather than the lover. So naturally you thought of Love as utterly beautiful; for the beloved is, in fact, beautiful, perfect, delicate, and prosperous—very different from the lover as I have described him."

"'Very well, dear lady,' I replied; "no doubt you're right. But in that case, what good can Love be to humanity?"

"'That's just what I'm coming to, Socrates,' she said. "So much, then, for the nature and the origin of Love; you were right in thinking that he was the love of what is beautiful. But suppose someone were to say: 'Yes, my dear Socrates; quite so, my dear Diotima; but what do you mean by the love of what is beautiful?—or, to put the question more precisely: What is it that the lover of the beautiful is longing for?'"

"'He is longing to make the beautiful his own,' I said.

"'Very well,' she replied; "but your answer leads to another question: What will he gain by making the beautiful his own?"

'This, as I had to admit, was more than I could answer on the spur of the moment.

'"Well, then," she went on, "suppose that, instead of the beautiful, you were being asked about the good. I put it to you, Socrates: What is it that the lover of the good is longing for?"

'"To make the good his own."

'"Then what will he gain by making it his own?"

'"I can make a better shot at answering that," I said; "he'll gain happiness."

'"Right," said she; "for the happy are happy inasmuch as they possess the good; and since there's no need for us to ask why men should want to be happy, I think your answer is conclusive."

'"Absolutely," I agreed.

'"This longing, then," she went on, "this love—is it common to all mankind? What do you think: do we all long to make the good our own?"

'"Yes," I said, "as far as that goes we're all alike."

'"Well then, Socrates, if we say that everybody always loves the same thing, does that mean that everybody is in love?—or do we mean that some of us are in love, while some of us are not?"

'"I was a little worried about that myself," I confessed.

'"Oh, it's nothing to worry about," she assured me; "you see, what we've been doing is to give the name of Love to what is only one single aspect of it; we make just the same mistake, you know, with a lot of other names."

'"For instance . . .?"

'"For instance, poetry. You'll agree that there is more than one kind of poetry in the true sense of the word—that is to say, calling something into existence that was not there before; so that every kind of artistic creation is poetry, and every artist is a poet."

'"True."

'"But all the same," she said, "we don't call them all poets, do we? We give various names to the various arts, and only call the one particular art that deals with music and metre by the name that should be given to them all: and that's the only art that we call poetry, while those who practise it are known as poets."

'"Quite."

'"And that's how it is with Love. For Love, 'that renowned and all-beguiling power', includes every kind of longing for happiness and for the good. Yet those of us who are subject to this longing in the various fields of business, athletics, philosophy, and so on, are never said to be in love, and are never known as lovers; while the man who devotes himself to what is only one of Love's many activities is given the name that should apply to all the rest as well."

'"Yes," I said, "I suppose you must be right."

'"I know it has been suggested", she continued, "that lovers are people who are looking for their other halves; but as I see it, Socrates, Love never longs for either the half or the whole of anything except the good; for men will even have their hands and feet cut off if they are once convinced that those members are bad for them. Indeed I think we only prize our own belongings in so far as we say that the good belongs to us, and the bad to someone else; for what we love is the good and nothing but the good. Or do you disagree?"

'"Good heavens, no!" I said.

'"Then may we state categorically that men are lovers of the good?"

'"Yes," I said, "we may."

'"And shouldn't we add that they long for the good to be their own?"

'"We should."

'"And not merely to be their own but to be their own for ever?"

'"Yes, that must follow."

'"In short, that Love longs for the good to be his own for ever?"

'"Yes," I said, "that's absolutely true."

'"Very well, then; and that being so, what course will Love's followers pursue, and in what particular field will eagerness and exertion be known as Love; in fact, what *is* this activity? Can you tell me that, Socrates?"

'"If I could, my dear Diotima," I retorted, "I shouldn't be so much amazed at *your* grasp of the subject; and I shouldn't be coming to you to learn the answer to that very question."

'"Well, I'll tell you, then," she said; "to love is to bring forth upon the beautiful, both in body and in soul."

'"I'm afraid that's too deep", I said, "for my poor wits to fathom."

'"I'll try to speak more plainly, then. We are all of us prolific, Socrates, in body and in soul; and when we reach a certain age our nature urges us to procreation. Nor can we be quickened by ugliness, but only by the beautiful. Conception, we know, takes place when man and woman come together; but there's a divinity in human propagation, an immortal something in the midst of man's mortality which is incompatible with any kind of discord; and ugliness is at odds with the divine, while beauty is in perfect harmony. In propagation, then, beauty is the goddess of both fate and travail; and so when procreancy draws near the beautiful it grows genial and blithe, and birth follows swiftly on conception. But when it meets with ugliness it is overcome with heaviness and gloom, and turning away it shrinks into itself and is not brought to bed, but still labours under its painful burden. And so, when the procreant is big with child, he is strangely stirred by the beautiful, because he knows that beauty's tenant will bring his travail to an end. So you see, Socrates, that Love is not exactly a longing for the beautiful, as you suggested."

'"Well, what is it, then?"

'"A longing, not for the beautiful itself, but for the conception and generation that the beautiful effects."

'"Yes. No doubt you're right."

'"Of course I'm right," she said. "And why all this longing for propagation?—because this is the one deathless and eternal element in our mortality. And since we have agreed that the lover longs for the good to be his own for ever, it follows that we are bound to long for immortality as well as for the good— which is to say that Love is a longing for immortality."

'So much I gathered, gentlemen, at one time and another from Diotima's dissertations upon Love. And then one day she asked me:

'"Well, Socrates, and what do you suppose is the cause of all this longing and all this Love? Haven't you noticed what an extraordinary effect the breeding instinct has upon both animals and birds; and how obsessed they are with the desire,

first to mate, and then to rear their litters and their broods;
and how the weakest of them are ready to stand up to the
strongest in defence of their young, and even die for them; and
how they are content to bear the pinch of hunger and every
kind of hardship, so long as they can rear their offspring?
With men," she went on, "you might put it down to the
power of reason; but how can you account for Love's having
such remarkable effects upon the brutes? What do you say to
that, Socrates?"

'Again I had to confess my ignorance.

'"Well," she said, "I don't know how you can hope to
master the philosophy of Love, if *that*'s too much for you to
understand."

'"But, my dear Diotima," I protested; "as I said before,
that's just why I'm asking you to teach me—because I realize
how ignorant I am. And I'd be more than grateful if you'd
enlighten me as to the cause not only of this but of all the
various effects of Love."

'"Well," she said, "it's simple enough, so long as you bear
in mind what we agreed was the object of Love. For here, too,
the principle holds good that the mortal does all it can to put
on immortality; and how can it do that except by breeding,
and thus ensuring that there will always be a younger generation to take the place of the old?

'"Now, although we speak of an individual as being the
same so long as he continues to exist in the same form, and
therefore assume that a man is the same person in his dotage
as in his infancy; yet, for all we call him the same, every bit of
him is different, and every day he is becoming a new man,
while the old man is ceasing to exist, as you can see from his
hair, his flesh, his bones, his blood, and all the rest of his body.
And not only his body: for the same thing happens to his soul;
and neither his manners, nor his disposition, nor his thoughts,
nor his desires, nor his pleasures, nor his sufferings, nor his
fears are the same throughout his life; for some of them grow,
while others disappear.

'"And the application of this principle to human knowledge
is even more remarkable; for not only do some of the things
we know increase, while some of them are lost, so that even in
our knowledge we are not always the same, but the principle

applies as well to every branch of knowledge. When we say we are studying, we really mean that our knowledge is ebbing away; we forget, because our knowledge disappears; and we have to study so as to replace what we are losing, so that the state of our knowledge may seem, at any rate, to be the same as it was before.

'"This is how every mortal creature perpetuates itself; it cannot, like the divine, be still the same throughout eternity; it can only leave behind new life to fill the vacancy that is left in its species by obsolescence. This, my dear Socrates, is how the body and all else that is temporal partakes of the eternal; there is no other way. And so it is no wonder that every creature prizes its own issue, since the whole creation is inspired by this love, this passion for immortality."

'"Well, Diotima," I said, when she had done; "that's a most impressive argument. I wonder if you're right."

'"Of course I am," she said, with an air of authority that was almost professorial. "Think of the ambitions of your fellow-men, and though at first they may strike you as upsetting my argument, you'll see how right I am if you only bear in mind that men's great incentive is the love of glory, and that their one idea is

To win eternal mention in the deathless roll of fame.

'"For the sake of fame they will dare greater dangers, even, than for their children; they are ready to spend their money like water and to wear their fingers to the bone; and, if it comes to that, to die. Do you think", she went on, "that Alcestis would have laid down her life to save Admetus, or that Achilles would have died for the love he bore Patroclus, or that Codrus, the Athenian king, would have sacrificed himself for the seed of his royal consort, if they had not hoped to win 'the deathless name for valour', which, in fact, posterity has granted them? No, Socrates, no. Every one of us, no matter what he does, is longing for the endless fame, the incomparable glory that is theirs; and the nobler he is, the greater his ambition, because he is in love with the eternal.

'"Well then," she went on, "those whose procreancy is of the body turn to woman as the object of their love, and raise a family, in the blessed hope that by doing so they will keep their memory green, 'through time and through eternity'. But those whose procreancy is of the spirit rather than of the flesh—and they are not unknown, Socrates—conceive and bear the things of the spirit. And what are they? you ask. Wisdom and all her sister virtues; it is the office of every poet to beget them, and of every artist whom we may call creative.

'"Now, by far the most important kind of wisdom", she went on, "is that which governs the ordering of society, and which goes by the names of justice and moderation. And if any man is so closely allied to the divine as to be teeming with these virtues even in his youth, and if, when he comes to manhood, his first ambition is to be begetting, he too, you may be sure, will go about in search of the loveliness—and never of the ugliness—on which he may beget. And hence his procreant nature is attracted by a comely body rather than an ill-favoured one; and if, besides, he happens on a soul which is at once beautiful, distinguished, and agreeable, he is charmed to find so welcome an alliance; it will be easy for him to talk of virtue to such a listener, and to discuss what human goodness is and how the virtuous should live—in short, to undertake the other's education.

'"And, so I believe, by constant association with so much beauty, and by thinking of his friend when he is present and when he is away, he will be delivered of the burden he has laboured under all these years; and what is more, he and his friend will help each other to rear the issue of their friendship —and so the bond between them will be more binding, and their communion even more complete, than that which comes of bringing children up, because they have created something lovelier and less mortal than human seed.

'"And I ask you, who would not prefer such fatherhood to merely human propagation, if he stopped to think of Homer, and Hesiod, and all the greatest of our poets; who would not envy them their immortal progeny, their claim upon the admiration of posterity? Or think of Lycurgus", she went on, "and what offspring he left behind him in his laws, which proved to be the saviours of Sparta and, perhaps, the whole of Hellas. Or think of the fame of Solon, the father of Athenian law; and think of all the other names that are remembered in Grecian cities and in lands beyond the sea for the noble deeds they did before the eyes of all the world, and for all the diverse virtues that they fathered. And think of all the shrines that have been dedicated to them in memory of their immortal issue; and tell me if you can of any *one* whose mortal children have brought him so much fame.

' "Well now, my dear Socrates, I have no doubt that even you might be initiated into these, the more elementary mysteries of Love; but I don't know whether you could apprehend the final revelation, for so far, you know, we are only at the bottom of the true scale of perfection. Never mind," she went on, "I will do all I can to help you understand, and you must strain every nerve to follow what I'm saying.

' "Well then," she began, "the candidate for this initiation cannot, if his efforts are to be rewarded, begin too early to devote himself to the beauties of the body. First of all, if his preceptor instructs him as he should, he will fall in love with the beauty of one individual body, so that his passion may give life to noble discourse. Next he must consider how nearly related the beauty of any one body is to the beauty of any other, when he will see that if he is to devote himself to loveliness of form it will be absurd to deny that the beauty of each and every body is the same. Having reached this point, he must set himself to be the lover of every lovely body, and bring his passion for the one into due proportion by deeming it of little or of no importance.

' "Next he must grasp that the beauties of the body are as nothing to the beauties of the soul; so that wherever he meets with spiritual loveliness, even in the husk of an unlovely body, he will find it beautiful enough to fall in love with and to cherish: and beautiful enough to quicken in his heart a longing for such discourse as tends towards the building of a noble nature. And from this he will be led to contemplate the beauty of laws and institutions; and when he discovers how nearly every kind of beauty is akin to every other he will conclude that the beauty of the body is not, after all, of so great moment.

' "And next, his attention should be diverted from institutions to the sciences, so that he may know the beauty of every kind of knowledge; and thus, by scanning beauty's wide horizon, he will be saved from a slavish and illiberal devotion to the individual loveliness of a single boy, a single man, or a single institution; and, turning his eyes towards the open sea of beauty, he will find in such contemplation the seed of the most fruitful discourse and the loftiest thought, and reap a golden harvest of philosophy; until, confirmed and strengthened, he will come upon one single form of knowledge, the knowledge of the beauty I am about to speak of. And here," she said, "you must follow me as closely as you can.

"'Whoever has been initiated so far in the mysteries of Love and has viewed all these aspects of the beautiful in due succession, is at last drawing near the final revelation. And now, Socrates, there bursts upon him that wondrous vision which is the very soul of the beauty he has toiled so long for. It is an everlasting loveliness which neither comes nor goes, which neither flowers nor fades; for such beauty is the same on every hand, the same then as now, here as there, this way as that way, the same to every worshipper as it is to every other.

"'Nor will his vision of the beautiful take the form of a face, or of hands, or of anything that is of the flesh; it will be neither words, nor knowledge, nor a something that exists in something else such as a living creature, or the earth, or the heavens, or anything that is, but subsisting of itself and by itself in an eternal oneness; while every lovely thing partakes of it in such sort that, however much the parts may wax and wane, it will be neither more nor less, but still the same inviolable whole.

"'And so, when his prescribed devotion to boyish beauties has carried our candidate so far that the universal beauty dawns upon his inward sight, he is almost within reach of the final revelation. And this is the way, the only way, he must approach, or be led towards, the sanctuary of Love: starting from individual beauties, the quest for the universal beauty must find him ever mounting the heavenly ladder, stepping from rung to rung, that is, from one to two, and from two to *every* lovely body; from bodily beauty to the beauty of institutions; from institutions to learning, and from learning in general to the special lore that pertains to nothing but the beautiful itself; until at last he comes to know what beauty is.

"'And if, my dear Socrates," Diotima went on, "man's life is ever worth the living, it is when he has attained this vision of the very soul of beauty. And once you have seen it you will never be seduced again by the charm of gold, of dress, of comely boys or lads just ripening to manhood; you will care nothing for the beauties that used to take your breath away and kindle such a longing in you, and many others like you, Socrates, to be always at the side of the beloved and feasting your eyes upon him; so that you would be content, if it were possible, to deny yourself the grosser necessities of meat and drink, so long as you were with him.

'"But if it were given to man to gaze on beauty's very self —unsullied, unalloyed, and freed from the mortal taint that haunts the frailer loveliness of flesh and blood—if, I say, it were given to man to see the heavenly beauty face to face, would you call *his*", she asked me, "an unenviable life, whose eyes had been opened to the vision, and who had gazed upon it in true contemplation until it had become his own for ever? And remember", she said, "that it is only when he discerns beauty itself through what makes it visible that a man will be quickened with the true, and not the seeming, virtue—for it is virtue's self that quickens him, not virtue's semblance. And when he has brought forth and reared this perfect virtue, he shall be called the friend of God; and if ever it is given to man to put on immortality, it shall be given to him."

'This, Phaedrus—this, gentlemen—was the doctrine of Diotima. I was convinced; and in that conviction I try to bring others to the same creed, and to convince them that, if we are to make this gift our own, Love will help our mortal nature more than all the world. And this is why I say that every man of us should worship the god of Love; and this is why I cultivate and worship all the elements of Love myself, and bid others do the same; and all my life I shall pay the power and the might of Love such homage as I can. So you may call this my eulogy of Love, Phaedrus, if you choose; if not, well, call it what you like.'

Socrates took his seat amid applause from everyone but Aristophanes, who was just going to take up the reference Socrates had made to his own theories, when suddenly there came a knocking at the outer door, followed by the notes of a flute and the sound of festive brawling in the street.

'Go and see who it is,' said Agathon to the servants. 'If it's one of our particular friends you can ask him in, but if not you'd better say the party's over and there's nothing left to drink.'

Well, it wasn't long before they could hear Alcibiades shouting in the courtyard, evidently very drunk, and demanding where Agathon was, because he *must* see Agathon at once. So the flute-girl and some of his other followers helped him stagger in, and there he stood in the doorway, with a mass of ribbons and an enormous wreath of ivy and violets sprouting on his head, and addressed the company.

'Good evening, gentlemen,' he said; 'I'm pretty well screwed already, so if you'd rather I didn't join the party, only say the word and I'll go away, as soon as I've hung this wreath on Agathon's head—which is what I really came for. I couldn't get along yesterday, so here I am tonight, with a bunch of ribbons on my head, all ready to take them off and put them on the head of the cleverest, the most attractive, and, I may say—well, anyway, I'm going to crown him. And now I suppose you're laughing at me, just because I'm drunk. Go on, have your laugh out, don't mind me; I'm not so drunk that I don't know what I'm saying, and you can't deny it's true. Well, what do you say, gentlemen? Can I come in on that footing? And shall we all have a drink together—or shan't we?'

At that they all cheered and told him to come in and make himself at home, while Agathon gave him a more formal invitation. And while his people helped him in he started pulling off the ribbons, so that he could transfer them to Agathon's head as soon as he was near enough. As it happened, the wreath slipped over his eyes and he didn't notice Socrates, although he sat down on the same couch, between him and Agathon—for Socrates had made room for him as soon as he came in. So down he sat, with a 'How d'you do!' to Agathon, and began to tie the ribbons round his head.

Then Agathon said to the servants: 'Here, take off Alcibiades' shoes, so that we can all three make ourselves comfortable.'

'Yes, do,' said Alcibiades; 'but just a minute, who's the third?' And when he turned round and saw who it was he leapt out of his seat and cried:

'Well, I'll be damned! You again, Socrates! So that's what

you're up to, is it?—the same old game of lying in wait and popping out at me when I least expect you. Well, what's in the wind tonight? And what do you mean by sitting *here*, and not by Aristophanes or one of these other humorists? Why make such a point of sitting next to the handsomest man in the room?'

'I say, Agathon,' said Socrates, 'I'll have to ask you to protect me. You know, it's a dreadful thing to be in love with Alcibiades. It's been the same ever since I fell in love with him: I've only got to look at anyone who's in the least attractive, or say a single word to them, and he flies into a fit of jealous fury, and calls me the most dreadful names, and behaves as if it was all he could do to keep his hands off me. So I hope you'll keep an eye on him, in case he tries to do me an injury. If you can get him to be friends, so much the better; but if you can't, and if he gets violent, you'll really have to protect me—for I shudder to think what lengths he might go to in his amorous transports.'

'Friends with *you*?' said Alcibiades. 'Not on your life! I'll be getting my own back on you one of these days; but at the moment—Agathon, give me back some of those ribbons, will you? I want to crown Socrates' head as well—and a most extraordinary head it is. I don't want him to say I wreathed a garland for Agathon and none for him, when *his* words have been too much for all the world—and all his life too, Agathon, not just the other day, like yours.'

So saying, he crowned Socrates' head with a bunch of ribbons, and took his seat again.

'And now, gentlemen,' he said, as he settled himself on the couch, 'can I be right in thinking that you're sober? I say, you know, we can't have this! Come on; drink up! You promised to have a drink with me. Now, I'll tell you, there's no one fit to take the chair at this meeting—until you've all got reasonably drunk—but me. Come on, Agathon, tell them to bring out something that's worth drinking out of; no, never mind,' he went on; 'here, you, just bring me that wine-cooler, will you?' (which he saw would hold a couple of quarts or so). He made them fill it up, and took the first drink himself, after which he told them to fill it again for Socrates, and remarked to the others:

'But I shan't get any change out of *him*. It doesn't matter *how* much you make him drink, it never makes him drunk.'

Meanwhile the servant had filled the wine-cooler up for Socrates and he had his drink; but here Eryximachus broke in:

'Is this the way to do things, Alcibiades?' he asked. 'Is there to be no grace before we drink? Are we to pour the wine down our throats like a lot of thirsty savages?'

'Why, there's Eryximachus,' said Alcibiades; 'the noblest, soberest father's soberest, noblest son, what?—Hallo, Eryximachus!'

'Hallo, yourself,' said Eryximachus. 'Well, what do you say?'

'What do *you* say?' retorted Alcibiades; 'we have to take *your* orders, you know. What's the tag?—"A good physician's more than all the world." So let's have your prescription.'

'Here it is, then,' said Eryximachus. 'Before you came in we had arranged for each of us in turn, going round from left to right, to make the best speech he could in praise of Love. Well, we've all had our turn; so since you've had your drink without having made a speech I think it's only right that you should make it now. And then, when you've finished, you can tell Socrates to do whatever you like and he can do the same to the next man on his right, and so on all the way round.'

'That's a very good idea, Eryximachus,' said Alcibiades, 'only you know it's hardly fair to ask a man that's more than half cut already to compete with a lot of fellows who are practically sober. And another thing, my dear Eryximachus; you mustn't believe a word of what Socrates has just been telling you. Don't you see that it's just the other way round? It's him that can't keep his hands off *me* if he hears me say a good word for anyone—god or man—but him.'

'Oh, do be quiet,' said Socrates.

'You can't deny it,' retorted Alcibiades. 'God knows I've never been able to praise anyone else in front of you.'

'Now there's a good idea,' said Eryximachus; 'why don't you give us a eulogy of Socrates?'

'Do you really mean that?' asked Alcibiades. 'Do you think I ought to, Eryximachus? Shall I go for him, and let you all hear me get my own back?'

'Here, I say,' protested Socrates; 'what are you up to now? Do you want to make me look a fool with this eulogy, or what?'

'I'm simply going to tell the truth—you won't mind that, will you?'

'Oh, of course', said Socrates, 'you may tell the truth; in fact, I'll go so far as to say you must.'

'Then here goes,' said Alcibiades. 'There's one thing, though: if I say a word that's not the solemn truth I want you to stop me right away and tell me I'm a liar—but I promise you it won't be my fault if I do. On the other hand, you mustn't be surprised if I tell them about you just as it comes into my head, and jump from one thing to another; you can't expect anyone that's as drunk as I am to give a clear and systematic account of all *your* eccentricities.

'Well, gentlemen, I propose to begin my eulogy of Socrates with a simile. I expect he'll think I'm making fun of him; but, as it happens, I'm using this particular simile not because it's funny but because it's true. What he reminds me of more than anything is one of those little Silenuses that you see on the statuaries' stalls; you know the ones I mean—they're modelled with pipes or flutes in their hands, and when you open them down the middle there are little figures of the gods inside. And then again he reminds me of Marsyas the satyr.

'Now I don't think even you, Socrates, will have the face to deny that you *look* like them; but the resemblance goes deeper than that, as I'm going to show. You're quite as impudent as a satyr, aren't you? If you plead not guilty I can call witnesses to prove it. And aren't you a piper as well? I should think you were; and a far more wonderful piper than Marsyas, who had only to put his flute to his lips to bewitch mankind. It can still be done, too, by anyone who can play the tunes he used to play; why, there wasn't a note of Olympus' melodies that he hadn't learnt from Marsyas. And whoever plays them, from an absolute virtuoso to a twopenny-halfpenny flute-girl, the tunes will still have a magic power, and by virtue of their own divinity they will show which of us are fit subjects for divine initiation.

'Now the only difference, Socrates, between you and Marsyas is that you can get just the same effect without any instrument at all; with nothing but a few simple words, not even poetry. Besides, when we listen to anyone else talking, however eloquent he is, we don't really care a damn what he says; but when we listen to you, or to someone else repeating what you've said, even if he puts it ever so badly, and never mind whether the person who's listening is man, woman, or child, we're absolutely staggered and bewitched. And speaking for myself, gentlemen, if I wasn't afraid you'd tell me I was completely bottled, I'd swear on oath what an extraordinary effect his words have had on me—and still do, if it comes to that. For the moment I hear him speak I am smitten with a kind of sacred rage, worse than any Corybant, and my heart jumps into my mouth and the tears start into my eyes—oh, and not only me, but lots of other men.

'Yes, I've heard Pericles and all the other great orators, and very eloquent I thought they were; but they never affected me like that; they never turned my whole soul upside down and left me feeling as if I were the lowest of the low; but this latter-day Marsyas here has often left me in such a state of mind that I've felt I simply couldn't go on living the way I did—now, Socrates, you can't say that isn't true—and I'm convinced that if I were to listen to him at this very moment I'd feel just the same again: I simply couldn't help it. He makes me admit that while I'm spending my time on politics I am neglecting all the things that are crying for attention in myself. So I just refuse to listen to him—as if he were one of those Sirens, you know—and get out of earshot as quick as I can, for fear he keeps me sitting listening till I'm positively senile.

'And there's one thing I've never felt with anybody else—not the kind of thing you'd expect to find in me, either—and that is a sense of shame. Socrates is the only man in the world that can make me feel ashamed. Because there's no getting away from it, I know I ought to do the things he tells me to; and yet the moment I'm out of his sight I don't care what I do to keep in with the mob. So I dash off like a runaway slave, and keep out of his way as long as I can; and then next time I meet him I remember all that I had to admit the time before, and naturally I feel ashamed. There are times when I'd honestly be glad to hear that he was dead; and yet I know that if he did die I'd be more upset than ever—so I ask you, what is a man to do?

'Well, that's what this satyr does for me, and plenty like me, with his pipings; and now let me show you how apt my comparison was in other ways, and what extraordinary powers he has got. Take my word for it, there's not one of you that really knows him; but now I've started on him I'll show him up. Notice, for instance, how Socrates is attracted by good-looking people, and how he hangs around them, positively gaping with admiration. Then again, he loves to appear utterly uninformed and ignorant—isn't that like Silenus? Of course it is. Don't you see that it's just his outer casing, like those little figures I was telling you about? But believe me, friends and fellow-drunks, you've only got to open him up and you'll find him so full of temperance and sobriety that you'll hardly believe your eyes. Because, you know, he doesn't really care a row of pins about good looks—on the contrary, you can't think how much he looks down on them—or money, or any of the honours that most people care about. He doesn't care a curse for anything of that kind, or for any of us either— yes, I'm telling you—and he spends his whole life playing his little game of irony, and laughing up his sleeve at all the world.

'I don't know whether anybody else has ever opened him up when he's been being serious, and seen the little images inside; but I saw them once, and they looked so god-like, so golden, so beautiful, and so utterly amazing, that there was nothing for it but to do exactly what he told me. I used to flatter myself that he was smitten with my youthful charms, and I thought this was an extraordinary piece of luck because I'd only got to be a bit accommodating and I'd hear everything he had to say—I tell you, I'd a pretty high opinion of my own attractions. Well, I thought it over, and then, instead of taking a servant with me as I always used to, I got rid of the man and went to meet Socrates by myself. Remember, I'm bound to tell you the whole truth and nothing but the truth; so you'd all better listen very carefully, and Socrates must pull me up if I begin telling lies.

'Well, gentlemen, as I was saying, I used to go and meet him, and then, when we were by ourselves, I quite expected to

E 418

hear some of those sweet nothings that lovers whisper to their
darlings when they get them alone—and I liked the idea of
that. But not a bit of it! He'd go on talking just the same as
usual till it was time for him to go; and then he said goodbye
and went.

'So then I suggested we should go along to the gymnasium
and take a bit of exercise together, thinking that something
was bound to happen there. And, would you believe it, we did
our exercises together and wrestled with each other time and
again, with not a soul in sight, and still I got no further. Well,
I realized that there was nothing to be gained in *that* direction,
but having put my hand to the plough I wasn't going to look
back till I was absolutely certain how I stood; so I decided to
make a frontal attack. I asked him to dinner, just as if I were
the lover trying to seduce his beloved, instead of the other way
round. It wasn't easy, either, to get him to accept, but in the
end I managed to.

'Well, the first time he came he thought he ought to go as
soon as we'd finished dinner, and I was too shy to stop him.
But next time I contrived to keep him talking after dinner, and
went on far into the night, and then, when he said he must be
going, I told him it was much too late and pressed him to stay
the night with me. So he turned in on the couch beside me—
where he'd sat at dinner—and the two of us had the room to
ourselves.

'So far I've said nothing I need blush to repeat in any
company; but you'd never have heard what I'm going to tell
you now if there wasn't something in the proverb: "Drunkards and children tell the truth"—drunkards anyway.
Besides, having once embarked on my eulogy of Socrates it
wouldn't be fair not to tell you about the arrogant way he
treated me. People say, you know, that when a man's been
bitten by a snake he won't tell anybody what it feels like
except a fellow-sufferer, because no one else would sympathize
with him if the pain drove him into making a fool of himself—
well, that's just how I feel, only I've been bitten by something
much more poisonous than a snake; in fact, mine is the most
painful kind of bite there is. I've been bitten in the heart, or
the mind, or whatever you like to call it, by Socrates' philosophy, which clings like an adder to any young and gifted

mind it can get hold of, and does exactly what it likes with it.
And looking round me, gentlemen, I see Phaedrus, and
Agathon, and Eryximachus, and Pausanias, and Aristodemus,
and Aristophanes, and all the rest of them; to say nothing of
Socrates himself; and every one of you has had his taste of this
philosophic frenzy, this sacred rage; so I don't mind telling
you about it because I know you'll make allowances for me—
both for the way I behaved with Socrates and for what I'm
saying now. But the servants must put their fingers in their
ears; and so must anybody else who's liable to be at all profane
or beastly.

'Well then, gentlemen, when the lights were out and the
servants had all gone, I made up my mind to stop beating
about the bush and tell him what I thought point-blank. So I
nudged him and said:

'"Are you asleep, Socrates?"

'"No, I'm not," he said.

'"Then do you know what I think?" I asked.

'"Well, what?"

'"I think", I said, "you're the only lover I've ever had
who's been really worthy of me; only you're too shy to talk
about it. Well, this is how I look at it: I think it'd be just as
absurd to refuse you *this* as anything else you wanted that
belonged to me or any of my friends. If there's one thing I'm
keen on it's to make the best of myself, and I think you're
more likely to help me there than anybody else; and I'm sure
I'd find it harder to justify myself to men of sense for refusing
to accommodate a friend of that sort than to defend myself to
the vulgar if I *had* been kind to him."

'He heard me out, and then said with that ironic simplicity
of his: "My dear Alcibiades, I've no doubt there's a lot in
what you say, if you're right in thinking that I have some kind
of power that would make a better man of you; because in that
case you must find me so extraordinarily beautiful that your
own attractions must be quite eclipsed. And if you're trying
to barter your own beauty for the beauty you have found in
me, you're driving a very hard bargain, let me tell you; you're
trying to exchange the semblance of beauty for the thing
itself—like Diomedes and Glaucus swopping bronze for gold.
But you know, my dear fellow, you really must be careful;

suppose you're making a mistake, and I'm not worth anything at all. The mind's eye begins to see clearly when the outer eyes grow dim—and I fancy yours are still pretty keen."

'To which I replied: "Well, I've told you exactly how I feel about it, and now it's for you to settle what's best for us both."

'"That sounds reasonable enough," he said; "we must think it over one of these days, and do whatever seems best for the two of us—about this and everything else."

'Well, by this time I felt that I had shot my bolt; and I'd a pretty shrewd idea that I'd registered a hit. So I got up, and, without giving him a chance to say a word, I wrapped my own cloak round him—for this was in the winter—and, creeping under his shabby old mantle, I took him in my arms and lay there all night with this godlike and extraordinary man—you can't deny that, either, Socrates. And after *that* he had the insolence, the infernal arrogance, to laugh at my youthful beauty and jeer at the one thing I was really proud of, gentlemen of the jury—I say "jury" because that's what you're here for, to try the man Socrates on the charge of arrogance—and believe it, gentlemen, or believe it not, when I got up next morning I had no more *slept* with Socrates, within the meaning of the act, than if he'd been my father or an elder brother.

'You can guess what I felt like after *that*: I was torn between my natural humiliation and my admiration for his manliness and self-control, for this was strength of mind such as I had never hoped to meet. And so I couldn't take offence and cut myself off from his society; but neither was there any way I could think of to attract him. I knew very well that I'd no more chance of getting at him with money than I had of getting at Ajax with a spear; and the one thing I'd made sure would catch him had already failed. So I was at my wits' end, and went about in a state of such utter subjection to the man as was never seen before.

'It was after all this, you must understand, that we were both sent on active service to Potidaea, where we messed together. Well, to begin with, he stood the hardships of the campaign far better than I did, or anyone else, for that matter. And if—and it's always liable to happen when there's fighting going on—we were cut off from our supplies, there was no one who put such a good face on it as him. But on the other hand, when there was plenty to eat he was the one man who really seemed to enjoy it; and though he didn't drink for choice, if we ever pressed him to he'd beat the lot of us; and, what's the most extraordinary thing of all, there's not a man living that's ever seen Socrates drunk. And I dare say he'll have a chance to show what he's made of before *this* party's over.

'Then again, the way he got through that winter was most impressive; and the winters over there are pretty shocking. There was one time when the frost was harder than ever, and all the rest of us stayed inside, or if we did go out we wrapped ourselves up to the eyes and tied bits of felt and sheepskins over our shoes; but Socrates went out in the same old coat he'd always worn, and made less fuss about walking on the ice in his bare feet than we did in our shoes. So much so, that the men began to look at him with some suspicion and actually took his toughness as a personal insult to themselves.

'Well, so much for that; and now I must tell you about another thing "our valiant hero dared and did" in the course of the same campaign. He started wrestling with some problem or other about sunrise one morning, and stood there lost in thought; and when the answer wouldn't come he still stood there thinking and refused to give it up. Time went on, and by about midday the troops noticed what was happening, and naturally they were rather surprised and began telling each other how Socrates had been standing there thinking ever since daybreak. And at last, towards nightfall, some of the Ionians brought out their bedding after supper—this was in the summer, of course—partly because it was cooler in the open air, and partly to see whether he was going to stay there all night. Well, there he stood till morning, and then at sunrise he said his prayers to the sun and went away.

'And now I expect you'd like to hear what kind of a show he made when we went into action; and I certainly think you ought to know. They gave me a decoration after one engagement, and do you know, Socrates had saved my life, absolutely single-handed; I'd been wounded and he refused to leave me; and he got me out of it, too, armour and all. And as you know, Socrates, I went straight to the General Staff and told them *you* ought to have the decoration; and you can neither deny that nor blame me for doing it. But the authorities thought they'd rather give it to me, because of my family connections and so forth, and you were even keener than they were that I should have it instead of you.

'And then, gentlemen, you should have seen him when we were in retreat from Delium. I happened to be in the cavalry, while he was serving with the line. Our people were falling back in great disorder and he was retreating with Laches when I happened to catch sight of them; I shouted to them not to be downhearted and promised to stand by them. And this time I'd a better chance of watching Socrates than I'd had at Potidaea—you see, being mounted, I wasn't quite so frightened. And I noticed for one thing how much cooler he was than Laches, and for another how—to borrow from a line of yours, Aristophanes—he was walking with the same "lofty strut and sideways glance" that he goes about with here in Athens. His "sideways glance" was just as unconcerned whether he was looking at his own friends or at the enemy; and you could see from half a mile away that if you tackled *him* you'd get as good as you gave—with the result that he and Laches both got clean away; for you're generally pretty safe if that's the way you look when you're in action; it's the man whose one idea it is to get away that the other fellow goes for.

'Well, there's a lot more to be said about Socrates, all very peculiar and all very much to his credit. No doubt there's just as much to be said about any of his little ways, but personally I think the most amazing thing about him is the fact that he is absolutely unique; there's no one like him, and I don't believe there ever was. You could point to some likeness to Achilles in Brasidas and the rest of them; you might compare Nestor and Antenor, and so on, with Pericles; there are plenty of such parallels in history; but you'll never find anyone like Socrates, or any ideas like his ideas, in our own times or in the past— unless, of course, you take a leaf out of my book and compare him, not with human beings, but with Silenuses and satyrs; and the same with his ideas.

'Which reminds me of a point I missed at the beginning; I should have explained how his arguments, too, were exactly like those Silenuses that open down the middle. Anyone listening to Socrates for the first time would find his arguments simply laughable; he wraps them up in just the kind of expressions you'd expect of such an insufferable satyr. He talks about pack-asses and blacksmiths and shoemakers and tanners; and he always seems to be saying the same old thing in just the same old way, so that anyone who wasn't used to his style and wasn't very quick on the uptake would naturally take it for the most utter nonsense. But if you open up his arguments, and really get into the skin of them, you'll find that they're the only arguments in the world that have any sense at all; and that nobody else's are so godlike, so rich in images of virtue, or so peculiarly, so entirely pertinent to those inquiries that help the seeker on his way to the goal of true nobility.

'And there, gentlemen, you have my eulogy of Socrates, with a few complaints thrown in about the unspeakable way he's treated me. I'm not the only one, either; there's Charmides, and Euthydemus, and ever so many more; he's made fools of them all, just as if he were the beloved, not the lover. Now, Agathon, I'm telling you this for your own good, so that you'll know what to look out for; and I hope you'll learn from our misfortunes, and not wait for your own to bring it home to you, like the poor fool in the adage.'

As Alcibiades took his seat there was a good deal of laughter at his frankness; especially as he seemed to be still in love with Socrates; but the latter said:

'I don't believe you're as drunk as you make out, Alcibiades, or you'd never have given the argument such a subtle twist and obscured the real issue; what you were really after—though you only slipped it in casually towards the end—was to make trouble between me and Agathon, so that I as your lover, and he as your beloved, should both belong to you and nobody else. But you can't humbug me; I can see what you're getting at with all this satyr and Silenus business. I only hope, Agathon, my dear, that he won't succeed; and I hope you'll be very careful not to let anybody come between us.'

'I'm inclined to think you're right, Socrates,' said Agathon; 'remember how he sat down in the middle so as to keep us apart. But I'll come round and sit next to you: so that won't help him very much.'

'Yes, do,' said Socrates; 'come round the other side.'

'Oh, God!' cried Alcibiades; 'look what I have to put up with! He's determined to drive me off the field. All the same, Socrates, I think you might let Agathon sit in the middle.'

'Oh, no,' said Socrates, 'that would never do. Now you've finished singing my praises I've got to do the same by the next man on my right; so you see, if he sat next to you, he'd have to start eulogizing me before he'd had my eulogy of him. So be a good chap and let the boy alone; you mustn't grudge him the praise I'm going to give him, because I'm dying to start my eulogy.'

'Aha!' cried Agathon. 'You don't catch me staying *here* much longer, Alcibiades; I shall certainly change places if it means a tribute from Socrates.'

'Oh, it's always the same,' said Alcibiades bitterly; 'no one else gets a look-in with the beauties when Socrates is there. Look how easily he trumped up an excuse for Agathon to sit beside him.'

And then, all of a sudden, just as Agathon was getting up to go and sit by Socrates, a whole crowd of revellers came to the door; and finding it open, as someone was just going out, they marched straight in and joined the party. No sooner had they sat down than the whole place was in an uproar; decency and order went by the board, and everybody had to drink the most enormous quantities of wine. By this time Eryximachus and Phaedrus and some of the others were beginning to leave, so Aristodemus told me; while he himself fell off to sleep.

He slept on for some time, for this was in the winter and the nights were long; and when at last he woke it was near daybreak and the cocks were crowing. He noticed that all the others had either gone home or fallen asleep, except Agathon and Aristophanes and Socrates, who were still awake and drinking out of an enormous bowl which they kept passing round from left to right. Socrates was arguing with the others; not that Aristodemus could remember very much of what he said, for, besides having missed the beginning, he was still more than half asleep; but the gist of it was that Socrates was forcing them to admit that the same man might be capable of writing both comedy and tragedy—that the tragic poet might be a comedian as well.

But as he clinched the argument, which the other two were scarcely in a state to follow, they began to nod: and first Aristophanes fell off to sleep and then Agathon, as day was breaking. Whereupon Socrates tucked them up comfortably and went away, followed, of course, by Aristodemus; and after calling at the Lyceum for a bath he spent the rest of the day as usual; and then, towards evening, made his way home to rest.

ION; OR, OF THE ILIAD

ST. I. 530–542

PERSONS OF THE DIALOGUE:

Socrates and Ion

SOCRATES. Hallo, Ion. Back among us again, I see. Been home to Ephesus, have you?

ION. No, Socrates, I've been to Epidaurus; they had a festival of Asclepius on there.

SOCR. Don't tell me they arrange rhapsody competitions at Epidaurus, too, to do the god honour?

ION. Oh yes they do—rhapsody, and all the other branches of music and literature.

SOCR. Well? Did you go in for it? And how did you get on?

ION. I took first prize, Socrates.

SOCR. That's good news; mind you carry off the Panathenaea as well now.

ION. I shall win that, too, God willing.

SOCR. You know, Ion, I've often envied you rhapsodist people your profession; because, besides being always beautifully got up, as your art demands, and looking your very best, you have to be grounded in a variety of good poets, especially Homer, the greatest and most inspired of them all, and have a thorough knowledge not merely of his verses but his meaning; that's something to make one envious. You see, no one can ever be a good rhapsodist unless he understands what the poet says. It's the rhapsodist's business to interpret the poet to his audience; and you can't do that properly if you don't know what the poet means. All that, surely, is something worth one's envy.

ION. You're right there, Socrates. It's that part of my profession which gives the most trouble—at least, it did to me, and I fancy there's no better man than myself when it comes to talking about Homer; so much so that neither Metrodorus

63

of Lampsacus, nor Stetimbrotus of Thasus, nor Glaucon nor
anyone else who has ever lived had such a wealth of beautiful
ideas to express about Homer as I have.

Socr. That's wonderful, Ion; I'm sure you won't refuse to give
me a demonstration.

Ion. It will certainly be worth your while, Socrates, to hear me
bringing out the beauties of Homer; I do it so well, you know;
I think I ought to be crowned with a golden crown by the
Homer Society.

Socr. Then I must certainly find time one of these days to give
you a hearing. But for the time being just answer me this: is
it only Homer you are good at, or Hesiod and Archilochus as
well?

Ion. No, just Homer; that's enough, so it seems to me.

Socr. Are there some subjects on which Homer and Hesiod both
speak alike?

Ion. I think there are; a good many of them.

Socr. Well now, to take these subjects, which could you explain
better, what Homer says about them, or what Hesiod does?

Ion. Both equally well, Socrates—at least, on those subjects
about which they both speak alike.

Socr. What about those where they differ? Prophecy, for
instance; Homer and Hesiod both say something about that.

Ion. Yes, I know.

Socr. Well now, taking all these two poets say about prophecy—
sometimes agreeing with one another, sometimes not—who
would give a better interpretation of it, you or a good prophet?

Ion. A prophet.

Socr. Now suppose you were a prophet; if you were able to
interpret these poets in passages where they agree, couldn't
you also explain them in places where they differ?

Ion. Of course I could.

Socr. Then how is it you are good at Homer but not at Hesiod
and the rest of the poets? Are Homer's themes any different
from those of other poets in general? Doesn't he usually tell of
warfare and the relations of men with one another, both good
and bad, the ordinary man and the professional? Doesn't he
describe the behaviour of the gods among themselves and in
regard to men, the way they behave? Events in the heavens
above and in the world beneath our own, and the origin of

gods and heroes? That's what Homer wrote his poetry about, isn't it?

Ion. Yes, that's true, Socrates.

Soc. Then what about the other poets? They use the same themes, don't they?

Ion. Yes, Socrates, but they haven't written poetry on the same level as Homer's.

Socr. Then how? Worse?

Ion. Very much so.

Socr. And Homer better?

Ion. Better? I should say so, by Zeus.

Socr. Now look, Ion, my dear fellow, when a lot of people are discussing a problem in arithmetic, and one of them gives the right answer, someone will know who is giving the right answer, won't he?

Ion. Yes, he will.

Socr. Well, who will it be, the same man who knows the others are wrong, or someone else?

Ion. The same man, of course.

Socr. Someone, that is, who knows his mathematics?

Ion. Yes.

Socr. Again, when a lot of people are discussing which kinds of food are wholesome, and one of them gives a sound opinion on the matter, will one person know that the man who is talking sense is in fact doing so, and another person know that the man who is talking nonsense is in fact wrong? Or will one and the same person know both?

Ion. The same person, naturally.

Socr. Who is this person? What do we call him?

Ion. A doctor.

Socr. In general, then, we may say that when a lot of people are discussing the same subjects, the same person will always know who is talking sense and who nonsense; or, turning it round, if he doesn't know who is talking nonsense, he won't know who is talking sense, either—at least, about the same subject.

Ion. That's right.

Socr. So the same person can judge equally well of either?

Ion. Yes.

Socr. Didn't you say that Homer and the other poets, including

Hesiod and Archilochus, speak of the same subjects, but not on the same level—one better, and the rest worse?

ION. That's what I said; and it's true.

SOCR. But if you knew the best speaker, you should also recognize the inferior speakers as such.

ION. So it would seem.

SOCR. Well then, my dear fellow, if we say that Ion is good at speaking about Homer and all the other poets, we shan't be wrong; because he himself admits that the same person is a fit judge of all who speak on the same subject, and that pretty well every poet writes on the same themes.

ION. Then why is it, Socrates, that whenever anyone is holding forth on some other poet, I pay no attention and can't put in a word worth talking about, but simply go to sleep; whereas, as soon as anyone mentions Homer, in a moment I'm wide awake and attentive and full of things to say?

SOCR. It's not hard to see why that is, my dear fellow. Anyone can see that your being able to expound Homer doesn't rest on any skill or understanding of yours, because if your ability were the outcome of art, you'd be able to expound all the other poets as well. Poetry, I take it, is something complete and whole in itself. Or don't you agree?

ION. I do.

SOCR. Well now, if you take any of the arts as a whole, will the same way of looking at it hold good for all the rest of the arts? Would you like to hear what I mean by that, Ion?

ION. I would, Socrates, by Zeus I would; I love listening to you wise people, you know.

SOCR. I wish what you say were true, Ion; but it is you rhapsodists and actors who are the wise ones, and those whose poetry you recite; I just tell the plain truth, as is only right for an unprofessional man like myself. Now, going back to what I asked you just now, look how ordinary and non-technical my statement was, the kind of thing anyone would know; I mean, about the way of looking at things being the same, whenever anyone took one of the arts as a whole. Let's think up an example . . . there's an art of painting as a whole, isn't there?

ION. Yes.

SOCR. And there are today, and have been before, many painters, both good and indifferent?

Ion. Certainly.

Socr. Well now, did you ever know of anyone who was clever at pointing out the good points and the bad ones in the pictures of Polygnotus, the son of Aglaophon, but was no good when it came to other painters? A man, I mean, who when called upon to give his verdict on Polygnotus or any other single painter you like, was wide awake and all attention, with plenty to say for himself?

Ion. No, by Zeus, certainly not.

Socr. Again, take sculpture; have you ever met anyone clever at explaining the merits of Daedalus the son of Metion—or Epeius the son of Panopeus, or Theodore the Samian, or any other individual sculptor—but who, given the works of other sculptors, is all at sea and falls asleep, unable to say a word?

Ion. No, by Zeus, I've never met anyone like that.

Socr. And if you take flute-playing, or playing the harp or singing to it, I don't imagine you've ever come across a man clever at giving his views on Olympus, or Thamyris or Orpheus, or Phemius the rhapsodist of Ithaca, but who when it comes to Ion of Ephesus is all at sea, unable to frame an opinion on the goodness or badness of his rhapsodizing.

Ion. Ah, there you have me, Socrates. All the same, I know very well in my own mind that I'm the best and most fluent talker about Homer in the world, and that everyone says I am, only not as regards other poets. Can you see why this should be so?

Socr. I do see, Ion; and I'm going to shew you what I think is the reason for it. As I said just now, this ability of yours to make fine speeches about Homer doesn't depend on any skill of yours; there's a divine power moving you, like the one in the stone that Euripides called a magnet, though most people call it the stone of Heraclea. Now this stone not only attracts iron rings but imparts to those rings the power to do what the stone itself does—to attract other rings in turn; so that sometimes you get a long chain of rings and bits of iron, all hanging one from the other, the power of all of them being dependent on that stone. In the same way the Muse first inspires men herself; and then from these men whom she inspires there is suspended a chain of others who catch the inspiration in their turn. All good epic poets, you know, compose all those lovely poems of theirs not by their own skill but in a state of inspiration and possession. It is the same with good lyric poets. Just as those who ape the Corybantes take leave of their senses and start dancing, so do lyric poets leave theirs when they compose those beautiful strains of theirs; when they fall beneath the spell of melody and the lilt of verse, they become frenzied and possessed, like priestesses of Bacchus, who when they are possessed draw milk and honey from the rivers, though unable to do so when in their right mind. The same effect is brought about by the soul of the lyric poet, as they themselves tell us. They tell us plainly, the poets, that they flit through the gardens and woody dells of the Muses, bringing us their songs from springs that flow with honey, like bees, and borne up, as they are, upon wings. What they say is true; for he's a lightsome thing, the poet is, a winged thing, a holy thing, unable to make poetry until he is inspired and bereft of his senses, his mind no longer within him. So long as a man retains dominion over his mind, he is powerless to make poetry or prophesy. But seeing that it's not by their own skill but by divine inspiration that they make poetry, using many beautiful expressions about heroic deeds, as you do about Homer, each of them can make poetry only of the kind to which the Muse urges them; this man dithyrambic verse, that man poems of praise, another man verses to be danced to, another epic verse or iambic. When it comes to other kinds of verse, none of them shews any ability. That's because it's not by their own skill that they speak but by divine power, since if they knew how to speak on one theme by their own skill, they'd know how to speak on every other. Because of this, God deprives the poets of their reason, using them as his ministers—as he does in the case of prophets and holy seers—so that we who hear them may know that it is not they who utter these inestimable words, they whose minds are gone; but God himself is the speaker, making his message known to us through their means. The most outstanding example of what I mean is Tynnichus the Chalcidian; he never wrote any other poem worth remembering except that paean which everybody sings, about the most beautiful of all poems, 'just something found by the Muses', as he himself

says. In his case particularly, I think, God is pointing out—
to prevent our doubting—that these lovely poems are not
human, not man's work, but divine, the work of the gods, and
that poets are simply the interpreters of the gods, each poet
being possessed by one or other of them; and to make the
point quite clear, the god in this case purposely sang his
loveliest melody through the lips of the most wretched of
poets. Don't you think that's true, what I say, Ion?

ION. It is, by Zeus. You know, Socrates, somehow you grip my
very soul with your words; and I look on good poets as men
sent by divine dispensation to interpret to us the mind of the
gods.

SOCR. Now don't you rhapsodists interpret the works of the
poets?

ION. Yes, you're right there.

SOCR. So you interpret the interpreters?

ION. Precisely.

SOCR. Now hang on to that, Ion, and give a straightforward
answer to what I'm going to ask you. When you're reciting
verse so beautifully and giving your audience their greatest
thrill—when you're singing of Odysseus, say, leaping to the
threshold, making himself known to the suitors and letting
fly with his arrows at their feet; or Achilles charging at
Hector, or one of those pathetic pieces about Andromache or
Hecuba or Priam—are you in your right mind at that moment?
Or are you beside yourself, your soul seeming to be carried off
in ecstasy to Ithaca or Troy or wherever else the scene of the
poem may be laid?

ION. What you say, Socrates, clearly bears out my own experience. Here is your straightforward answer. When I recite
something sad, my eyes fill with tears; when I say something
likely to cause fear or terror, my hair stands on end with
fright and my heart begins pounding.

SOCR. Now look, Ion, when a fellow dresses up in an embroidered
robe and golden crowns and starts bursting into tears at
festivals and banquets, although he hasn't lost any of his
trappings; or starts trembling with terror when he's standing
up among twenty thousand men, all friendly towards him, and
none of them robbing him of his clothes or doing him wrong
—can we say that at that moment he's in his right mind?

Ion. No, by Zeus, Socrates, we can't; he's not quite himself, and that's the truth.

Socr. I suppose you know you affect most of your audience in same way?

Ion. Know it? I should think I do. You see, I always take a look at them from up there on the platform, bathed in tears or with faces grimly set, so carried away they are by whatever's being recited. I've got to keep them well before my mind's eye, you know; because if I make them cry, I laugh and pocket my money; whereas if I make them laugh, it's my turn to cry, because then I'm the one to lose money.

Socr. You can see now, then, that the man in the audience is the last of those rings I spoke of as taking their power from one another by means of the stone of Heraclea? In the middle comes the rhapsodist and actor—yourself; the first ring is the poet himself. Now by means of all these God draws men's souls in whichever direction he wants, making each man's power depend on that of another. And just as the rings hang down from that stone, so from the Muse hangs suspended—at an oblique angle—a great long chain of members of the dancing-chorus, their instructors and sub-instructors. One poet will depend on one Muse, another on a different one—being possessed, we call it, and that's just about what it is, because the poet is held fast. Others in turn hang from those first rings—the poets, I mean—and get their inspiration from them, some from Orpheus, some from Musaeus; most of them, however, are possessed and inspired by Homer, including you, Ion. You are possessed by Homer, and whenever anyone recites anyone else's poetry, off you go to sleep, with not a word to say, whereas when anyone utters a line from that poet, in a moment you're wide awake, your heart leaps up, you have plenty to say. You see, it's not by any skill or understanding of yours that you say what you do, but by divine dispensation and possession. The Corybantes, you know, have a keen ear only for the music of the god they are possessed by, and have a wealth of expressions and gestures to suit that particular music; other kinds make no impression on them. In the same way, you, Ion, have plenty to say whenever anyone mentions Homer, but nothing in the case of other poets. There you have the answer to what you asked me, about your having plenty to say about Homer but nothing about other poets—your ability to interpret Homer is due to no skill of yours, but to divine dispensation.

Ion. An eloquent speech, Socrates. All the same, I'd be surprised if your eloquence could convince me that when I'm expounding Homer I'm possessed and out of my mind. I don't think you'd take me for a madman if you heard me talking about Homer.

Socr. But that's just what I want to do, to hear you; only first answer me this: of all the subjects Homer mentions, which are you best at speaking about? I mean, you're surely not equally good at them all.

Ion. You can take it from me, Socrates, there's nothing I can't talk about.

Socr. But surely you can't talk about subjects you know nothing about, but which come in Homer?

Ion. And what, may I ask, are these subjects which come in Homer and which I know nothing about?

Socr. Well, doesn't Homer mention the arts a number of times, and say a good deal about them? Chariot-driving, for instance; if I remember the lines, I'll quote them for you.

Ion. No, I'll do that; I remember how they go.

Socr. Very well, tell me what Nestor says to his son Antilochus when he warns him to mind the turning-post in the chariot-race—you know, the one held in honour of Patroclus.

Ion. He says:

> Do thou in thy fair-fashioned chariot lean but a space
> To the left of thy pair; but shout at the horse on the right
> And lay on the goad, the while that thy hands give him rein;
> But suffer the horse on the left to draw nigher the post
> Till the nave of the well-wrought wheel seems even to graze
> Its outermost edge; but see thou touch not the stone.

Socr. That will do. Now, Ion, who would know better whether Homer is correct in those lines or not—a doctor or a charioteer?

Ion. A charioteer, of course.

Socr. Is that because he's a master of the art, or for some other reason?

Ion. No, it's because he's a master of the art.

Socr. Hasn't each of the arts been divinely appointed to have a certain work as the sphere of its knowledge? What we know by the pilot's art we shan't by the doctor's?

ION. No, of course not.

SOCR. Nor know by the builder's art what we do by the doctor's?

ION. No, of course not.

SOCR. Isn't that how it is with all the arts, that what we know by one of them we shan't by another? But before we go on to that, just answer me this question: do you admit that any given art is different from the rest?

ION. Yes.

SOCR. Now I argue thus: when one branch of knowledge covers certain subjects and another branch covers others, I call one branch by one name and the other by a different one—don't you do the same?

ION. Yes.

SOCR. Yes, because if our knowledge covered the same subjects, what would be the point of giving those arts different names, if we got the same knowledge from both of them? For instance, I know that these fingers of mine are five in number; so do you. Now supposing I were to ask if you and I knew this fact by the same art—arithmetic, I mean—or by some other, you'd certainly say it was by the same art.

ION. Yes.

SOCR. Then tell me what I was going to ask you just now—do you think that this holds good for all the arts, that one must know certain things by one art and not by another? And that if a different art is in question, one must know different things by it?

ION. That's the way I see it, Socrates.

SOCR. So a man who hasn't mastered any given art will be unable to judge its terms and the practical side of it?

ION. That's right.

SOCR. Now, going back to those lines you were reciting, which would know better whether Homer was correct in them or not, you or a charioteer?

ION. A charioteer.

SOCR. That's because you're a rhapsodist and not a charioteer?

ION. Yes.

SOCR. Is the rhapsodist's art different from the charioteer's?

ION. Yes.

Socr. And, being different, it imparts a knowledge of different things?

Ion. Yes.

Socr. Then what about where Homer tells how Hecamede, Nestor's concubine, gives the wounded Machaon a drink to take? Something like this, it goes:

> Into Pramnian wine she grated a goatsmilk cheese
> With a grater of brass, and sprinkled barley-meal white.

Whose business is it to know really and truly whether Homer is right or wrong in saying that, the doctor's or the rhapsodist's? Is Homer correct in those lines or not? Which art has the better claim to make a proper decision on it, medicine or rhapsody?

Ion. Medicine.

Socr. What about when Homer says:

> Then down to the bottom she went, like a plummet of lead
> That, mounted upon the horn of an ox of the field,
> Goes down to the ravening fish with its burden of death?

To decide what is meant by these lines and pronounce them correct or not, are we to say they come under fishing rather than rhapsody?

Ion. Of course they come under fishing, Socrates.

Socr. Now look, suppose you were to question me and ask me this: 'See here, Socrates, since you can find passages in Homer for criticism in the light of one or other of the arts, see if you can find me something about prophecy and the prophet; the sort of things, I mean, he should have a knowledge of to be able to decide whether the poet has written about them well or badly'—see how easily and truly I could answer you. You see, Homer often mentions the subject in the Odyssey; for instance, where Theoclymenus, the prophet of the Melampians, says to the suitors:

> Poor wretches, what evil is this that ye suffer? In night
> Are shrouded the heads of you, shrouded your faces and limbs,
> And wailing flares forth, and tears lie wet on your cheeks.
> Crowded with ghosts is the porch and crowded the hall,
> That in darkness haste to the underworld. Aye, and the sun
> Is fled from the sky, and an evil mist spread about.

There are many passages in the Iliad, too—in the Fight by the
Walls, for instance. Homer says there:

> As they eagerly sought to pass on, came nigh them a bird,
> An eagle, flying aloft on the left of the host,
> With a monstrous snake in its claws, of the colour of blood,
> Still alive and gasping, and still with a mind to fight;
> For, writhing backward, it gave its captor a bite
> On the breast, by the neck. The eagle, stricken with pain,
> Losing its hold on the snake, let it fall to the ground,
> Where it dropped in the midst of the throng below, while
>   the bird
> With a screaming cry took wing with the breath of the wind.

It's passages like that, I'd say, that call for a prophet's attention
and await his verdict.

ION. And you're quite right to say so, Socrates.

SOCR. You're right to say so, too, Ion. Now come on, Ion; I've
been choosing you passages out of the Odyssey and the Iliad
dealing with the kind of things which concern prophets and
doctors and fishermen. So now you choose me some passages
—because you know much more Homer than I do—about
rhapsodists and the art of rhapsody; the kind of things that a
rhapsodist, more than any other man, should pay attention to
and give his verdict upon.

ION. Well, Socrates, I say that means everything.

SOCR. No you don't Ion; not everything. Or are you as forgetful
as all that? Though it doesn't do for a rhapsodist to be
forgetful, you know.

ION. What is it I'm forgetting, then?

SOCR. Don't you remember you said the rhapsodist's art was
different from the charioteer's?

ION. Yes, I remember that.

SOCR. And didn't you admit that, differing as it does, the subjects
of its knowledge will be different, too?

ION. Yes.

SOCR. According to what you say, then, the art of rhapsody will
not know everything, nor will the rhapsodist, either.

ION. Well, Socrates, everything except possibly the kind of
thing we've been quoting.

SOCR. By which you mean everything except what is closely connected with the other arts. But what *will* a rhapsodist know, if
he doesn't know everything?

Ion. He will know—at least, that's what I think—the proper sort of speech for a man to use, and for a woman, too; for the slave and the freeborn, for the man who is subject to authority as well as for the man who is in charge of things.

Socr. Well, take the man who is in charge of a ship when there's a storm at sea: will the rhapsodist know better than the pilot the proper sort of things the latter should say?

Ion. No, there it would be the pilot.

Socr. Then take the man who's in charge of an invalid; will the rhapsodist know better than the doctor the proper thing to say?

Ion. No, he wouldn't in that case, either.

Socr. But he will know the right sort of speech for a slave, didn't you say?

Ion. Yes.

Socr. Take a slave who looks after cattle; will the rhapsodist know better than the cowhand the proper things to say for calming down infuriated cows?

Ion. Of course not.

Socr. But will he know the right sort of things for a woman who spins wool to say about woolworking?

Ion. No.

Socr. Will he know the sort of thing a general haranguing his men should say?

Ion. Yes, that's the kind of thing a rhapsodist will know.

Socr. Now why? Is rhapsody one and the same as the art of war?

Ion. Well, at any rate, I should know the sort of things a general should say.

Socr. Perhaps that's because you're keen on army affairs, Ion. Now suppose you happened to be a horseman and a harpist into the bargain, you would know who rode well and who badly. But if I were to ask you, 'By what art do you tell which riders ride well? Is it a horseman or as a harpist?'—what answer would you give me?

Ion. 'As a horseman', I should say.

Socr. And if you could tell those who played the harp well, wouldn't you admit that you could tell it as a harpist, not as a horseman?

Ion. Yes.

Socr. Well, then, since you're well up in army matters,

do you know them as a student of strategy or as a good
rhapsodist?

Ion. I don't see that there's any difference.

Socr. What's that? You say there's no difference? Do you mean
that the art of rhapsody and the art of war are one thing, or
two?

Ion. One, I'd say.

Socr. So whoever is a good rhapsodist will be a good general as
well?

Ion. Certainly.

Socr. And whoever happens to be a good general will be a good
rhapsodist, too?

Ion. Well, no, I don't think that's right.

Socr. But you do hold that other principle, about a good
rhapsodist's being a good general, too?

Ion. Certainly I do.

Socr. Well now, you're the best rhapsodist in Greece, aren't
you?

Ion. Absolutely, Socrates.

Socr. And are you the best general in Greece, too, Ion?

Ion. You can be sure of that, Socrates; I learned it from Homer.

Socr. Then why in heaven's name, Ion, if you're the best
rhapsodist and the best general in Greece, do you go about
Greece rhapsodizing, but never command an army? Or do you
fancy there's a large demand among the Greeks for a rhapsodist crowned with a golden crown, and none for a general?

Ion. Well, Socrates, for one thing, our city is governed by yours
and under its command, and has no need of a general; and for
another, your city and the Lacedamonians would never choose
me for their general, because you both think yourselves
sufficient.

Socr. Ion, my good friend, have you ever heard of Apollodorus
of Cyzicum?

Ion. And who might he be?

Socr. A man the Athenians often chose for their general,
foreigner though he was. Then there's Phanosthenes of
Andros and Heraclides of Clazomenae, non-Athenians both of
them; but, when they shewed themselves to be worthy of
notice, this city of ours appointed them to lead her armies and
to fill other positions of authority. So if Ion of Ephesus seems

worth her notice, won't she choose him to lead her armies and shew him honour? After all, you Ephesians were Athenians to start with, weren't you? And Ephesus isn't a second-rate city, is it? But look here, Ion, if you're speaking the truth when you say that your ability to expound Homer is based on knowledge and skill, you're a fraud. Why? Because after assuring me of the variety and beauty of your Homeric lore and promising to give me a demonstration, you let me down, because you're nowhere near giving this demonstration of yours; and though I've been begging you for hours, you won't tell me what it is you're clever at, but, changing your shape as often as Proteus, you've been turning into this and that, till at last you give me the slip and emerge as a general, to avoid having to display your cleverness in the matter of Homeric wisdom. Now, as I said just now, if your performance is based on skill and if, after promising to give me a demonstration of Homer, you let me down, you're a fraud; if, on the other hand, you're not skilled, but utter all that wealth of beautiful words about Homer because by divine dispensation you are, unknown to yourself, possessed by the poet, you're not a fraud at all. So choose which you want us to think you—a fraud, or a man inspired.

ION. There's a lot of difference, Socrates. It's far better to be thought inspired.

SOCR. Very well, Ion, we'll allow you the better verdict of the two, and pronounce your interpretation of Homer to come not from skill but from inspiration.

MENO

ST. II. 70–100

PERSONS OF THE DIALOGUE:

Meno.   *Boy (one of Meno's slaves).*
Socrates.   *Anytus.*

Scene: Athens, *c.* 402 B.C.

MENO. Tell me, Socrates, is virtue something that can be taught, or is it a habit acquired by practice? If neither, is it innate in its possessor, or is it produced in some other way?

SOCRATES. You Thessalians, Meno, have long been one of the most remarkable of Greek peoples. You have always been admired for your splendid horsemanship, and celebrated for your great wealth; but in my opinion you have now won equal fame for your intelligence. Among those of you who have distinguished themselves in this last respect are the citizens of Larissa, one of whom is your lover Aristippus. This intellectual pre-eminence is entirely due to Gorgias.[1] In the course of his travels he visited Larissa, where his learning attracted the leading members of the Aleuadae (including Aristippus), and indeed all the most prominent people elsewhere in Thessaly. He taught you the art of supplying an immediate answer to any question proposed; and the magnificent confidence with which you do so is such as might be expected of men who are fully acquainted with the matter under discussion, whatever it may be. His method of teaching was to offer himself for free interrogation by any Greek who cared to question him; and he never failed to reply, no matter what he was asked. But here in Athens, my dear Meno, we have a very different state of affairs. With us there is what you might call a drought of

---

[1] Gorgias of Leontini (fifth century B.C.), one of the most famous of Greek sophists. He travelled widely, settled at Athens *c.* 427, but spent his last years in Thessaly.

wisdom; it seems as though wisdom has forsaken our borders in favour of yours. You have only to ask one of our people the question you have just put to me, and he will merely laugh and say: 'My good sir, you must think me a highly favoured mortal if you imagine I can tell you whether virtue is teachable or by what other means it is acquired; I am so far from knowing whether or not it can be taught, that I don't even know what it is.' Well, Meno, that is exactly my situation: I am just as badly off as my fellow citizens in this matter. I confess myself totally ignorant concerning the nature of virtue; so how can I possibly tell what attributes belong to it? Surely you don't suppose that a man utterly ignorant of who Meno is could say whether he is honourable, rich, magnanimous, or the reverse?

MENO. No, I don't. But look here, Socrates: don't you even know what virtue is? Are we to return home and tell my countrymen such a thing about you?

SOCR. Not only that, my friend. You can tell them this too: I have never come across a man anywhere whom I considered to possess knowledge of that kind.

MENO. What? Did you never meet Gorgias during his residence here?

SOCR. Oh indeed I did.

MENO. Well, did you come to the conclusion that he knew nothing about the matter?

SOCR. My memory is a little vague, Meno, so I can't say definitely what I thought of him at the time. It may be that he did know, and that you know what he said. Please, therefore, remind me of his teaching or, if you prefer, let me have your own opinion, which I imagine agrees with his.

MENO. Oh yes, it certainly does.

SOCR. Then let us leave Gorgias out of the discussion, especially as he is no longer with us. Tell me, in heaven's name, what *you* think virtue is. Speak out quite frankly; I should be delighted to be shown up as having uttered a patent untruth in saying I had never met anyone who knew what virtue is, when all the time both you and Gorgias were so well acquainted with its nature.

MENO. Why, Socrates, there is no difficulty in that. First, as regards the virtue of a man, it is quite plain that it consists in his ability to manage the affairs of his city, and in so doing to benefit his friends and harm his enemies, and to take care to avoid suffering harm himself. Then as regards the virtue of a woman: here again the particulars are not far to seek. Her virtue is looking after the house properly, keeping a watchful eye on everything indoors, and obeying her husband. Another kind of virtue belongs to a child, differing again in boys and girls; so too in the case of old folk. If you wish to go further still, there is a difference between the virtue of a freeman and that of a slave. There are many other kinds of virtue too; so one cannot be at a loss for an answer to the question, What is virtue? Some special form of virtue is peculiar to each individual at every stage of life and in every one of his activities. In the realm of vice also, Socrates, I imagine there are the same respective differences and the same variety.

SOCR. Meno, I consider myself highly favoured by Fortune; for while seeking one virtue I appear to have found a whole swarm of virtues hiving in your mind. Let me carry on with this metaphor from the world of bees. Supposing, Meno, I had asked you what is the real nature of the bee, and you had replied that there are many different kinds of bees, what would you have said if I had gone on to ask whether you described them as 'many and various' (i.e. differing one from another) *qua* bees, or whether you thought they differed in some other and purely accidental respect, e.g. beauty or size? How would you have answered this latter question?

MENO. I would have answered by saying that *qua* bees they differ in no way at all.

SOCR. Suppose I then said: 'Tell me now, Meno, what do you call this quality in respect of which they do not differ but are all exactly alike?' You could find me an answer, I presume.

MENO. Yes, I could.

SOCR. Well, the same principle applies in the case of the virtues; however many and various they may be, they all have one common character whereby they are virtues, and upon which, of course, one would do well to keep an eye when giving a definite answer to the question of what virtue really is. You see my point, don't you?

MENO. Fairly well, I think; but I don't understand you as clearly as I could wish.

SOCR. Well, look at it this way. You take the view that a man's virtue is one thing, a woman's another, and so on. Now do you think in that way about virtue alone, or would you say the same, for example, about the health, size, and strength of the body? I mean, do you think a man's health is one thing, a woman's another; or is it of the same character universally, wherever we find it, in a man or in anyone else?

MENO. I think that health is the same both in man and in woman.

SOCR. Then presumably you think in the same way about size and strength; you would hold that if a woman is strong, she is strong by reason of the same form, i.e. with the same strength. When I say 'the same' I mean that whether strength is in a man or in a woman it is, *qua* strength, identical in either case. But perhaps you think there is some difference.

MENO. No I don't.

SOCR. Well then, will there be any difference in virtue, *qua* virtue, according as it resides in a child or in an elderly person, in a man or in a woman?

MENO. This matter of virtue, Socrates, appears somehow to be not exactly parallel with your other examples.

SOCR. Why? Didn't you tell me that the virtue of a man consists in the good management of public affairs, and that of a woman in the good management of a house?

MENO. I did.

SOCR. I ask you then: Is it possible to manage a city-state well, or a house or anything else, unless one manages it temperately and justly?

MENO. Of course it's not.

SOCR. Then whoever manages temperately and justly will manage with temperance and justice?

MENO. That must be so.

SOCR. In which case both the man and the woman must have the same attributes of justice and temperance if they are to be good.

MENO. Evidently.

SOCR. Then how about a child or an old man? Can they ever be good if they are intemperate and unjust?

MENO. Certainly not.

SOCR. Only if they are temperate and just?

MENO Yes.

SOCR. So all mankind is good in the same way; for they become good when they acquire the same qualities?

MENO. Apparently.

SOCR. But if virtue were not the same thing in each and every one of them, they would *not* be good in the same way?

MENO. No.

SOCR. Seeing then that virtue is the same thing in all cases, try to remember and tell me what Gorgias had to say about it; his account, it seems, tallies with your own view.

MENO. Well, if you are looking for a single description to cover every case, I would say that it is simply the power of governing human beings.

SOCR. Just what I wanted! But is virtue the same in a child, Meno, and in a slave—an ability to govern each his master? And do you think one who governed would still be a slave?

MENO. I'd say most certainly not, Socrates.

SOCR. No, my excellent friend, most unlikely. And here is another point: you say that virtue is 'the ability to govern'; but ought we not to add 'justly, not unjustly'?

MENO. Yes, I think so; for justice, Socrates, is virtue.

SOCR. Virtue, Meno, or *a* virtue?

MENO. What do you mean by that?

SOCR. What I would in any other case. Take roundness, for example. I would call it *a* shape, not shape pure and simple; and I would do so because there are other shapes as well.

MENO. You would be quite right too. Indeed I myself call justice *a* virtue, and say there are other virtues besides.

SOCR. What are they? Tell me, just as I would tell you if you asked me for a list of shapes other than the round. Let me hear, then, what are the virtues other than justice.

MENO. Well, I suppose courage is a virtue, and temperance another; then there is wisdom, magnanimity—oh, and a whole lot more.

SOCR. There we are again, Meno! While seeking for one virtue we have once more run across a plurality of virtues, though in a different way. We cannot find what it is that makes all these things virtues.

MENO. No, Socrates; that is because I cannot follow your line of search, and discover a single virtue common to all, as one can in other cases.

Socr. No wonder; but I will do my best to help the discussion on its way. You understand of course that this principle of mine applies to everything. If someone asked you the question I put to you just now: 'What is shape, Meno?' and you replied: 'Roundness'; and then he said, as I did: 'Is roundness shape, or *a* shape?' I suppose you would answer: '*A* shape'?

Meno. Certainly I would.

Socr. And you would do so because there are other shapes in addition to the round.

Meno. Exactly.

Socr. Would you have an answer ready if he asked you this further question: 'What are those other shapes?'?

Meno. I would.

Socr. Suppose again that he asked you 'What is colour?' and on your answering 'White' he proceeded to inquire, 'Is "white" colour or *a* colour?' you would reply: '*A* colour', because there happen to be other colours besides?

Meno. I would.

Socr. And if he bade you enumerate other colours, you would tell him of others that are colours no less than is white?

Meno. Yes.

Socr. Suppose he pressed the argument, as I do, and said: 'We are always reaching plurality; don't take that line with me. You give a common name to each instance of shape; I mean, you enumerate a series of things and tell me that every one of them is shape, even though some of them are the contrary of others. Very well then, *what is it* that comprises the round as well as the straight—this thing which you call shape, telling me that the round is no more shape than is the straight?' That's what you say, is it not?

Meno. It is.

Socr. I ask you then: Do your words mean that round is no more round than straight, or straight no more straight than round?

Meno. No, Socrates, I don't mean that.

Socr. What you mean then is that the round is no more a shape than the straight, or the straight than the round.

Meno. True.

Socr. Well, see if you can tell me what it is that is described by this word 'shape'. Suppose that in reply to such a question, either about shape or about colour, you had answered: 'Sir, I don't understand what you are looking for, or even what you mean.' The questioner might well have been surprised, and exclaimed: 'Don't you understand that I am seeking for that which is the same common element in all these things—the round, the straight, and all the rest?' Would you still be stuck for an answer, Meno, if you were questioned about other terms and asked: What is it that is common to the round and the straight and everything else that you call shapes—the same in all? Try to tell me; it will help you to an answer about virtue.

MENO. No, Socrates. Tell me yourself what shape is.

SOCR. You wish me to do you the favour?

MENO. Please.

SOCR. If I do so, will you tell me what virtue is?

MENO. I will.

SOCR. Let us then do our best; it is worth our while.

MENO. It certainly is.

SOCR. Come now; let me see if I can tell you what shape is. I wonder if you'll agree to the following description: Shape, let us say, is the one and only thing that always accompanies colour. Does that satisfy you, or are you looking for something else? I must say, I'd be content if you gave me a similar account of virtue.

MENO. But, Socrates, it is a silly description.

SOCR. How so?

MENO. According to you, shape is that which always accompanies colour. That is all very well; but if someone said that he did not know what colour is—that he was just as ignorant about colour as about shape—what sort of answer would you have given him?

SOCR. I would have told the truth; and if my questioner happened to be one of those eristic and contentious professors, I would say to him: 'You've had my answer; if it is wrong it is up to you to examine and refute it.' But if, like you and me here now, we were friends and felt inclined for debate, I should have to reply in some less peremptory tone more suited to dialectic. The more dialectical way, I suppose, is not merely to give a true answer, but also to make use of those points which the person questioned admits he knows. I shall

G 418

therefore now attempt to argue with you in that way. Tell me, is there something you call an end; such a thing, I mean, as a limit or extremity? I use all these terms in the same sense, though I dare say Prodicus [1] might quarrel with us. But you, I feel certain, would refer to a thing as terminated or ended; something of that kind is what I mean—nothing complicated.

MENO. Yes, I do, and I believe I understand what you have in mind.

SOCR. Well then, there is something you call a surface, and another thing you call a solid—two terms employed in geometrical problems?

MENO. I do call certain things by those names.

SOCR. Very good; from all this you are now able to infer what I mean by shape. In every instance of shape I call that 'shape' in which the solid ends; briefly I should define shape as the 'limit of solid'.

MENO. And what do you say colour is?

SOCR. Now that, Meno, is most unkind. You set an old man the task of answering questions, yet you yourself won't try to remember and tell me what account Gorgias gives of virtue.

MENO. I will do so after you have told me what colour is.

SOCR. Meno, a blindfolded man could tell from your manner of discussing that you are handsome and still have lovers.

MENO. How so?

SOCR. Because you invariably speak in that peremptory fashion, after the manner of spoilt beauties, who wield despotic power so long as they are in the heyday of their charms. You have also, I dare say, noticed my weakness for handsome men. So I will indulge you and reply.

MENO. Oh, you must.

SOCR. Would you like me to answer you in the style of Gorgias, which you would most easily follow?

MENO. Yes, indeed I would.

SOCR. Am I not right in saying that you both accept the doctrine of Empedocles that there are certain effluences [2] of existent things?

---

[1] An expert in fine verbal distinctions. Cf. *Protag.* 337.
[2] According to Empedocles, material objects are known to us through effluences or films given off by them and adapted in various ways to our sense-organs.

MENO. We hold that view strongly.

SOCR. And passages into which and through which the effluences pass?

MENO. Certainly.

SOCR. And some of the effluences fit into various passages, while others are too large or too small?

MENO. That is so.

SOCR. You admit also that there is something you call sight?

MENO. Yes.

SOCR. Very well then, 'conceive my meaning', as Pindar says: colour is an effluence of shapes, commensurate with sight and sensible.

MENO. Socrates, I don't think you could find a better answer.

SOCR. You may think so because you are accustomed to its terminology, and at the same time I fancy you detect that it enables you to tell what sound and smell are, and many other things of the kind.

MENO. Certainly.

SOCR. The answer I gave you, Meno, was in the lofty poetic style, and it therefore satisfied you more than my definition of shape.

MENO. It certainly did.

SOCR. And yet, son of Alexidemus, I feel pretty sure that the other was in fact the better. I think you would come round to the same view were you not obliged, as you were saying yesterday, to leave Athens before the Mysteries, and could stay to be initiated.

MENO. If you would tell me a lot of other things like this, I would certainly stay.

SOCR. I will do my very best to continue in the same style, for my own sake as well as for yours, though I fear I may not succeed in maintaining that level. But it is now your turn to see whether you can fulfil your part of the agreement by telling me what virtue is—virtue in general. Don't go on producing a plural from the singular, as the wits say whenever one breaks something. Leave virtue whole and sound, and tell me what it is. I have already given you the pattern.

MENO. Well, Socrates, I think virtue is, in the poet's words, 'to rejoice in things honourable and be able for them'; and that, I say, is virtue—to desire what is honourable and be able to procure it.

SOCR. Then do you say that he who desires what is honourable
desires what is good?

MENO. Certainly.

SOCR. Implying that there are some who desire what is evil,
others who desire what is good? Don't you think, my friend,
that *all* men desire what is good?

MENO. No, I don't.

SOCR. There are some who desire the evil?

MENO. Yes.

SOCR. Thinking the evil to be good, do you mean, or recog-
nizing it as evil and yet desiring it?

MENO. I answer Yes to both those questions.

SOCR. Do you really believe, Meno, that anyone knows the evil
to be evil and desires it nevertheless?

MENO. Undoubtedly.

SOCR. What do you mean by 'desires'? Desires to possess it?

MENO. Yes. What else could I mean?

SOCR. Does he imagine that the evil benefits its possessor, or
does he know that it harms him?

MENO. There are some who think the evil is advantageous, and
others who know it to be harmful.

SOCR. And, in your opinion, do those who imagine the evil to be
advantageous know that it is evil?

MENO. I don't think that at all.

SOCR. Obviously those who are ignorant of the evil do not
desire it, but only what they imagine to be good, though
it is in fact evil. Consequently those who are ignorant
of it and believe it to be good are really desiring the good.
Isn't that so?

MENO. That would appear to be the case.

SOCR. But now as regards those who, as you say, desire what is
evil and consider that the evil is harmful to its possessor; do
they know that they will suffer harm from it?

MENO. They must indeed.

SOCR. But do they not hold that those who suffer harm are
miserable in proportion to the harm they suffer?

MENO. Yes, they must hold that too.

SOCR. And don't they believe as well that the miserable are ill-
starred?

MENO. I presume they do.

Socr. Then is there anyone who chooses to be ill-starred and miserable?

Meno. Surely not, Socrates.

Socr. No one, therefore, Meno, desires evil, if no one desires to be in that unhappy plight; for what is being miserable but desiring evil and obtaining it?

Meno. I think what you say, Socrates, is true; no one desires evil.

Socr. Were you not saying just now that virtue consists in the desire and ability for good?

Meno. Yes, that is what I said.

Socr. One part of the statement—the desire—is present in all human beings, and in this respect one man is no better than another?

Meno. Apparently.

Socr. But clearly, if one man is not better than another in this respect, he must be superior in the ability.

Meno. Undoubtedly.

Socr. According to you, then, virtue is ability to procure goods.

Meno. You seem to me, Socrates, to be perfectly right.

Socr. Let us inquire then as to whether your account of virtue is true in another respect; for you may quite possibly be correct. You say that virtue is the ability to procure goods?

Meno. I do.

Socr. And do you mean by goods such things as health and wealth?

Meno. Yes, and I include the acquisition of gold and silver, and of state honours and offices.

Socr. Is there anything else that you class as goods?

Meno. No; I refer only to all things of that kind.

Socr. Well then, obtaining gold and silver is virtue, says Meno, the ancestral friend of the Great King. Tell me, do you qualify this procuring with the added statement that it must be done justly and piously? Or is this indifferent to you, so that even though a man procures these things unjustly, you call them virtue all the same?

Meno. Certainly not.

Socr. Rather vice?

Meno. Yes, of course.

SOCR. Then it appears that the procuring of these things must be accompanied by justice or temperance or holiness or some other part of virtue; otherwise it will not be virtue, despite the fact that it provides one with goods.

MENO. Quite. How else could it be virtue?

SOCR. And not to procure gold and silver, when to do so would be unjust—what we call the lack of such things—is virtue, is it not?

MENO. Clearly.

SOCR. So the procuring of this sort of goods will be no more virtue than the want of them; it seems that whatever comes accompanied by justice will be virtue, and whatever comes without any such quality, vice.

MENO. I think you must be right.

SOCR. Didn't we say a little while ago that justice, temperance and so on are parts of virtue?

MENO. We did.

SOCR. Then, Meno, you are pulling my leg?

MENO. How so, Socrates?

SOCR. I asked you just now not to split virtue into small change, and I gave you a pattern upon which you should reply. Yet now you completely ignore all this, and tell me that virtue is the ability to procure good things with justice; and this, you say, is a part of virtue.

MENO. I do.

SOCR. Then it follows from your own admission that doing whatever one does with a part of virtue is itself virtue; for according to you justice and so forth are parts of virtue. You ask the meaning of my remark? It is that after my requesting you to speak of virtue as a whole, you say not a word about what it is in itself, but tell me that every action is virtue, provided it is performed with a part of virtue; as though you had told me what virtue is in the whole and I must understand it forthwith—when you are really splitting it into fragments. I think therefore that you must face the same question all over again, my dear Meno—What is virtue?—if we are to be told that every action accompanied by a part of virtue is virtue; for that is the meaning of the statement that every action accompanied by justice is virtue. Do you not agree that you have to meet the same question all over again? Do you suppose that anyone can know a part of virtue when he doesn't know virtue itself?

MENO. No, I don't think one can.

SOCR. You doubtless remember how, a little while ago when I answered your question about shape, we rejected the sort of answer that tries to proceed by way of terms which are still open to dispute and have not yet been admitted.

MENO. We did right, Socrates, in rejecting any such answer.

SOCR. Please do not imagine, then, that you will be able to explain the nature of virtue by replying in terms of its parts, or by any other statement on the same lines. You will merely have to face the same question once again—What *is* the virtue to which you continually refer? Or do you think I am talking nonsense?

MENO. I think you are absolutely right.

SOCR. Well then, begin again and tell me what you and your friend Gorgias take virtue to be.

MENO. Before I ever talked with you, Socrates, I used to be told that yours was just a case of being in doubt yourself and making others doubt as well. It seems to me that you are doing the same now, bewitching me with your spells and incantations, which have reduced me to utter perplexity. If you'll allow me a small jest, I think you are, not only in looks but in other respects as well, very like the cramp-fish,[1] a denizen of the sea which benumbs anyone who approaches and touches it. You appear to have done something like that to me. For in truth I feel my soul and my tongue quite benumbed, so that I just cannot give you an answer. I have so often made long speeches about virtue to various people—and very good speeches they were, so I thought—yet now I am unable to say one word as to what it is. I think you have acted with the utmost good sense in never travelling far from home either by land or sea. For if you were to behave in this way in any other city, you would run the risk of being arrested as a wizard.

SOCR. You're a cunning fellow, Meno; you nearly caught me out.

MENO. How was that, Socrates?

SOCR. I know why you introduced that simile.

MENO. Why was it?

[1] i.e. the electric ray.

SOCR. You were hoping that I might compare *you* to something.
I know one thing about handsome young men: they all love
being compared to something. And they do well out of it,
since fine faces, I suppose, require fine similes. But I shall do
nothing of the sort. As to your picture of me, if the cramp-fish
itself is torpid while benumbing others, then I am like it, but
not otherwise. For it is not from any self-sufficiency that I
cause others to doubt; it is through being in more doubt than
anyone else that I raise doubts in others. I am in that position
here as regards virtue. I have no idea what it is, while you,
though you may have known before you came into contact
with me, are now virtually ignorant of it also. Nevertheless I
am willing to consider it along with you and see if we can
together find out what it is.

MENO. But, Socrates, how are you going to look for something
of whose nature you know nothing at all? Pray, what sort of
thing, among those that you know not, are you going to
suggest as the object of your search? Even supposing, at the
best, that you manage to fall in with it, how will you recognize
it as the thing you did not know?

SOCR. I see your point, Meno; but don't you realize how
captious your argument is? You are saying in effect that a man
cannot inquire about what he knows or about what he does not
know. For he cannot inquire about what he knows, because he
already knows it, and in that case has no need of inquiry; nor
again can he inquire about what he does not know, since he
does not know about what he is to inquire.

MENO. Don't you think then, Socrates, that my argument is
sound?

SOCR. I certainly do not.

MENO. Can you tell me how it is wrong?

SOCR. I can; for I have heard from wise men and women who
told of things divine that——

MENO' What was it they said?

SOCR. Something true, as I thought, and admirable.

MENO. What was it, and who were the speakers?

SOCR. They were certain priests and priestesses who have
studied so as to be able to give a rational account of their
ministry; and Pindar also, and many other inspired poets. As
to their words, they are these; mark now, if you judge them to

be true. They declare that the human soul is immortal; that at one time it comes to an end, which is called dying, and at another is born again; but that it never perishes. Consequently one ought to live all one's life in the utmost holiness.

> For from whomsoever Persephone accepts requital for ancient wrong, the souls of these she restores in the ninth year to the upper sun. From them arise glorious kings and men of noble might and surpassing wisdom, and for all remaining time they are called holy heroes among mankind.[1]

Seeing then that the soul is immortal and has been often reborn, and has beheld all things both in this world and in Hades, there is nothing of which she has not acquired knowledge; so no wonder she is able to recollect what she knew before about virtue and other things. For as all nature is akin, and the soul has learned all things, there is no reason why we should not, by recollecting one single thing—an act which men call learning—discover everything else, if we have courage and tire not in the search; since, it appears, research and learning are nothing but recollection. We must therefore take no notice of that captious argument—it would make us indolent, and is pleasing only to the indolent ear, whereas the other makes us energetic and inquiring. Now since I believe it to be the right way, I am willing, with your assistance, to inquire into the nature of virtue.

MENO. By all means, Socrates. But what do you mean by saying that we do not learn, and that what we call learning is recollection? Can you convince me that this is so?

SOCR. I told you just now, Meno, what a crafty fellow you are; and here you are asking me to teach you. I am to *teach* you— I who maintain that there is no such thing as teaching, but only recollection! You were hoping to make me contradict myself.

MENO. Good lord, no, Socrates! What I said had no such purpose; it was only a manner of speaking. But if you can somehow prove to me that your theory is correct, then do so.

SOCR. This is by no means an easy matter, but for your sake I am ready to do my level best. Please call one of your numerous attendants—any one you like—and I will use him to demonstrate the truth of what I say.

[1] Probably from the *Dirges* of Pindar.

MENO. Certainly. [*To* BOY] Come here, you!

SOCR. Is he a Greek? Can he speak the language? [*Enter* BOY].

MENO. Perfectly. He was born in my own household.[1]

SOCR. Pay attention now, and see whether he appears to recollect of his own accord or to learn anything from me.

MENO. I will.

SOCR. Tell me, boy, do you know that a figure like this [*draws a square*] is a square?

BOY. Yes.

SOCR. A square figure then has all these four lines equal.

BOY. Certainly.

SOCR. [*drawing the diagonals*] Then these lines [AC, BD] drawn through the middle of it are also equal to one another, are they not?

BOY. Yes.

SOCR. And a figure of this sort may be larger or smaller?

BOY. Indeed it may.

SOCR. Now if this side [AB] and that [AD] were each two feet long, how many feet would the whole be? Look at it this way. If one of those lines were two feet long and the other only one foot, the space would of course be two feet taken once?

BOY. It would.

SOCR. But since in fact both lines are two feet long, it must be twice two feet?

BOY. Just so.

SOCR. Then the space is twice two feet?

BOY. Exactly.

SOCR. Well, how many are twice two feet? Do the sum and tell me.

BOY. Four, Socrates.

SOCR. And might there not be another figure twice the size of this, but of the same sort, that is to say, having all its sides equal?

BOY. Yes, sure.

SOCR. Then how many feet will it be?

BOY. Eight.

---

[1] The Greek 'household', like the Roman *familia*, included the slaves.

SOCR. Come now, try to tell me how long each side of that figure will be. The other square, remember, was supposed to have two-foot sides; how long then are the sides of this new square, which is twice as large as the other?

BOY. Obviously, Socrates, twice as long.

SOCR. There you are, Meno. I'm not teaching the lad anything, but only asking him questions. And now he imagines that he knows the length of the lines enclosing eight square feet. Do you think he imagines he does?

MENO. I do.

SOCR. But does he *really* know?

MENO. Certainly not.

SOCR. He just imagines it, from the double size required?

MENO. Yes.

SOCR. Now observe his progress in recollecting, by the proper use of memory. Tell me, boy, do you say that the double space is generated from the double line? The space to which I refer is not longer in one direction than in the other, but must be equal each way like the original one, while being double its size—eight square feet. I wonder now whether you still think we obtain this from a double length of line?

BOY. I do.

SOCR. Very well; [*draws* BE] this line [AB] is doubled if we add to it here another of the same length?

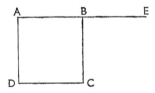

BOY. Definitely.

SOCR. And you say we shall obtain our eight-foot space from four lines of this length?

BOY. Yes.

SOCR. Then let us describe the square [AEFG], drawing four equal lines of that length. This will be what you say is the eight-foot figure, won't it?

BOY. Quite.

SOCR. [*Draws* CK, CH] And here, contained in it, have we not four squares [ABCD, BEHC, CHFK, DCKG], each of which is equal to the original four-foot space?

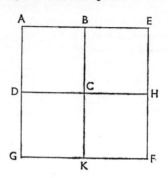

BOY. Yes.

SOCR. Then how large is the whole [AEFG]? Four times that space, isn't it?

BOY. It must be.

SOCR. And is four times equal to double?

BOY. No, of course not.

SOCR. But how much is it?

BOY. Fourfold.

SOCR. Thus from a double-sized line, boy, we get a space not of double but of fourfold size.

BOY. True.

SOCR. And if it is four times four it is sixteen, isn't it?

BOY. Yes.

SOCR. What line will generate a space of eight feet? This one [AE] yields a fourfold space, doesn't it?

BOY. It does.

SOCR. And a space of four feet arises from this line [AB] of half the length?

BOY. Yes.

SOCR. Very good; and isn't a space of eight feet double the size of this one [ABCD] and half the size of this other [AEFG]?

BOY. Yes.

SOCR. Will it not be made from a line longer than the one of these [AB], and shorter than the other [AE]?

Boy. I think so.

Socr. Splendid; always answer exactly what you think. Now tell me, didn't we take this line [AB] to be two feet, and that [AE] four?

Boy. Yes.

Socr. Then the side of the eight-foot figure should be longer than two feet and less than four?

Boy. It should.

Socr. Try to tell me how long you would say it is.

Boy. Three feet.

Socr. In that case we shall add on a half [BL] to this one [AB], and so make it three feet. For here [AB] we have two feet, and here [BL] one more, and so again on that side [AD—DM] there are two and another one; and that makes the figure of which you speak.

Boy. Yes.

Socr. Now if it is three this way [AL] and three that way [AM], the entire space will be three times three feet, won't it?

Boy. Apparently.

Socr. And how many are three times three feet?

Boy. Nine.

Socr. And how many feet did we say that double one was to be?

Boy. Eight.

Socr. So an eight-foot figure is not generated from this three-foot line?

Boy. No indeed.

Socr. Then from what length of line shall we obtain it? Try to tell us exactly; if you prefer not to reckon it out, just show us what line it is.

Boy. Good lord, Socrates, I really don't know.

Socr. There now, Meno, do you see the progress he has already made in recollection? At first he did not know what line forms a figure of eight feet, and even now he does not know. But at any rate he fancied he knew then, and answered boldly as though he knew, and was conscious of no difficulty; whereas

now he recognizes the difficulty he is in, and besides not
knowing does not imagine he knows.

MENO. True.

SOCR. Well, has not his attitude towards the subject of his
ignorance improved?

MENO. There again I agree with you.

SOCR. By causing him to doubt and giving him the cramp-
. fish's shock, have we done him any harm?

MENO. No, I don't think we have.

SOCR. We certainly appear to have given him some help
towards arriving at the truth of the matter. For now he will
pursue the search gladly, as one lacking knowledge; whereas
then he would have readily supposed himself right in declaring
over and over again before any number of people that the
double space must have a side of double the length.

MENO. Very likely.

SOCR. Now do you believe he would have attempted to inquire
about or learn what he thought he knew (when in fact he *did
not* know it) until he had been reduced to the perplexity of
realizing that he did not know, and had begun to feel a
longing to know?

MENO. I think not, Socrates.

SOCR. In which case he has benefited by the cramp-fish's shock?

MENO. Agreed.

SOCR. You should observe how, in consequence of this perplexity, he will proceed to discover something by joint
inquiry with me, while I teach him nothing but simply ask
questions. Watch out, too, and see if at any stage you detect
me instructing him or explaining anything to him, instead of
questioning him about his own views.

[*To* BOY] Now then, my lad: here we have a square [ABCD] of
four feet, have we not? Do you understand?

BOY. Yes.

SOCR. And here we have another square [BEHC] equal to it?

BOY. Yes.

SOCR. And here a third [DCKG], equal to each of them?

BOY. Yes.

SOCR. Now shall we fill up this vacant space [CHFK] in the
corner?

BOY. Why not?

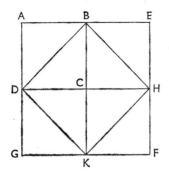

Socr. Here then we must have four equal spaces?

Boy. Yes.

Socr. Well now, how many times larger is this whole space [AEFG] than this other [ABCD]?

Boy. Four times.

Socr. But we wanted it only *twice* as large; do you remember?

Boy. Sure, I do.

Socr. [*drawing the diagonals*]. Do these four lines [BD, BH, DK, HK] cut in half each of those four spaces?

Boy. Yes.

Socr. And have we then four equal lines containing this space [DBHK]?

Boy. We have.

Socr. Now consider how large that space is.

Boy. I don't understand.

Socr. Has not each of the inside [diagonal] lines cut off half of each of those four spaces?

Boy. Yes.

Socr. And how many spaces of that size are there in this part [DBHK]?

Boy. Four.

Socr. And how many in this [ABCD]?

Boy. Two.

Socr. And how many times two is four?

Boy. Twice.

Socr. And how many feet is this space [DBHK]?

Boy. Eight feet.

SOCR. From what line is this figure generated?

BOY. From this.

SOCR. From the line [BD] drawn corner-wise across the four-foot figure [ABCD]?

BOY. Yes.

SOCR. The professors call this the diagonal; so if the diagonal is its name, then according to you, Meno's boy, the double space is the square of the diagonal.

BOY. Yes, it is indeed, Socrates.

SOCR. What do you think, Meno? Was there a single one of his answers that did not proceed from his own thoughts?

MENO. No, they were all his own.

SOCR. But you see, he did not know, as we were saying just now.

MENO. True.

SOCR. He then who does not know about any given matter may have true opinions about it, concerning which he knows nothing?

MENO. Apparently.

SOCR. And in these last few minutes such opinions have been stirred up in that boy, like a dream. But if he were repeatedly asked those same questions in various forms, you know that he would eventually have as exact an understanding of them as anyone else.

MENO. So it seems.

SOCR. Without anyone having taught him, but only through questions put to him, he will understand, recovering the knowledge out of himself?

MENO. Yes.

SOCR. And is not this recovery of knowledge, in himself and of his own accord, recollection?

MENO. Undoubtedly.

SOCR. Must he not, then, have either once acquired or always possessed the knowledge he now has?

MENO. Yes.

SOCR. Well, if he always had it he was always in a state of knowing; and if he acquired it at some time he could not have done so in this present life. Or has someone taught the lad geometry? You see, he can do the same as this with all geometry and every other branch of knowledge. Now has anyone taught him all this? You ought to know, especially as he was born and bred in your household.

MENO. Oh no, I'm certain no one ever taught him.

SOCR. And has he these opinions, or not?

MENO. He must have them, Socrates; that much is quite clear.

SOCR. And if he did not acquire them in this present life, is it not immediately evident that he had them and learnt them during some other period of time?

MENO. Apparently.

SOCR. Mustn't this have been the time when he was not a human being?

MENO. Yes.

SOCR. If therefore in both these periods—when he was and when he was not a human being—he has had within himself true opinions which require only to be awakened by questioning in order to become knowledge, then his soul must have had this cognizance throughout all time, eh? For clearly he has always been or not been a human being.

MENO. Evidently.

SOCR. And if the truth of all things that are is always in the soul, it follows that the soul is immortal; so that you should take heart and, whatever you do not happen to know at present—that is, what you do not remember—you must endeavour to search out and recollect?

MENO. Somehow or other, Socrates, I find what you say most satisfying.

SOCR. So do I, Meno. Most of the points with which I have supported my argument I cannot assert with any confidence; but that the belief in the duty to seek after what we do not know will make us better and braver and less helpless than will the notion that there is not so much as a possibility of discovering what we do not know, nor any duty of seeking after it—this is a point for which I am resolved to fight to the bitter end, as far as I am able, both in word and deed.

MENO. Once again, Socrates, I think you are perfectly right.

SOCR. Then since we are agreed upon the duty of seeking after what we do not know, are you willing that we should attempt a joint inquiry into the nature of virtue?

MENO. Most certainly I am. Nevertheless, Socrates, I myself would most enjoy examining that question I asked at first, and

hearing your opinion as to whether in pursuing it we are to
look upon it as a thing to be taught, or as a gift of nature to
mankind, or as available to them by some other means which
I should be glad to know.

SOCR. Meno, if I had control of you, as I have of myself, we
should not have begun by considering whether virtue can or
cannot be taught until we had first inquired into the more
important question of what it is. Since, however, you are so
fond of your freedom that you do not even make an effort to
control yourself, but at the same time manage to exercise
control over me, I will bow to your request—what else am I
to do? It seems then that we are to consider what sort of thing
it is of which we do not as yet know what it is! Well, you might
at all events relax a little of your authority and permit the
question—whether virtue comes by teaching or some other
way—to be examined by means of hypothesis. I mean by
hypothesis what geometers often do in handling a problem
submitted to them; for example, whether a certain area can be
inscribed as a triangular space in a given circle. 'I cannot yet',
they reply, 'tell whether that can be done; but I think, if I
may so express myself, that I have a hypothesis that is
relevant to the problem. It is as follows. If an area [ABCD] is
such that when you apply it to a given line [the diameter] of
the circle you find it falls short by a space similar to that which
you have just applied, then I take it you have one consequence,
and if it cannot fall so, then some other. I therefore wish to put
a hypothesis, before stating my conclusion as regards inscrib-
ing this figure in a circle, by saying whether or not it is
impossible.' [1] In the same way with regard to our question
about virtue, since we do not know either what it is or what
kind of thing it may turn out to be, let us employ a hypothesis in considering whether or not it can be taught. Here we
go, then. Supposing virtue is some kind of thing belonging to
the class of mental properties, will it or will it not be teachable?
To begin with, if it is something dissimilar or similar to
knowledge, is it taught or not—or, as we were saying just now,

[1] The problem is solved as shown on page 103 by converting the given area
ABCD into an equivalent triangle A'BC. This right-angled triangle is then
inscribed in a circle O' which has a common chord A'B with the given
circle O. The parallel drawn through C gives A'BC' as an 'inscribed triangular space in a given circle'.

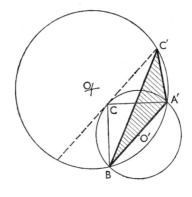

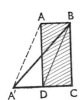

recollected? Let us have no quarrelling about the choice of a
name: is it taught? Or is not this fact clear to everyone—that
the one and only thing taught to men is knowledge?

MENO. I agree to that.

SOCR. Then if virtue is a kind of knowledge, obviously it must
be taught?

MENO. Indubitably.

SOCR. There you are, we have taken a short cut; if virtue belongs
to one class of entities it is teachable, and if to another, it is not.

MENO. Exactly.

SOCR. Next, it would seem, we have to consider whether virtue
is knowledge, or of a kind other than knowledge.

MENO. Yes, I think that is our next subject.

SOCR. Well now, surely we call virtue a good thing, do we not,
and our hypothesis stands, that it is good?

MENO. Yes indeed.

SOCR. Then if there is some good apart and separable from
knowledge, virtue may perhaps not be a kind of knowledge;
but if there is no good that is not comprised in knowledge, we
should be justified in suspecting that virtue is a kind of
knowledge.

MENO. True.

SOCR. Listen now: is it by virtue that we are good?

MENO. Yes.

SOCR. And if good, profitable; for all good things are profitable, are they not?

MENO. Yes.

SOCR. So virtue is definitely profitable?

MENO. That follows from what we have admitted.

SOCR. Then let us see, by taking particular instances, what sort of things they are that profit us: health, for example, and strength, and beauty, and wealth; these and their like we call profitable, do we not?

MENO. Yes.

SOCR. But we admit that these very things actually harm us on occasion; or do you take a different view?

MENO. No, I agree.

SOCR. Ask yourself now, what is the criterion in each case that enables us to recognize them as at one time profitable and at another harmful? Are they not profitable when rightly used, and harmful when abused?

MENO. That is perfectly correct.

SOCR. Well, let us next consider the goods of the soul. Among these, I take it, you would include temperance, justice, courage, intelligence, memory, magnanimity, and so on.

MENO. Yes.

SOCR. Look now at those of them which you think are not knowledge, but different therefrom: do they not sometimes harm us, and at other times profit us? Courage, for example, if it is divorced from prudence and is only a brand of boldness: when a man is senselessly bold he suffers harm, but when he is at the same time sensible he is profited. Is that right?

MENO. Yes.

SOCR. The same holds of temperance and intelligence: things learnt and co-ordinated with the help of good sense are profitable, otherwise they are harmful?

MENO. There is no doubt about that.

SOCR. And in brief, all the undertakings and endurances of the soul, when guided by practical wisdom, lead to ultimate happiness, but, when folly guides, to the opposite.

MENO. Apparently.

SOCR. Then if virtue is something that is in the soul, and is inevitably profitable, it ought to be wisdom, seeing that all the soul's properties are in themselves neither profitable nor harmful, but become either one or the other by the accompaniment of wisdom or folly; and so according to this argument virtue, being profitable, must be a kind of wisdom.

MENO. Yes, I think so.

SOCR. Then as regards the other things, wealth and suchlike, that we described just now as being sometimes good and sometimes harmful, are they not also rendered profitable or harmful by the soul according as she uses and guides them rightly or wrongly; just as, in the case of the soul generally, we saw that the guidance of wisdom makes profitable the properties of the soul, while that of folly makes them harmful?

MENO. Indeed yes.

SOCR. And the wise soul guides rightly, and the foolish erratically?

MENO. That is so.

SOCR. Then are we entitled to declare this as a universal rule, that in man all else is dependent upon the soul, while the properties of the soul herself depend upon wisdom, if they are to be good; and so by this account the profitable will be wisdom, and virtue, we say, is profitable?

MENO. Certainly.

SOCR. We are therefore led to conclude that virtue is either wholly or partially wisdom?

MENO. Socrates, I think you have expressed it very well indeed.

SOCR. In that case good men cannot be good by nature.

MENO. Presumably not.

SOCR. No, for then of course we should have had this result: if good men were so by nature, we should undoubtedly have had men capable of discerning which of our young people were good by nature; and as soon as they had pointed them out we should have taken them in charge and laid them up for safety in the Acropolis, stamping them in preference to our gold and silver,[1] so that no one might tamper with them, and so that when they came of age they might be useful to the state?

MENO. Yes, Socrates, we most probably would.

SOCR. Well, since it is not by nature that the good become good, is it by means of education?

MENO. I think the time has now come for us to conclude that it

---

[1] The Athenian treasury was in the Acropolis.

is; and clearly, Socrates, on our hypothesis that virtue is knowledge, it must be taught.

SOCR. Yes, no doubt that is so; but suppose we were mistaken in accepting that?

MENO. Oh come, the statement appeared correct only a moment or two ago.

SOCR. That is all very well; it needs to be correct not only in the immediate past, but now and in the future, if it is to be at all sound.

MENO. Why, what have you in your mind's eye that makes you hesitate to recognize virtue as being knowledge?

SOCR. I will tell you, Meno. I do not withdraw as incorrect the statement that virtue is taught, provided that it really is knowledge; but ask yourself whether I have not some reason to doubt of its being knowledge. For tell me this: if anything at all (not only virtue) is teachable, must there not be teachers and learners of it?

MENO. Yes, I see that.

SOCR. Then also, conversely, if something had neither teachers nor learners, we should rightly surmise that it could not be taught?

MENO. Fair enough; but do you think there are no teachers of virtue?

SOCR. Well, I have certainly made frequent inquiry as to whether any existed, but try as I will I simply cannot find one. Yet many have taken part in the search along with me, and particularly a number of men whom I consider best qualified for the task. [*Enter* ANYTUS] But look, Meno, here and now, just when we needed him, we have Anytus [1] sitting down beside us; so let us ask him to join in our quest. We shall do well to invite his assistance; for our friend Anytus, in the first place, is the son of a wise and wealthy father, Anthemion, who became rich not by mere accident or in consequence of a gift —like that fellow Ismenias [2] the Theban, of whom we heard the other day as having come into Polycrates' [3] fortune—but as a result of his own skill and industry; and secondly he has the reputation of being generally a well-behaved and polite

---

[1] Afterwards one of the accusers of Socrates. He was the son of a tanner.
[2] Theban demagogue who aided the Athenian exiles in 403 B.C.
[3] Tyrant of Samos, 533–522 B.C.

sort of person, not insolent towards his fellow citizens or arrogant and intrusive; and finally he gave his son a good up-bringing and education, the people of Athens think, for they elect him to the highest offices. This is the sort of man from whom one may expect help in the inquiry as to whether or not there are teachers of virtue, and who they may be. So please, Anytus, join with me and your family friend Meno in our investigation of this matter—who can be the teachers. Look at it this way: suppose we wanted Meno here to become a good doctor, to whom should we send him for instruction? Wouldn't it be to the doctors?

ANYTUS. Certainly.

SOCR. And if we wanted him to become a good shoemaker, wouldn't we send him to the shoemakers?

ANYT. Yes.

SOCR. And likewise as regards all other trades and professions?

ANYT. Of course.

SOCR. Now tell me something more about these same examples. We should do right, we say, in sending him to the doctors if we wanted him to be a doctor. But when we say this, do we mean that common sense would demand that we send him to those who profess the art of medicine rather than to those who do not—to those, in other words, who charge a fee for their services, as self-declared teachers of anyone who desires to come and learn? If these were our reasons, should we not be right in sending him?

ANYT. Yes.

SOCR. And the same principle would apply in the case of flute-playing, and so forth? It is the height of folly, when one wants to turn someone into a flute-player, not to agree to send him to the professed teachers of the art, who charge a regular fee, but to besiege with requests for instruction other people who neither profess to be teachers nor have so much as one pupil in that branch of study which we expect him, when sent, to pursue. Don't you think this would be most irrational?

ANYT. My goodness, I do, and stupid into the bargain.

SOCR. Hear! hear! And now you have a chance to join me in a consultation upon friend Meno. He has been telling me for some while, Anytus, that he would like to possess that wisdom and virtue whereby men keep their house or their city in good order, and honour their parents, and know when to welcome and when to dismiss citizens and foreigners as befits a good man. Now I want to know from you to whom we ought to send him for instruction in that virtue. Or is it sufficiently clear, from what we said just now, that he should go to those men who profess to be teachers of virtue and proclaim themselves as the common educators of the Greeks, and are prepared to give lessons to anyone who cares to pay the advertised fees?

ANYT. To whom are you referring, Socrates?

SOCR. Surely *you* know, if anyone does; they are the men whom people call sophists.

ANYT. God bless my soul, Socrates! Hold your tongue. May no friend or relative of mine, either here in Athens or anywhere else, be seized with such madness as to let himself be infected with the company of those creatures; they are a manifest and lethal plague to those who frequent their schools.

SOCR. What a thing to say, Anytus! Of all the people who claim to understand how to do us good, do you mean to single out these as conferring not only no profit, such as other professionals can give, but actually corruption to anyone entrusted to their care? Is it for such villainy that they openly demand payment of fees? Personally, I cannot bring myself to believe you; for I know one man, Protagoras,[1] who earned more money by his craft than Pheidias [2] (so famous for the noble works that came from his hands) or any ten other sculptors. And yet how amazing that menders of old shoes and repairers of clothes should not be able to go undetected for thirty days if they returned the clothes or shoes in worse condition than they received them, and that such conduct on their part would quickly starve them to death, whereas for more than forty years all Greece failed to observe that Protagoras was corrupting his pupils and sending them out into the world in a worse state than when he took charge of them. For I believe he died at the age of about seventy years, forty of which he had spent in the practice of his skill; and his reputation continues untarnished to this very day. As much might be

---

[1] First and one of the most famous of Greek sophists; born at Abdera in Thrace, *c.* 485, died *c.* 415 B.C.

[2] Athenian sculptor (*c.* 500–*c.* 417 B.C.). He and his school were responsible for the sculptures of the Parthenon, which were completed in 432.

said not only of Protagoras, but of a host of others too—some earlier than he, others still alive. Now are we to take it, in accordance with your view, that all these men wittingly deceived and corrupted the youth, or that they were themselves unconscious of it? Are we to put down those who are often called the wisest of mankind as having been so crazy?

ANYT. Crazy! Not they, Socrates; far rather the lads who pay their fees, and even more so the relatives who entrust young men to their care; but above all, the cities that grant them admission or fail to banish them, according as the offenders are aliens or natives.

SOCR. Tell me, Anytus, has any of the sophists wronged you, that you disapprove of them so strongly?

ANYT. Good heavens, no! I've never had dealings with any of them, and would not allow a member of my family to do so either.

SOCR. Then you have no experience whatever of these people?

ANYT. God forbid that I ever may.

SOCR. But how, my dear sir, can you know whether a thing is good or evil if you have no experience of it?

ANYT. Easily; the fact is, I know what these people are, irrespective of my having experience of them.

SOCR. You must be a soothsayer, Anytus; for I just cannot see, from what you yourself say, how else you can know anything about them. However, we are not at present asking who the teachers are whose instruction would cause Meno to deteriorate; let us grant, if you like, that they are the sophists. I invite you simply to tell us, and do Meno a kindness as a friend of your family by letting him know, to whom in all this great city he should apply in order to become pre-eminent in the virtue I described a few moments ago.

ANYT. Why don't you tell him yourself?

SOCR. I did mention to him certain men whom I supposed to be teachers of such things; but it appears from what you say that I am at fault, and I daresay you are on the right track. Now you take your turn and tell him to whom of the Athenians he should go. Name somebody—anyone you please.

ANYT. Why single out individuals? Any Athenian gentleman he happens to meet will do him more good, if he will follow the advice he receives, than the sophists.

SOCR. Well, did those gentlemen grow spontaneously into what
they are? Can they, without lessons from anyone, teach others
what they themselves did not learn?

ANYT. I presume they must have learned in their turn from the
older generation, who were also gentlemen; or do you fancy
that we have had no good men in this city?

SOCR. Oh yes, Anytus, I'm sure we have; we have also many
distinguished politicians, as we have had them in the past.
But have they, in addition, proved good teachers of the virtue
they themselves possessed? That is the question with which
our discussion is actually concerned; not whether there are or
have been good men in our midst, but whether virtue is
something that can be taught. That has been our problem all
the time. And our inquiry may be reduced to this one question: Did the good men of our own and of former generations
understand how to transmit to another person the virtue in
respect of which they were good, or is that virtue something
not to be transmitted or taken over from one human being to
another? That is the question Meno and I have been discussing all this while. So just consider it from your own point of
view: would you not say that Themistocles [1] was a good man?

ANYT. I would indeed, most certainly.

SOCR. And if any man was ever a teacher of his own virtue, he
was an outstandingly good teacher of his?

ANYT. I would say so, assuming that he wished to be.

SOCR. But can you imagine that he would not have wished
others to become good, honourable men—above all, I
presume, his own son? Or do you fancy he was jealous of him,
and deliberately refrained from imparting to him the virtue of
his own goodness? Have you never heard how Themistocles
had his son Cleophantus taught to be a good horseman? Why,
he could keep his balance standing upright on the back of a
horse, and hurl a javelin from that position, and perform a
number of other remarkable feats in which his father had had
him trained, so as to make him skilled in all that could be
learned from good teachers. Surely you must have heard all
that from your elders?

---

[1] Themistocles (c. 528–c. 460 B.C.), Athenian soldier and statesman, to
whose efforts and advice the Greek victory over the Persians in 480 was
largely due.

ANYT. I have.

SOCR. Then no one could complain of an evil streak in the son's nature?

ANYT. Perhaps not.

SOCR. But tell me: did you ever hear anyone, old or young, say that Cleophantus, son of Themistocles, was as good and wise a man as his father?

ANYT. Certainly not.

SOCR. Then, assuming that virtue was teachable, can we believe that his father decided to have his son trained in those feats, and yet made him no better than his neighbours in his own particular accomplishments?

ANYT. Indeed, I think not.

SOCR. Well, there's a fine teacher of virtue for you—a man whom you admit to have been one of the noblest figures of the past! Let us look at another, Aristeides,[1] son of Lysimachus: don't you admit that he was a good man?

ANYT. Yes, yes; of course.

SOCR. Well, did he not have his son Lysimachus trained better than any other Athenian in all that masters could teach him? But as things have turned out do you think he is better than anyone else? I know you have been closely acquainted with him, and you see what kind of fellow he is. Or, if you like, take another example: the brilliant Pericles; he, as you are aware, brought up two sons, Paralus and Xanthippus.

ANYT. Yes.

SOCR. And you know as well as I do that he taught them to be the finest horsemen in Athens, and trained them to excel in music, gymnastics, and everything else that can be described as an art. With all that, had he no desire to make them good men? Surely he must have, but presumably it is not a thing that can be taught. And lest you should imagine it was only a few of the meanest class of Athenians who failed in this respect, let me remind you that Thucydides [2] also brought up two sons, Melesias and Stephanus, and that in addition to giving them a first-rate education he made them the best

_____

[1] Aristeides (d. 468 B.C.), nicknamed 'the Just'. He was the great rival of Themistocles, who secured his ostracism c. 484.

[2] Son of Melesias. A man of strongly conservative views, who led the aristocratic opposition to Pericles. He was no relation of the historian.

wrestlers in Athens. One he placed with Xanthias, and the other with Eudorus—instructors who were supposed to be the most eminent practitioners of that art. You remember them, don't you?

ANYT. Yes, by hearsay.

SOCR. Well, is it not obvious that Thucydides would never have spent money on having his children taught such things, and then have omitted to teach them at no cost whatever certain others things which, if virtue had been teachable, would have made them good men? You are surely not going to say that he was one of the meaner sort, and had few friends among the Athenians and their allies? After all, he belonged to a great family and had much influence here and throughout the Greek states; so if virtue were something that can be taught he would have discovered the man most likely to make his sons good—either one of our own people or a foreigner—if affairs of state kept him too busily employed. Ah no, my dear Anytus, it seems as though virtue is not teachable.

ANYT. Socrates, I consider you are too ready to speak ill of people. I for one, if you will take my advice, would warn you to be careful. In most cities it is probably easier to do people harm than good, and particularly here in Athens. I believe you realize that yourself. [*Exit.*]

SOCR. Meno, I think Anytus is angry, and I am not in the least surprised; for he imagines, in the first place, that I am denigrating these gentlemen, and in the second place he considers himself one of them. Yet, should the day come when he knows what 'speaking ill' means, his anger will subside; at present he does not know. Now you tell me this: are there not good and honourable men among your people too?

MENO. Certainly.

SOCR. Well then, are they ready to offer themselves as teachers of the young, declaring that virtue can be taught and that they are qualified to teach it?

MENO. Heavens no, Socrates; sometimes one hears them describe it as teachable, but sometimes as not.

SOCR. Then are we entitled to call those persons teachers of the subject in question, when they do not even agree to that much about it?

MENO. Hardly, Socrates.

SOCR. Well, and what of the sophists? Do you regard them, its only professors, as teachers of virtue?

MENO. That is a point, Socrates, for which I particularly admire Gorgias; you will never hear him promising this, and he laughs at others whom he hears doing so. Eloquence is what he takes as their business to inculcate.

SOCR. Then you don't think the sophists are teachers of virtue?

MENO. I don't know what to say, Socrates. I'm in the ranks of the majority: sometimes I think that they are, sometimes that they are not.

SOCR. Are you aware that not only you and other statesmen are in doubt as to whether virtue can be taught, but the poet Theognis [1] too says, you remember, exactly the same.

MENO. In which of his poems?

SOCR. In the elegy where he says:

> Drink and eat with these men; sit with them, and be pleasant to them, for they wield great power. From the good you will learn goodly things; but mix with the bad, and you'll lose even what sense you have.

You realize, don't you, that these words of his imply that virtue is teachable?

MENO. Evidently they do.

SOCR. But in some other lines he shifts his ground a little, saying:

> If understanding could be created and instilled into a man [I think this is how it goes] they would obtain many high rewards [he is referring to the men who could do that].

And again:

> A bad son would never have sprung from a good father, for he would have followed the precepts of wisdom; but never by teaching will you make the bad man good.

Do you notice how in the second passage he contradicts himself on the same point?

MENO. He appears to do so.

SOCR. Well, can you name any other subject in which self-professed teachers are not only refused recognition as teachers of others, but are regarded as not even understanding it themselves, and indeed as inferior in the very quality which they

[1] Theognis of Megara (sixth century B.C.).

claim to impart; while those who are themselves acknowledged as men of worth and honour say at one time that it is
teachable, and at others that it is not? When people are so
confused about a particular subject, would you call them
teachers of it in the proper sense of the word?

MENO. Indeed I would not.

SOCR. Well, if neither the sophists nor those who are themselves
good and honourable are teachers of the subject, clearly no
others can be. Isn't that so?

MENO. Agreed.

SOCR. And if there are no teachers, there can be no pupils
either?

MENO. True enough.

SOCR. And we have admitted that a thing of which there are
neither teachers nor pupils cannot be taught?

MENO. We have.

SOCR. Well, is it a fact that no teachers of virtue are to be found
anywhere?

MENO. That is so.

SOCR. And if no teachers, then no pupils?

MENO. Quite.

SOCR. Virtue, therefore, cannot be taught.

MENO. That would appear to be the case, if we have pursued
our quest along the right lines. I wonder therefore, I must say,
Socrates, whether perhaps there are no good men at all, or
what on earth can be the process whereby people become
good.

SOCR. Alas, Meno, you and I are rather second-rate creatures,
and Gorgias has trained you as poorly as Prodicus did me. So
first of all we must take stock of ourselves, and try to find
someone who will manage to improve us. I say this with
special reference to our recent inquiry, in which I see that we
absurdly failed to note that it is not only by following the lead
of knowledge that human conduct is right and good. It is
doubtless for this reason that we fail to detect by what means
good men can be produced.

MENO. What exactly do you mean by that, Socrates?

SOCR. I mean that good men must be useful; were we not right
in agreeing that this must needs be so?

MENO. Yes.

Socr. And I suppose we were likewise correct in thinking that they will be useful if they give us right guidance in matters of conduct, eh?

Meno. Yes.

Socr. But we seem to have been wrong in maintaining that it is impossible to give right guidance unless one has knowledge.

Meno. Meaning, again——?

Socr. I will explain. If a man knew the way to Larissa, or anywhere else you please, and led others on a walk thither, would he not give right and good guidance?

Meno. Certainly.

Socr. Well, might not sound guidance be afforded by a person who had a correct opinion as to the way, but had never been there?

Meno. Certainly.

Socr. Presumably then, so long as he has a right opinion about that which the other man really knows, he will prove just as satisfactory a guide—if he *thinks* the truth instead of *knowing* it—as the man who possesses the knowledge.

Meno. Just as satisfactory.

Socr. True opinion therefore is as good a guide to right conduct as is knowledge; and this is a point which we overlooked just now in our consideration of the nature of virtue, when we stated that knowledge is the only guide of right conduct. We find now that there is also true opinion.

Meno. So it seems.

Socr. Then right opinion is no less useful than knowledge.

Meno. Except of course, Socrates, that he who has knowledge will *always* hit on the right way, whereas the man with right opinion will *sometimes* do so, but *sometimes* not.

Socr. Come, come; will not he who always has right opinion be always right, so long as he opines rightly?

Meno. Yes, I suppose he must; and therefore I wonder, Socrates, that knowledge should ever be more highly valued than right opinion, and why they should be regarded as two separate things.

Socr. Do you know just why you wonder, or shall I tell you?

Meno. Please tell me.

Socr. It is because you have not carefully observed the statues made by Daedalus.[1] But perhaps there are none in your part of the world.

MENO. What is your point?

SOCR. That if they are not fastened up they play truant and run away; but if fastened they remain in place.

MENO. So what?

SOCR. I mean to say that they are not very valuable possessions if they are at liberty; they will walk off just like runaway slaves. But provided they are fastened up they are worth a lot of money, for they are really beautiful works of art. Now what does all this signify? Why, true opinions. For these, so long as they remain with us, are a splendid possession and bring about all that is good; but they are unwilling to stay for long—they escape from the human soul and are thus of little value until one makes them fast with causal reasoning. And this process, dear Meno, is recollection, as we agreed earlier in our conversation. When once they are fastened, in the first place they are transformed into knowledge; in the second, they are permanent. And this is why knowledge is more prized than right opinion: the one differs from the other by its fixity.

MENO. Beyond a doubt, Socrates, that is almost certainly true.

SOCR. I myself indeed speak as one who does not know but only conjectures; nevertheless that there is a difference between right opinion and knowledge is by no means a conjecture of mine, but something I would strongly assert that I know. There are few things about which I would say that, but this one at all events I will rank among the things that I do know.

MENO. What you say, Socrates, is quite correct.

SOCR. Well then, am I not also correct in saying that true opinion, leading the way, renders the consequence of any action as worthy as knowledge does?

MENO. Once again, Socrates, I believe you speak the truth.

SOCR. Right opinion, then, will be in no wise inferior to knowledge in worth or usefulness as regards our conduct, nor will a man who has right opinion be inferior to one who has knowledge.

MENO. Agreed.

[1] According to legend Daedalus, the first sculptor, equipped his statues with mechanism which enabled them to move.

Socr. And you remember we have admitted that a good man is useful?

Meno. Yes.

Socr. Since therefore it is not only on account of knowledge that men will be good and useful to a country where such are to be found, but also on account of right opinion; and since neither of these two things is a natural property of mankind, being acquired—or do you think that either of them is natural?

Meno. No, I don't.

Socr. Then if they are not natural, good people cannot be good by nature either.

Meno. Of course not.

Socr. And seeing they are not an effect of nature, we went on to consider whether virtue can be taught.

Meno. Yes.

Socr. And we decided it was teachable if virtue was wisdom?

Meno. Yes.

Socr. And if teachable it must be wisdom?

Meno. Certainly.

Socr. And if there were teachers, it could be taught, otherwise not?

Meno. Exactly.

Socr. But did we not acknowledge that it had no teachers?

Meno. We did.

Socr. Then we acknowledged it neither to be taught nor to be wisdom?

Meno. Yes, indeed.

Socr. But we admitted it was good.

Meno. Yes.

Socr. And that that which gives right guidance is useful and good?

Meno. Certainly.

Socr. And that there are only two things—true opinion and knowledge—that give right guidance, and a man guides rightly if he possesses these; for chance occurrences are not due to human guidance, but where a man is a guide to what is right we find these two things—true opinion and knowledge.

Meno. I agree.

SOCR. Well now, since virtue is not taught, we no longer recognize it as knowledge?

MENO. Apparently not.

SOCR. So one of two useful things has been rejected: knowledge cannot be our guide in public affairs.

MENO. I assume it cannot.

SOCR. Consequently it was not by any wisdom, nor because they were wise, that the sort of men we spoke of governed their states—Themistocles and the rest, to whom our friend Anytus was referring a short time ago. It was for this reason that they were incapable of making others like unto themselves—because their endowments were not the fruit of knowledge.

MENO. You are probably right there, Socrates.

SOCR. Well, if it was not by knowledge, it can have been only by sound opinion. This is the means that statesmen employ for the direction of city-states, and they have no more to do with wisdom than have soothsayers and diviners, who utter many a truth when inspired, but have no knowledge of anything they say.

MENO. That is very likely so.

SOCR. May we then, Meno, fairly call those men divine who, though they have no understanding, often achieve great success in word and deed?

MENO. Certainly.

SOCR. So we shall be right in calling those divine of whom we spoke just now as soothsayers, prophets and so forth; and in particular we can say of the statesmen that they are divine and enraptured, as being inspired and possessed of God when they manage to speak a number of highly significant things, while knowing naught of what they say.

MENO. We certainly can.

SOCR. And women too, Meno, as I am told, call good men divine. And the Spartans, when they extol a good man, say: 'He is a divine person.'

MENO. And there is every reason, Socrates, to believe them right; though our friend Anytus might take umbrage at what you say.

SOCR. I don't care one little bit. As for him, Meno, we'll have a talk with him some other time. The point now is this: If throughout this discussion our queries and assertions have been correct, virtue is found to be neither natural nor taught, but is imparted by a heavenly dispensation without understanding in its recipients, unless there happens to be somebody among the statesmen capable of making a statesman of another. If there is any such person, he might be said to be among the living what Homer says Teiresias was among the dead: 'He alone has comprehension; the rest are flitting shadows.' [1] In the same way he on earth, in respect of virtue, will be a real substance among shadows.

MENO. Magnificently expressed, Socrates!

SOCR. Very well then, Meno, the upshot of our conversation turns out to be that virtue comes to us by divine dispensation, when it comes at all. But we shall attain the certainty of this only when, before asking how virtue comes to mankind, we set about inquiring what exactly virtue is, in and by itself.

I must be getting along now. You must try to convince our friend Anytus of that whereof you yourself are now persuaded, and thus allay his wrath; for if you can manage to do that, you will confer a benefit on the people of Athens too.

---

[1] *Odyssey*, x. 494.

LACHES

ST. II. 178–201

PERSONS OF THE DIALOGUE:

Lysimachus.
Melesias.
Nicias.
Laches.

Sons of Lysimachus and
 Melesias.
Socrates.

LYSIMACHUS. You have witnessed the demonstration of the man fighting in armour, Nicias and Laches; but my friend Melesias did not tell you at the time our reason for inviting you to come along and see it with us. However, we will do so now; for we think we ought to speak quite openly to friends like you. Some people, of course, ridicule such motives as have prompted us to ask you here; when called upon to give advice they will say something quite different from what they really think, aiming to satisfy the inquirer and speaking against their own judgment. But you, we consider, not merely have the requisite discernment but will favour us with your candid views; and therefore we have enlisted your counsel on the matter we are going to lay before you.

Now the subject about which I have made this long preamble is as follows. Melesias and I have two sons here: that one, my friend's, is called Thucydides after his grandfather; this one, my own, is likewise named after my father, and we call him Aristeides. Well, we are determined to give them our unflagging care, and not—as most fathers do when their boys are growing into young men [1]—allow them to run loose as their fancy leads them, but start from today doing the utmost we can for them. And, knowing that you have sons of your own, we thought that you, if anyone, must have concerned yourselves with the problem of what kind of upbringing

[1] The Greek word *meirakion*, used here, was applied to youths between the ages of fifteen and twenty-one.

would be best for them; if, on the other hand, you have not given much thought to the question, we would remind you that it ought not to be ignored, and we invite you to join us in working out some method for the care of our sons.

The origin of our decision, Nicias and Laches, is worth hearing, even though the story be rather long. My friend Melesias and I take our meals together, and the lads share our table. Now, as I said a moment ago, we are going to be quite frank with you. Each of us has many splendid deeds of his own father to relate to these youngsters—their numerous achievements both in war and in peace, when they administered the affairs of our allies or of our own state; but neither of us has any deeds of his own to tell. We are ashamed that our boys cannot help noting this fact, and we blame our fathers for letting us indulge ourselves on the threshold of manhood while they attended to other people's business; and we show the significance of it all to these lads, telling them that if they disregard their own interests and reject our advice they will get absolutely nowhere, but that if they behave sensibly they have every chance of becoming worthy of the names they bear. Well, they themselves say they will do as we ask; so we are now wondering what lessons or pursuits will lead them to the highest attainable accomplishment. Someone told us about this particular skill of fighting in armour, as being just the thing for a young man to learn; he spoke in high praise of that fellow whose demonstration we have just been watching, and then strongly advised us to go and see him. So we decided we ought to go along and have a look at him ourselves, and to have you with us not merely as fellow spectators, but also as counsellors and co-partners, if you will be so kind, in the matter of our sons' training. That is the problem we wanted to discuss with you; and we invite you now, on your part, to let us have your views, first as to whether you believe this skill should be learned or not; secondly as regards any other such accomplishment or exercise that you can recommend for a young man; and finally, what attitude you take towards our partnership.

NICIAS. So far as I'm concerned, Lysimachus and Melesias, I thoroughly approve of your idea, and am ready to lend a hand; and I'm sure that that goes for Laches here too.

LACHES. Certainly, Nicias. You know, I think what Lysimachus said a little while ago about his own father and Thucydides was very much to the point, not only as regards them but also in relation to ourselves and to everyone in public life. As he says, it is practically the rule with such people to treat their private affairs, whether connected with children or anything else, in an offhand sort of way. You are absolutely right in saying that, Lysimachus; but it seems very odd that you should appeal to us for advice upon the education of your boys without referring to our friend Socrates here. To begin with, he belongs to your district, and then he is always preoccupied with such important questions as you have raised in connection with youthful studies or pursuits.

LYS. How do you mean, Laches? Has Socrates ever considered matters of this kind?

LACH. Indeed he has, Lysimachus.

NIC. I believe I'm as well qualified as Laches to assure you on that point. Only the other day he put me in touch with a music master for my sons—Damon, pupil of Agathocles, who is not only the most accomplished of musicians, but in every other way as profitable a companion as one could find for young men of that age.

LYS. It is impossible, gentlemen, for men of my years to keep up to date with our juniors, because old age compels us to spend most of our time at home; but if you, son of Sophroniscus,[1] have any sound advice to give our friend, who belongs to your district, you should not withhold it. I say this with all the more confidence because you happen to be closely connected with us through your father; he and I were constant companions and friends, and he died without ever having had a single difference with me. Yes, memory is awakened by what I have just heard. For these lads, talking with each other at home, often speak of one Socrates in the most complimentary terms; but I have never asked them whether they meant the son of Sophroniscus. Tell me, my boy, is this the Socrates whose name you have so frequently mentioned?

SON. Indeed, father, it is.

LYS. Upon my word, Socrates, it is good to know that you carry on your father's most honourable reputation, especially

[1] i.e. Socrates.

because of the intimate relationship in which both you and we shall feel that we stand.

LACH. Indeed, Lysimachus, he is someone with whom you must not lose touch; for I have observed him elsewhere upholding not only his father's but his country's honour. He was with me in the retreat from Delium, and I assure you that if others had chosen to follow his example, Athens would not have suffered such a terrible disaster and would be firmly on her feet today.

LYS. Socrates, this is really high praise which you are now receiving from men whose word is of great weight, and for such conduct as merits their admiration. So let me tell you how delighted I am to hear it and to know that you have so splendid a reputation; in return, you must reckon me as one of your warmest friends. You should indeed have paid us a visit long before this, and treated us on familiar terms, as you have a right to do; however, now that we have made one another's acquaintance, you must from this day forward make a point of sharing our thoughts and getting to know us and our young people also, so that you and they may in turn perpetuate the friendship of our families. But you will do that, I'm sure; and in any case we shall remind you of it another time. For the present, what do you say of the matter with which this conversation began? What is your view? Is the accomplishment of fighting in armour a suitable one for our boys to learn, or not?

SOCRATES. As to that, Lysimachus, I will try my best to advise you, so far as I can, and also to do all the rest that you so kindly ask. But, as I am so much younger and less experienced than you and your friends, I think I ought first to hear what they have to say, and learn from them; afterwards, if I disagree with what they say and have anything else to suggest, I might try to explain it and persuade you and them to adopt my opinion. Now then, Nicias, let one or other of you make a start.

NIC. No difficulty in that, Socrates. I take the view that this accomplishment is in many ways a useful thing for young men to possess. It is good for them, instead of wasting their time on the usual things to which young fellows enjoy devoting their leisure hours, to spend it on this, which not only has the inevitable effect of building up their physique—since it is as respectable and strenuous as any athletic pursuit—but is also a form of exercise which, with riding, is particularly fitting for a gentleman. After all, only men practised in handling these weapons can claim to be trained for the contest in which we are competitors—I mean for that exacting strife [1] in which we are expected to play a part. Further, this accomplishment will prove of some benefit also in actual battle, when it comes to fighting in line with a number of other men; but its greatest advantage will be felt when the ranks are broken, and you have to fight man to man, either in chasing someone who is trying to beat off your attack, or in retreating yourself and beating off the attack of another. Anyone who possessed this accomplishment could come to no harm so long as he had only one opponent to deal with, nor even, perhaps, if he had several; it would give him an advantage in any situation. Furthermore, it is something that arouses a desire for another splendid accomplishment. For everyone who has learned how to fight in armour will be anxious to acquire the still higher gift of being able to manage troops; and when he has that, and has once taken pride in his work, he will press on to attain the whole art of generalship. It is already clear that all accomplishments and purs ts in the military sphere are both honourable and well wortl a man's while, both in acquisition and in practice; and this particular one may serve as an introduction to them. And we can make an important addition to the claims of this science, namely that it will make any man individually far bolder and braver in war. Nor let us disdain to mention, even though some think it a rather trivial matter, that it will give him a smarter appearance in the place where it behoves a man to look smartest, and where at the same time he will appear more terrible to the enemy on account of his smartness. So my opinion is, Lysimachus, as I say, that we ought to have our young men taught this drill, and I have told you my reasons for so thinking. If Laches disagrees, I shall be as glad as anyone to hear what he has to say.

LACH. Well, Nicias, one hesitates to say of any sort of knowledge that it should not be learned; for all knowledge appears to be good. If this skill in the handling of weapons is really a species of knowledge, as maintained by those who teach it, and as

---

[1] Regular warfare.

Nicias describes it, then it ought to be learned; but if it is not a species of knowledge, and those who undertake to impart it are deceiving us, or if it is a species of knowledge but not a very important one, then what can be the good of learning it? I say this because I think that if there were anything in it, it would not have been overlooked by the Spartans, whose sole purpose in life is to seek out and devote themselves to any study or pursuit that will give them an advantage over others in war. And if they have overlooked it, at any rate these teachers of it cannot have overlooked the obvious fact that the Spartans are more intent on such matters than any other Greek people, and that anyone who had distinguished himself among them as a practitioner of this art would amass a fortune elsewhere, just as a tragic poet does who has achieved renown among ourselves (which is the reason why he who thinks himself a good writer of tragedy does not take his show on a tour of the outlying Attic towns, but makes a bee-line for Athens and stages his show here, as one might expect). But I notice that these fighters in armour consider Sparta as holy ground where none may tread; they do not set foot on it even with the tips of their toes, but circle round it and prefer to give demonstrations to any other people, espe ially to those who would admit that they are inferior to man in the arts of war. Furthermore, Lysimachus, I have come across quite a number of these gentry in the field, and have taken their measure. Indeed, one can assess it offhand; for, as though of set purpose, not one of these self-styled experts in the use of arms has ever distinguished himself in war. In all other arts, the men who have made a name are to be found among those who have specialized in one or other of them, whereas these individuals, apparently, stand out from the rest by the futility of their profession. Take this fellow Stesilaus, whom you watched with me in that huge crowd as he gave his demonstration and blew his own trumpet in our presence; I've watched him elsewhere giving a finer entertainment in the form of a very real though quite involuntary exhibition. Once while serving on board ship he was armed with a sickle tied to the end of a spear—an extraordinary weapon worthy of so extraordinary a man. Well, his ship collided with a transport; and although his part in the ensuing action was otherwise undistinguished, you simply must hear what happened as regards that proud sickle-spear. In the heat of battle it managed to get entangled in the transport's rigging, and stuck fast. Stesilaus tugged at the thing, in the hope of freeing it; but he failed, and the two vessels were drifting past one another. For a few moments he ran along in his own ship, clinging to the spear; but as the transport sheered off, pulling him with it, he let the spear slip through his hand until he grasped only the butt-end of the shaft. From the crew of the transport there came laughter and clapping at his posture; and when someone aimed a stone at him (it hit the deck near his feet), and he let go the spear, the troops in the warship in their turn could no longer restrain their laughter, as they saw the wonderful sickle-spear dangling from the transport.

Now there may be something in this art of theirs, as Nicias maintains; but at all events that is my impression of it, derived from cases within my own experience. Therefore, as I began by saying, it is not worth the trouble of learning, whether it be a true but rather useless accomplishment, or merely claimed and represented as such. Yes, I believe that if a man who was a coward imagined he possessed it, his only gain would be in rashness, which would render his true character all the more conspicuous. On the other hand, if he were brave, people would be on the look-out for even his slightest mistake, and he would become the victim of much grievous slander; for the claim to possess such skill arouses jealousy, so that unless a man is vastly superior to the rest in valour he is bound to be made a laughing-stock through professing to be so skilled. That, Lysimachus, is my opinion of the interest taken in this accomplishment. But, as I told you at the start, you must not let our friend Socrates go: you must ask him to advise us according to his view of the matter under discussion.

Lys. Yes, please do so, Socrates; for the members of our council (if I may thus describe them) seem to me to require someone who will decide between them. Had these two agreed, we should have had less need of your help; but as things stand—Laches, you see, has voted on the opposite side to Nicias—it is right that we should hear you and see on which side you cast your vote.

SOCR. What, Lysimachus? Are you going to come down on the side that obtains the approval of the majority of us?

LYS. Well, what can one do, Socrates?

SOCR. And would you do the same, Melesias? Suppose you held a consultation to decide how your son should train for some contest, would you be guided by the majority of us, or by the one who happened to have had a thorough training under a real expert?

MELESIAS. By the latter, of course, Socrates.

SOCR. Would you be guided by him alone rather than by the four of us?

MEL. I imagine so.

SOCR. Naturally; for any justifiable decision must be based upon knowledge rather than on numbers.

MEL. Quite.

SOCR. Very well then, as regards the question you have raised, we must begin by asking whether any of us here has expert skill in the subject of our deliberations. If so, then we must be guided by him alone, and ignore the rest; if not, we must look for someone else. Or do you think that the matter now at issue between you and Lysimachus is a mere trifle rather than something that is really your greatest possession? After all, I assume that the whole future of a man's house depends upon the result of his sons' education; their character will determine its fate for better or for worse.

MEL. True enough.

SOCR. So the problem requires most careful forethought.

MEL. Indeed yes.

SOCR. How then (to take the case I suggested just now) should we set to work if we wanted to consider which of us was best qualified as a trainer for some particular contest? Should we not have recourse to him who had learned and practised the art in question and had had the best teachers?

MEL. I think so.

SOCR. And even before that, should we not ask ourselves what exactly is this thing for which we require teachers?

MEL. How do you mean?

SOCR. Perhaps I can explain myself more clearly in this way. I think that, in approaching the question as to which of us is a properly trained expert, we have not started by agreeing upon a definition of the subject under debate.

NIC. Look here, Socrates, what we're talking about is the art of fighting in armour—whether or not it is something that young men ought to learn.

SOCR. Of course, Nicias. But take the case of a man inquiring whether or not a particular medicine should be used as an eye-salve: do you think his concern is with the medicine or with the eyes?

NIC. With the eyes.

SOCR. And if one wants to know whether or not a horse should be bridled, and when, I presume one's inquiry centres on the horse—not on the bridle?

NIC. True.

SOCR. Briefly therefore, when we consider a thing for any purpose, we are deliberating in fact about the ultimate end in view, and not about the means to that end?

NIC. Indubitably.

SOCR. So we must consider our adviser too, asking ourselves whether he is expert in the treatment required for the end which is our concern?

NIC. Certainly.

SOCR. And we say that our present subject is an accomplishment studied for the sake of young men's souls?

NIC. Yes.

SOCR. So what we have to consider is whether one of us is skilled in treatment of the soul: does the instruction he has received enable him to give it the treatment it requires?

LACH. One moment, Socrates. Have you never noticed that some people become more skilled in certain arts without teachers than others with them?

SOCR. Indeed I have, Laches; people, that is, whom you would not care to trust on the strength of their mere claim to be sound practitioners, unless they could offer some example of their personal skill: some work well performed—not in an isolated case, but repeatedly.

LACH. Fair enough.

SOCR. Well now, Laches and Nicias, Lysimachus and Melesias have invited us to a consultation on their sons, whose souls they are anxious to have as good as possible. Those of us, therefore, who can claim to have had teachers must let them know who those teachers were who, being themselves good to begin with, and having treated the souls of many young men, taught us also in due course and are known to have done so. Any of us, on the other hand, who has had no teacher, but can mention some achievements of his own—that is to say, can point to a number of Athenians or foreigners, either slaves or freemen, who are acknowledged to owe their goodness to him —should do so. But if none of us falls under either category, let us bid them look elsewhere; for we cannot take risks with the sons of our good friends when there are chances of our ruining them, and of thus bringing upon ourselves the gravest charges from our nearest and dearest. Now I, Lysimachus and Melesias, am the first to admit that I've never had a teacher in this respect, although I have longed for such instruction since my boyhood days. You see, I really hadn't the wherewithal to pay fees to the sophists, who alone professed to be able to turn me out a complete gentleman; and to this hour I am powerless to discover the art myself. However, I would not be surprised if Nicias or Laches had discovered or learned it; they have more money than I to enable them to learn from others, and they are older too, and have had time to discover it for themselves. Indeed I regard them as qualified to teach a man; for they would never reveal their thoughts so candidly on pursuits that are beneficial or harmful to a youth unless they felt confident of possessing the requisite knowledge. And I myself have full confidence in them, except that I was surprised at their differing from one another. In my turn, therefore, Lysimachus, I have a favour to ask you: just as Laches urged you a moment ago not to release me but to ask me questions, so I now bid you not to release Laches or Nicias but to question them as follows: ' Socrates says that he has no understanding of the matter, and that he is not competent to decide which of your statements is true; that he has never been either a discoverer or a learner of any such thing. But you, Laches and Nicias, are each to tell us who is the authority from whom you've received the art of bringing up youth; whether you have knowledge of it by learning from someone else or by discovering it yourselves; and if you learned it, who were your respective teachers, and what other colleagues they

had. We require this information so that, in the event of your
being too busy with public affairs, we may approach them and
induce them either with gifts or services (or both) to undertake the care of our and your children together, and so prevent
them from turning out knaves and disgracing their ancestors.
But if you have made the glorious discoveries yourselves, give
us an example to show what other persons you have managed
to alter, by your care of them, from knaves to honest gentlemen. For if you are now going to make your first venture into
the field of education, you must take care lest you find yourselves experimenting, not on a *corpus vile*, but on your sons and
the children of your friends, and you prove to be a mere case,
as the saying goes, of "starting pottery on a wine jar". Tell us
then what you claim, or do not claim, as your resources and
qualifications in this sphere.' Now, Lysimachus, demand that
information from these gentlemen, and do not let them go
scot-free.

Lys. Sirs, to my way of thinking Socrates has spoken sound
    sense; but it is for you, Nicias and Laches, to decide for your-
    selves whether you are ready to be questioned and offer some
    explanation. I and my friend Melesias would certainly be
    delighted if you would agree to deal point by point with all
    that Socrates puts to you. As I said at the outset of this dis-
    cussion, we invited you to join our deliberations precisely
    because we very naturally fancied that you had given serious
    thought to this kind of problem, especially as your boys, like
    ours, are almost of an age to begin their education. So if you
    have no objection, discuss it now by joint inquiry with
    Socrates, exchanging views with him; for he quite rightly says
    that we are here concerned with the greatest of all our
    interests. Come, see if you believe this to be the proper course.

Nic. Upon my soul, Lysimachus, I have an idea that you must
    have known Socrates only at second hand—through his father
    —and have never before talked with him personally except in
    his childhood, when you may have chanced to meet him
    among the good folk of his district, accompanying his father
    at some shrine or local gathering. You have evidently had no
    dealings with the man since he reached maturity.

Lys. What makes you so sure of that, Nicias?

Nic. You seem to be unaware of the fact that anyone who gets to know Socrates well and talks with him face to face is inevitably led round and round by him in the course of argument—which may have originated from an altogether different topic —and cannot call a halt until he has been trapped into giving an account of himself, of the manner in which he now spends his days, and of the kind of life he has lived hitherto; and when once he has fallen into that snare, Socrates will never let him go until he has well and truly criticized all his ways. Now I am used to him; I know that one is bound to be thus treated by him, and also that I too shall receive the same sort of handling. For, Lysimachus, I enjoy conversing with the man, and see nothing wrong in our being reminded of any past or present fault. Nay, one is driven to take more careful thought for the remainder of one's life, if one does not flee from his words—but is willing, as Solon said, and eager to learn as long as one lives, and does not expect to attain sound sense by the mere arrival of old age. As far as I'm concerned, then, there is nothing unpleasant, or unusual either, in being cross-examined by Socrates. In fact I had a shrewd idea from the start that our discussion would not centre upon our boys if Socrates were present, but upon ourselves. So, as I say, there is no objection on my part to debating with Socrates in the way he likes best; but you must see how our friend Laches feels about it.

Lach. Personally, Nicias, in my attitude to debate I am single-minded, or if you prefer, double-minded. You might consider me a lover, and yet also a hater, of discussion. For when I hear a man holding forth on virtue or any kind of wisdom, one who is truly a man and worthy of his argument, I am delighted beyond measure; I take the speaker and his speech together, and note how they are adapted to and harmonize with each other. Such a man is exactly what I understand by 'musical'; he has tuned himself to the fairest harmony, not that of a lyre or other instrument of entertainment, but has made of his own life a true concord between words and acts, not in the Ionian nor in the Phrygian nor in the Lydian, but simply in the Dorian mode, which is the sole Hellenic harmony. Such a man makes me rejoice with his utterance, and I would appear to anyone then as a lover of debate, so eagerly do I welcome all that he says. But a man who reveals the opposite character causes me pain; and the better speaker he is the more I am offended, with the result, in this case, that I am thought to hate discussion. Now I have no experience of Socrates as a debater, but I have assuredly in the past made trial of his deeds; and these I found consistent with the finest and most freely spoken words. So if he has that gift as well, his wish is mine, and I should be delighted to be scrutinized by such a man, and should not begrudge to learn. Yes, I too agree with Solon, but, adding just one rider to his remark, I would like, as I grow old, to learn more and more, *but only from honest folk*. Let him grant me that my teacher is himself good, otherwise I shall dislike my schooling and be put down as a dunce; once I have that assurance I shall not mind in the least if my teacher is to be a younger man or one who as yet has no reputation, or anything of that sort. I therefore invite you, Socrates, both to teach and to refute me to your heart's content, and to learn too what I myself know. Such is the position you have held in my eyes since that day on which we survived a common danger [1] and you gave proof of your own valour, which is to be expected of anyone who proposes to justify his reputation. So say whatever you like, regardless of the discrepancy between our ages.

SOCR. It appears that we shall have no cause for complaint on the score of you two not being ready to join us in considering this question and tendering advice.

LYS. No, but the matter now rests with *us*, Socrates; for I venture to reckon you as one of ourselves. So take my place in making this investigation on behalf of the young men; decide what it is that we want our friends here to tell us, and serve as our adviser by discussing it with them. For I find that in consequence of my age I quickly forget most of the questions I intend to put, and also the answers I receive; and if the discussion alters course my memory fails me altogether. Please therefore debate and elucidate our problem among yourselves; I will listen, and then with my friend Melesias I will act immediately upon whatever decision you reach.

SOCR. Well, Nicias and Laches, let us oblige Lysimachus and Melesias. The questions upon which we touched a little while ago—'Who have been our teachers in this sort of training?' 'What other men have we improved?'—are perhaps of a kind on which we might well examine ourselves. But I believe there

[1] At Delium. See *Symposium*, iii. 221.

is another line of inquiry, one that will lead to the same result and is probably more fundamental in its starting-point. If we know of a certain thing that it makes another thing better by being united thereto, and further, if we can effect that union, we obviously know the thing whose surest and easiest attainment is the object of any deliberation in which we might be engaged. I daresay you don't grasp my meaning; but you will do so more readily through the following example. If we happen to know that sight united with eyes makes those eyes so much the better, and further if we are able to effect its union with the eyes, we obviously know what this faculty of sight is, on which we might be consulting as to how it might be best and most easily acquired. For unless we knew beforehand what sight or hearing is, we should hardly prove ourselves reliable consultants or physicians in the matter of eyes or ears, and the surest way of acquiring sight or hearing.

LACH. You are quite right, Socrates.

SOCR. And you realize, Laches, that our friends have just invited us to a consultation as to the way in which virtue may be united to their sons' souls, and so make them better?

LACH. Yes indeed.

SOCR. Then we need first to know what virtue [1] is, eh? For surely, if we have no notion at all of what virtue actually is, we cannot possibly discuss with anyone the best means of acquiring it.

LACH. I definitely think not, Socrates.

SOCR. Then we may assume, Laches, that we know the nature of virtue.

LACH. I suppose we may.

SOCR. And that which we know, I presume, we can also tell.

LACH. Undoubtedly.

SOCR. Let us not, therefore, my good friend, look into the subject of virtue as a whole, since that may very likely prove too much for us; let us first see whether we have sufficient knowledge about some part of it. This will most probably facilitate our inquiry.

LACH, Yes, Socrates, let us do as you suggest.

SOCR. Then which of the parts of virtue shall we choose?

[1] The word 'virtue' here and in the following pages includes the accomplishments and merits of a good citizen.

Clearly, I think, that which the technique of fighting in armour is alleged to promote; and that, of course, is generally recognized to be courage, is it not?

LACH. Yes, it generally is, to be sure.

SOCR. Then let us first endeavour, Laches, to say what courage is. We can then go on to inquire in what way young men may acquire it, so far as it can be acquired at all by means of learning and practical exercise. Come, do as I say, and try to tell me what courage is.

LACH. Good gracious, Socrates, that is easy enough. Anyone who is willing to stand fast in face of the enemy, and does not run away, is courageous; no doubt about that.

SOCR. Well said, Laches; but I daresay it's my own fault, through not expressing myself clearly, that you did not answer the question I had in mind, but something different.

LACH. What do you mean by that, Socrates?

SOCR. I will do my best to explain. We will assume for the moment that a man is courageous if, as you yourself put it, he remains at his post and fights the enemy.

LACH. That is certainly my view.

SOCR. So it is mine. But what about this other fellow—one, I mean, who does not stand fast but fights while fleeing?

LACH. How fleeing?

SOCR. You know, as the Scythians are said to fight, no less in flight than in pursuit. Again, Homer says in praise of Aeneas's horses, that they knew 'how to pursue and how to flee in fright full swiftly in all directions'; and he extols Aeneas himself for this same knowledge of fright, calling him 'prompter of fright'.[1]

LACH. And rightly too, Socrates; for he was speaking of chariots, and you are speaking similarly of Scythian horsemen. That is the way cavalry *do* fight; but infantry tactics are as I have stated.

SOCR. Except perhaps, Laches, in the case of the Spartans. It is said that at Plataea, when the Spartans found themselves confronted with a line of wicker shields, they dared not stand and fight, but turned tail; when, however, the Persian ranks were broken, the Spartans kept turning round and fighting like cavalry, and so won that great battle.[2]

[1] *Iliad*, viii. 107–8.
[2] *See* Herodotus, ix. 61–2.

LACH. Perfectly true.

SOCR. Well, this is what I meant just now by saying that I myself was to blame for your incorrect answer, by framing my question wrongly. I wanted your view not only of brave infantrymen, but also of courage in cavalry and indeed among soldiers generally; also of the courageous not only in warfare but amid the perils of the sea; of all who are courageous in poverty and disease, or again in public life; and further of all who are not merely brave in face of pain or fear, but resolute opponents of appetites and pleasures, whether standing their ground or turning their backs upon the foe. That is what I wanted; for I presume, Laches, there are courageous people in all such circumstances.

LACH. Most definitely there are, Socrates.

SOCR. All these then are courageous. But some have acquired courage amid pleasures, some in the throes of pain, some in face of appetite and some in despite of fear; while others, I imagine, have acquired cowardice in these respects.

LACH. Of course.

SOCR. What courage and cowardice *are*—that is what I wanted to know. So try once more: tell me first what is this thing, courage, which is identical in all the cases I have mentioned. Or do you still not understand my meaning?

LACH. Not very clearly.

SOCR. Well, listen now. Suppose, for example, I were asking you to define quickness, as it occurs in running and playing the harp, in speaking, learning and many other activities, and as possessed by us in almost every movement worth mentioning, whether of arms or legs, or mouth or voice, or mind; or do you not use the word so?

LACH. Certainly I do.

SOCR. Well then, if someone asked me: 'Socrates, what do you mean by this thing which in all cases you term quickness?' I would answer: 'The faculty that accomplishes a great deal in a little time is what I call quickness, whether in a voice or in a race or in any of the other instances.'

LACH. Your reply would be perfectly correct.

SOCR. Very good; now try to tell me, Laches, in the same way about courage; what faculty is it—the same whether in pleasure or pain, or in any of the circumstances in which we described it just now as occurring—that has been given the name courage?

LACH. Well, it seems to me to be a certain constancy or persistence of the soul, if we are to speak of the natural quality that is manifested in them all.

SOCR. Why, of course we must, if we are to answer one another's question. Now it seems to me that by no means *all* constancy, as I conceive it, can be regarded by you as courage. My reason for thinking so is this: I am almost sure, Laches, that you reckon courage among the nobler qualities.

LACH. Nay, among the very finest, you may be certain.

SOCR. And constancy joined with prudence is noble and good?

LACH. Very much so.

SOCR. But what when it is joined with foolhardiness? Is it not then, on the contrary, harmful and mischievous?

LACH. Yes.

SOCR. And can you maintain that such a thing is noble, when it is both mischievous and harmful?

LACH. Not rightly, Socrates.

SOCR. Then you will not admit that such constancy is courage, seeing that it is not noble, whereas courage is something noble.

LACH. True.

SOCR. So, according to you, prudent constancy will be courage.

LACH. Apparently.

SOCR. Now let us see *in what* it is prudent. In all matters, both great and small? For example, if a man persists in laying out money prudently, because he knows that by doing so he will earn more, would you call him courageous?

LACH. Good heavens, no.

SOCR. Or how about the case of a doctor who, when his son or anyone else is suffering from pleurisy and begs for something to eat or drink, resolutely and persistently refuses?

LACH. That is no instance of courage, in any sense, either.

SOCR. Well, take a man who is constant in war, and is willing to fight, on a prudent calculation whereby he knows that others will lend him their support and that the enemy will be less numerous and weaker than his own side, and when he has also the advantage of position. Now which would you say is the more courageous, this man who is constant on the strength of such prudence and preparation, or a man in the opposing army who is ready to stand fast against him?

LACH. The latter, I should say, Socrates.

SOCR. And yet his constancy is more foolhardy than that of the first man?

LACH. True.

SOCR. So you would say that an expert horseman who is constant in a cavalry action is less courageous than a man who is so without that skill?

LACH. Yes, I think so.

SOCR. And likewise in the case of an expert slinger, bowman or other such fighter?

LACH. Certainly.

SOCR. And anyone who agrees to go down a well and dive, and to persist in this or other such action, without having the appropriate skill, you would describe as more courageous than those who have it?

LACH. Yes, for what else can one say, Socrates?

SOCR. Nothing, if that is what one thinks.

LACH. Well, I do think so.

SOCR. It is also a fact, I presume, Laches, that persons of this sort are more foolhardy in constantly taking risks than those who are adepts?

LACH. Manifestly.

SOCR. Have we not already agreed that persistence in fool-hardiness is base and harmful?

LACH. Exactly.

SOCR. But courage was admitted to be something noble?

LACH. Yes, it was.

SOCR. Yet now, on the contrary, we are saying that this base thing—foolhardy persistence—is courage.

LACH. So it seems.

SOCR. Then do you think our statement is correct?

LACH. On my word, Socrates, no.

SOCR. It would seem then, Laches, on your own showing, that you and I are not tuned to the Dorian mode; for there is dis-cord between our deeds and our words. Judged by our deeds, we should quite likely be said to have our share of courage, but I fancy our words would make a very different impression if someone heard us talking as we are now.

LACH. Too true.

SOCR. Well, does it seem right that we should be in that position?

LACH. Indeed it does not.

SOCR. Then do you mind if we accept our statement up to a certain point?

LACH. What statement, and to what point do you mean?

SOCR. That which enjoins constancy. And, please, let us also be constant and persistent in our inquiry, so as not to be laughed at by courage herself for failing to be courageous in our search for her, when it is possible we may find after all that this very constancy is courage.

LACH. Personally, Socrates, I'm ready to continue undaunted; at the same time, I'm not used to discussions of this kind. However, I am in the grip of a certain ambitious zeal after hearing what has been said, and feel quite annoyed at finding myself unable to express offhand what I think. For I believe I have a notion of what courage is, but somehow or other she has momentarily escaped me, with the result that I fail to capture her in words and state what she is.

SOCR. Well, my dear sir, the good huntsman must follow the hounds and not abandon the chase.

LACH. I'm with you there, all the way.

SOCR. Then how about asking our friend Nicias to join us in the hunt? He may be more resourceful than we are.

LACH. I'm most willing, of course.

SOCR. Come now, Nicias; come and do your best to help your friends who are caught in a storm of argument and don't know what to do. You see the difficulty of our situation; you must now tell us what *you* think courage is, and thereby free us from our dilemma by giving your own thoughts the stability of words.

NIC. Well, Socrates, I have been thinking for some while that you two are not defining courage in the right way; you are not acting up to a very sound observation I have heard you make in the past.

SOCR. What is that, Nicias?

NIC. I have often heard you say that every one of us is good in that wherein he is wise, and bad in that wherein he is unlearned.

Socr. Well, that is quite true, Nicias.

Nic. Hence, if the brave man is good, clearly he must be wise.

Socr. Do you hear him, Laches?

Lach. I do, without understanding exactly what he means.

Socr. But I think I understand; our friend appears to mean that courage is a branch of wisdom.

Lach. What branch of wisdom, Socrates?

Socr. Won't you put that question to our friend here?

Lach. I do.

Socr. Good. Now tell him, Nicias, what branch of wisdom courage is, by your account. Not that of flute-playing, I presume?

Nic. Not at all.

Socr. Nor yet that of harping?

Nic. No, no.

Socr. But what is this knowledge then, or of what?

Lach. I must say you are questioning him on exactly the right lines, Socrates; so let him tell us what he thinks it is.

Nic. I say, Laches, that it is this: the knowledge of what is to be dreaded or dared, either in war or in any other circumstances.

Lach. How strangely he talks, Socrates!

Socr. What makes you say that, Laches?

Lach. Why, surely, wisdom is distinct from courage.

Socr. Well, Nicias denies that.

Lach. Upon my word, indeed he does; that is where he just talks nonsense.

Socr. Then let us enlighten instead of abusing him.

Nic. No, Socrates, I believe Laches wants to have me shown up as talking nonsense, because he was proved a little while ago to be in the same position himself.

Lach. Very true, Nicias, and I will try to make it evident. You *are* talking nonsense; for example, don't doctors know what is to be dreaded in disease? Or do you fancy the courageous know this? Or do you call doctors as such courageous?

Nic. Not at all.

Lach. Nor, I imagine, farmers either. And yet they, I presume, know what is to be dreaded in farming, just as any other skilled worker knows what is to be dreaded and dared in his particular craft; but they are none the more courageous for that.

SOCR. What do you think Laches is saying, Nicias? There *does* seem to be something in his remarks.

NIC. Yes, there is something, but it happens not to be true.

SOCR. How so?

NIC. Because he supposes that doctors, in treating their patients, know something more than how to recognize what is healthy and what is diseased. This, surely, is in fact all they know; do you think, Laches, that it is within a doctor's knowledge to tell whether health itself is to be dreaded by someone rather than sickness? Do you not realize that in many cases it is better that a man should never rise again from his sick bed? Honestly, do you say that it is invariably better to live? Is it not often preferable to die?

LACH. Yes, I agree with that.

NIC. And do you think that the same things are to be dreaded by those who would be better off dead, as by those who were better alive?

LACH. No, I don't.

NIC. Well, do you attribute the decision on this matter to doctors or to any other skilled worker except one who has knowledge of what is to be dreaded and what is not—in other words, to the man whom I describe as courageous?

SOCR. Do you grasp his meaning, Laches?

LACH. I do: seers are the people whom he calls courageous; for who else can know for which of us it is better to be alive than dead? And yet, Nicias, do you claim to be a seer, or to be neither a seer nor courageous?

NIC. What's that? Are you now suggesting that the gift of deciding what is to be dreaded and what dared belongs to a seer?

LACH. Indeed I am; to whom else could it belong?

NIC. Much rather to the man of whom I speak, my dear sir; for a seer's business is to judge only the signs of what portends: whether So-and-so is to meet with death or disease or loss of property, or victory or defeat in war or some other contest. Which of these things it is better for a man to suffer or escape can surely be no more for a seer to decide than for anyone else.

LACH. Well, Socrates, it is beyond me to understand what he is driving at. He assures us that the man to whom he refers as courageous is neither a seer nor a doctor nor anybody else, unless perhaps he has in mind some god. Now it seems to me that Nicias is unwilling to admit frankly that his words have no meaning at all, but twists and turns in the hope of concealing his own perplexity. Why, you and I could have played the same trick just now, had we wished to avoid the appearance of inconsistency. Of course, if we were arguing in a court of law there would be some reason for behaving like that; but here, in a gathering such as this, why waste time in decorating oneself with empty words?

SOCR. I agree there is no point in doing that, Laches; but let us see whether Nicias thinks he does mean something, and is not indulging in talk for its own sake. So let us ask him to explain more clearly what he has in mind. If he can show that he means something, we will agree with him; if not, we will mistrust him.

LACH. Well, Socrates, if you care to ask him, go ahead. Perhaps I've asked too many questions already.

SOCR. There is no reason why I should not; after all, the question will come as from us both.

LACH. Very good.

SOCR. Now tell me, Nicias, or rather tell *us*—for Laches and I are sharing the argument—do you say that courage is the knowledge of what is to be dreaded or dared?

NIC. I do.

SOCR. And that such knowledge is not the property of everyone, since neither a doctor nor a seer as such possesses it, and cannot be courageous unless he adds this particular brand of knowledge to his own? Wasn't that what you said?

NIC. Yes, it was.

SOCR. And so what is to be dreaded or dared is not in fact a thing which, as the proverb says, 'any pig would know'; and therefor a pig cannot be courageous.

NIC. I think not.

SOCR. Indeed it is obvious, Nicias, that you at any rate do not believe that even the Crommyonian sow could have been courageous. I say this not in jest, but because I am sure that anyone propounding your theory must refuse courage to any brute beast, or else admit that an animal like a lion or a leopard or even a boar is so wise as to know what only a few men know because it is so hard to discern. Why, he who subscribes to your account of courage is in the position of having to agree that a lion, a stag, a bull and a monkey have all by their very nature an equal share of courage.

LACH. Ye gods, how brilliantly you argue, Socrates! Now answer us candidly, Nicias, and say whether those animals, which we all admit to be courageous, are wiser than ourselves; or whether you are so rash, in face of everyone else, to describe them as not even courageous.

NIC. No, Laches, I do not describe brute beasts, or anything else that from lack of intelligence has no fear of the dreadful, as courageous, but rather as fearless or foolhardy. Surely you do not suppose that I apply the epithet courageous to little children, whose fearlessness is due to lack of forethought? No, I maintain that fearlessness and courage are not the same thing. In my opinion very few people are endowed with courage and forethought, whereas rashness, boldness and fearlessness, without forethought to guide them, occur in a great number of men, women, children and animals. So you see, the acts that you and most people call courageous, I call rash; it is the prudent acts of which I speak that are courageous.

LACH. Look there, Socrates! See how grandly, as he imagines, my friend dresses himself up in words; and how he endeavours to tear the honourable badge of courage from those whom all mankind acknowledge to be courageous!

NIC. Don't be scared, Laches; I am not referring to you. I grant that you, and Lamachus also, are wise since you are courageous, and I say the same of many other Athenians.

LACH. I'll not say what I *could* say in reply to that, lest you call me a true son of Aexone.[1]

SOCR. No—say nothing, Laches. You seem to me not to have noticed that he has acquired his wisdom from old Damon; and Damon is a constant associate of Prodicus, who is alleged to be the cleverest of the sophists at distinguishing terms like these.

LACH. Yes, and it better becomes a sophist to parade such refinements than a man whom the state deems worthy to govern her.

SOCR. It is fitting, of course, for a man in the highest seat of

[1] An Attic *deme*, whose people were famed for their acid tongues.

government to possess the highest degree of wisdom. However, I think Nicias deserves further examination, so that we may discover in what connection he uses the word 'courage'.

LACH. Then examine him yourself, Socrates.

SOCR. That is just what I'm going to do, my dear sir; but please don't imagine that I shall excuse you from your proper share in the argument. No, you must apply your mind to it and join in, weighing carefully what is said.

LACJ. Fair enough, if you think I ought.

SOCR. Indeed I do. Now, Nicias, kindly go back to the beginning and answer us: you know we started our debate by considering courage as a part of virtue?

NIC. Quite so.

SOCR. And you were one of those who agreed in saying that it is one of several parts, which taken together have been called 'virtue'?

NIC. Certainly.

SOCR. Now do you mean the same as I do by those parts other than courage—temperance, justice and so forth? I'm sure you do.

NIC. Yes, yes.

SOCR. So much for that; so far we agree. But let us pass on to what is to be dreaded and what to be dared, and make sure that you and we do not view them from two different standpoints. Let me tell you our view of them, and if you don't agree with it you shall enlighten us. We maintain that dreadful things are those that cause fear, while the safely ventured are those that do not; and fear is caused not by past or present, but by expected evils. You hold the same opinion, don't you, Laches?

LACH. Entirely, Socrates.

SOCR. Well, there you have our view, Nicias: coming evils are to be dreaded, whereas things not evil, or good things, that belong in the future are to be safely dared. Would you describe them so, or in some other way?

NIC. No, just like that.

SOCR. And the knowledge of these things is what you term courage?

NIC. Exactly.

SOCR. There is still a third point on which we must see whether you agree with us.

NIC. What point is that?

SOCR. I will tell you. Taking the various subjects of knowledge, your friend and I are of the opinion that there is not one knowledge of how an event has happened in the past, another of how things are happening in the present, and another of how a thing that has not yet happened might or will come to pass most favourably in the future, but that the knowledge is identical in all cases. For example, in the case of health, it is medicine always and alone that takes cognizance of present, past and future processes alike; and farming is in the same position as regards the products of the soil. Now as regards warfare: I feel sure you yourself will support me when I say that in such matters generalship makes the best forecasts by and large, particularly of future results, and is mistress rather than handmaiden of the seer's art, because it knows better what is happening or is about to happen in the operations of warfare. Hence the law provides that the seer shall take his orders from the general, and not *vice versa*. May we say this, Laches?

LACH. We may.

SOCR. Well now, do you agree with us, Nicias, that the same science takes cognizance of the same things, whether present, past or future?

NIC. I do; that is my own view, Socrates.

SOCR. And courage, my friend, is knowledge of what is to be dreaded and dared? Isn't that what you say?

NIC. Yes.

SOCR. And we have admitted that things to be dreaded and things to be dared are future evils and future goods?

NIC. Certainly.

SOCR. And the same science is concerned with the same objects, whether in the future or at any particular stage?

NIC. That is so.

SOCR. Then courage is knowledge not only of what is to be dreaded and what dared; for it covers evils and goods not merely in the future but also in the present and the past—in fact at any stage—like other kinds of knowledge.

NIC. Apparently.

SOCR. So the answer you gave us, Nicias, deals with only about
a third part of courage, whereas our question asked what
courage is as a whole. And it now appears, on your own showing, that courage is knowledge not simply of what is to be
dreaded and what dared, but practically a knowledge concerning all evils and goods at every stage. That is your latest
account of what courage must be. What do you say to this new
theory, Nicias?

NIC. I accept it, Socrates.

SOCR. Well, do you think, my good sir, there could be anything
lacking in the virtue of a man who knew all good things, and
all about their occurrence in the present, the future and the
past, and all about evil things likewise? Do you suppose that
such a man could be wanting in temperance or justice, and
holiness, when he alone is capable first of taking due pre-
cautions, in his dealings with gods and men, as regards what
is to be dreaded and what is not, and secondly of procuring
good things, thanks to his knowledge of the right behaviour
towards them?

NIC. I think, Socrates, there is something in what you say.

SOCR. Therefore, Nicias, what you are now describing will be
not a part but the whole of virtue.

NIC. So it seems.

SOCR. But remember, we said courage is *a part* of virtue.

NIC. Yes, we did.

SOCR. And what we now describe is manifestly different.

NIC. Apparently.

SOCR. There you are, Nicias: we have failed to discover what
courage really is.

NIC. Well, well.

LACH. Aha! And I imagined, my dear Nicias, that you were
going to discover it, when you sneered at the answers I gave
to Socrates. Indeed I entertained high hopes that the wisdom
you received from Damon would enable you to make the
discovery.

NIC. That's all very fine, Laches. You think you can now disregard the fact that you yourself were proved a little while ago
as knowing nothing about courage; when my turn comes to be
shown up in the same light, that is all you care, and it seems
you will not mind at all if I share your ignorance of things

about which any self-respecting man should have knowledge. Honestly, you strike me as following the all-too-common practice of keeping an eye on others rather than oneself. But I fancy that for the time being I have said enough on the subject of our discussion, and that later on I shall have to make good any shortcomings in my statement upon it with the help of Damon—whom, of course, you choose to ridicule without ever having met the man himself—and with the help of others too. When I am thoroughly prepared I shall not hesitate to enlighten you; for I think you have grave need of instruction.

LACH. I know you are a wise fellow, Nicias. Nevertheless I advise Lysimachus here and Melesias to dismiss you and me, retaining our friend Socrates, as I originally suggested, for the education of their boys. If my own sons were old enough I would do the same.

NIC. Fair enough; if Socrates will consent to take charge of these young people, I will look for no one else. I should be delighted to entrust him with my lad Niceratus, if he is willing; but whenever I broach the subject he declines and recommends other tutors. I wonder, Lysimachus, if Socrates will lend a more ready ear to you.

LYS. He certainly ought to, Nicias; for I assure you I'd be willing to do for him a great deal that I wouldn't do for a host of other men. Well, what do you say, Socrates? Will you comply, and do what you can for the highest improvement of these boys?

SOCR. Why, how strange it would be, Lysimachus, to withhold one's efforts for the highest improvement of anyone! If the discussion we have just finished had shown me to know what our friends did not, it would be only proper to invite my co-operation in this work; but as it is, we all find ourselves in the same difficulty, so why should one of us be preferred to another? In my opinion, none of us should; in which case I will venture to give you some advice. I tell you gentlemen, between ourselves, that all of us should seek out the best available teacher, first for ourselves—for we need one—and then for our boys, sparing neither money nor anything else we can provide. I certainly do not advise that we should leave ourselves in our present condition. If anyone laughs at us for seeing fit to go to school at our time of life, I think we should

have recourse to Homer, who said that 'shame is no good
mate for a needy man'.[1] So let us not mind what anyone may
say, but unite in arranging for our own and our sons' tuition.

Lys. That is a most welcome suggestion, Socrates; and, as I am
the senior in years, so I am most eager to take lessons with the
youngsters. Now this is what I beg you to do: come to my
house tomorrow at dawn; don't fail to turn up, and then we
can consult on this matter. For the present, let us break up our
meeting.

Socr. God willing, Lysimachus, I'll be with you for certain
tomorrow.

---

[1] *Odyssey*, xvii. 347.

EUTHYDEMUS

PERSONS OF THE DIALOGUE:

Crito.   Dionysodorus.
Socrates.   Cleinias.
Euthydemus.   Ctesippus.

Scene: Athens, c. 400 B.C.

CRITO. I say, Socrates, who was that you were talking to
yesterday at the Lyceum? There was such a crowd standing
around you that when I came up intending to listen I could
hear nothing distinctly. However, by craning over I got a
glimpse, and you appeared to be in conversation with a
stranger. Who was he?

SOCRATES. Which one do you mean, Crito? There were two of
them.

CRI. The man I'm referring to was sitting two away from you,
on your right. Between you was Axiochus's boy, who seemed
to have grown a good deal. He looked about the same age as
my Critobulus; Critobulus is rather puny, but this lad has
come on splendidly—a fine-looking fellow.

SOCR. Oh, you mean Euthydemus. The one on my left was his
brother Dionysodorus; he too takes part in our discussions.

CRI. I don't know either of them, Socrates. A pair of new
sophists, I suppose. Where do they come from, and what
science do they profess?

SOCR. Well, I believe they are natives of Chios; they went out
as colonists to Thurii, but were exiled from there and have
spent several years now in various parts of this country. As to
their profession, it's an amazing one, Crito. These two men
are absolutely omniscient; I never knew until now what 'all-
round sportsmen' were. They are a couple of regular all-
round contestants—not in the style of those two famous

L 418   149

Acarnanian brothers, whose efforts were confined to athletic prowess. These two, in the first place, are very powerfully built and tremendous fighters; they take on all comers, being highly skilled in the handling of weapons, and can also impart that skill—for a fee—to others. Secondly, they are more than competent in an action at law, and teach others how to deliver, or to get composed for them, speeches that are sure to prove successful. There was a time when their ability in this latter respect was only moderate; but now they have given the final polish to their skill as all-round sportsmen. The one feat of arms hitherto unperformed by them they have now accomplished, so that no one dares stand up to them for a moment; such is the faculty they have acquired in wielding words as their weapons and refuting any argument, whether it be true or false, with equal ease. Therefore, Crito, I have a mind to place myself in these two gentlemen's hands; for they claim it would take them only a little while to make anyone else clever in exactly the same way.

CRI. Good heavens, Socrates! Aren't you afraid that, at your time of life, you may now be too old for that?

SOCR. Not at all, Crito; I have sufficient assurance, and indeed proof, to the contrary. These two fellows were themselves already in late middle age when they took up this science of disputation, which I desire to possess. Last year, or the year before, they were as yet without their science. All I'm afraid of is that I may bring the same discredit on our two visitors as upon Connus the harper, who is still trying to teach me the harp; the lads who attend his classes with me make fun of me and call Connus 'the old boys' master'. This makes me fear that someone may likewise ridicule the two strangers. So, Crito, just as I have persuaded some elderly men to come along and take harping lessons with me, in this latest matter I am going to try and recruit another lot. Now I'm sure you will come with me to school; and we'll take your sons as a bait, for I have no doubt that the attraction of these youngsters will make them include us also in the class.

CRI. I don't see why not, Socrates, if you think it's all in order. But you must explain to me what is the science these men profess, so that I may know what it is we are going to learn.

SOCR. You shall hear without delay. I cannot plead that I did not give them my attention; for I not only listened carefully, but also remember everything that was said, and will try to give you a full account of the whole business.

Providence had decreed that I should be sitting alone in the place where you saw me, in the undressing room.[1] I was just intending to get up and go; but the moment I did so I was visited, as so often, by that spiritual sign.[2] So I resumed my seat, and presently these two persons entered—Euthydemus and Dionysodorus—accompanied by what seemed to me quite a number of their pupils. At all events, in they came and began walking round the cloister. They had hardly taken two or three turns when along came Cleinias, who, as you rightly say, has grown into such a fine specimen. Behind him walked a whole troop of admirers, among them Ctesippus—a young fellow from Paeania, of gentle birth and upbringing, but rather insolent in a youthful way. As he entered, Cleinias noticed me sitting there alone; he came straight across to me and sat beside me—on my right, just as you say. Dionysodorus and Euthydemus, when they saw him, stood for a while in conversation, though casting an occasional glance in our direction —I saw that because I was watching them closely. Then one of them, Euthydemus, took a seat by the lad, and the other next to me on my left; the rest where each happened to find a place.

Well, I greeted the two brothers, as not having seen them for some time. After that: 'My dear Cleinias,' I said, 'these two men, you know, are skilled not in mere trifles but in things of paramount importance. They understand all about warfare—as much, at least, as is likely to be required by a good general; I mean military tactics and strategy, and the training of troops under arms. They can also enable you to obtain redress in the courts for any wrong you may have suffered.'

Having said that, I could see they despised me for it; they both laughed, looking at each other. Then Euthydemus spoke:

[1] The Lyceum at this time was a public gymnasium.
[2] Socrates believed that he was occasionally directed by an inner voice. According to Plato its bidding was always negative (see *Apology*), so that in this case it would have said: 'Do not go.' Xenophon (*Memorabilia*) says its orders were sometimes positive.

'No, no, Socrates, we are not interested in such things now; we treat them as mere diversions.'

I was surprised at this and said: 'Your business must be sublime indeed if you regard matters of that sort as diversions. So do please tell me: what is this lofty concern?'

'Virtue, Socrates,' he replied, 'is what we deem ourselves able to purvey in a pre-eminently excellent and speedy fashion.'

'Heavens above!' I exclaimed. 'A mighty affair indeed! When did you have the good fortune to discover it? As I said just now, I still thought of you as chiefly skilled in fighting under arms, and so spoke of you in those terms; for that, I recall, was your profession when you were last here in Athens. However, if you really possess this other kind of knowledge also, please forgive me—you see I address you as though you were a couple of gods, imploring you to pardon my earlier remarks. But are you sure, Euthydemus and Dionysodorus, that you spoke the truth? The magnitude of your promise gives me some excuse for disbelief.'

'Have no fear, Socrates,' they replied; 'what we say is perfectly true.'

'Then I congratulate you on your acquisition far more than the Persian monarch on his empire; only tell me whether you intend to give a demonstration of this science, or what you have resolved to do.'

'We are here for the very purpose, Socrates, of demonstrating and expounding it to whoever wishes to learn.'

'Well, I guarantee that all who do not possess it will be anxious to do so—myself first, then Cleinias here, not forgetting Ctesippus and all these others,' I said, indicating Cleinias's admirers. All these fellows were by this time standing around us. Ctesippus, you see, happened to be sitting some distance from Cleinias; and as Euthydemus leaned forward in talking to me he accidentally obscured Ctesippus's view of Cleinias, who was between us. Whereupon Ctesippus, longing to gaze on his favourite, and being also an eager listener, led the way by jumping up and taking his stand opposite us; and this caused the others, on seeing what he did, to gather around us, both Cleinias's admirers and the disciples of Euthydemus and Dionysodorus. Pointing to this group, I told Euthydemus they were all ready to learn; to which Ctesippus assented enthusiastically, and so did the rest; and they all joined in urging the two men to exhibit the potentialities of their wisdom.

On this I remarked: 'Euthydemus and Dionysodorus, please do your level best to satisfy my friends, and for my sake let us have a demonstration. This, of course, is going to be very far from a trifling performance. But tell me something: will you be able to make a good man of him only who is already convinced that he ought to learn from you, or of him also who is not yet so convinced, owing to an absolute disbelief that virtue can be learned or that you are qualified to teach it? Come now, is it the function of this same art to persuade a man that virtue is teachable and that you are the men from whom one may best learn it, or does this require some other art?'

'No, this same one will do it, Socrates,' said Dionysodorus.

'Then you two, Dionysodorus,' I said, 'must be of all men alive today the best qualified to incite one to the pursuit of wisdom and the practice of virtue.'

'We think so, at all events, Socrates.'

'Well, kindly postpone the rest of your demonstration to some future occasion,' I went on, 'and prove this one point. You are to persuade this young man here that he ought to pursue wisdom and practise virtue; by doing so you will oblige me and indeed all of us. This youth happens to be in exactly the state of mind to which I referred; and I and all the rest of us here are anxious for him to become thoroughly good. He is the son of Axiochus, son of the late Alcibiades,[1] and is first cousin to the latter's present namesake. His name is Cleinias. He is young; and so we feel uneasy about him, as is only natural in the case of a young man, lest someone steal a march on us, incline him to some other course of life, and thereby corrupt him. Your arrival at this juncture is therefore most fortunate. Come now, if it is all the same to you, make a trial of the lad and talk to him in our presence.'

When I had finished speaking, in almost those very words, Euthydemus answered boldly and without hesitation: 'Oh,

[1] The famous Alcibiades, who died in 404 B.C.

it's all the same to us, Socrates, provided the young man is willing to answer our questions.'

'Of course he is,' I said; 'he's quite used to doing that. People here are constantly approaching him and plying him with questions, so there's not much timidity about him when it comes to answering.'

I hardly know, Crito, how to give you a satisfactory account of what followed. It is no slight task to evoke in words such vast knowledge as theirs. Consequently, like the poets, I must begin my tale by invoking Memory and the Muses. At all events, Euthydemus set to work, so far as I remember, in more or less these terms: 'Cleinias, which group of men are learners—the wise or the foolish?'

Now this was an awkward question; the young man blushed and glanced at me in his confusion. Observing his dilemma I said: 'Don't be frightened, Cleinias; answer bravely and tell him exactly what you think, for he is perhaps doing you the greatest service possible.'

Meanwhile Dionysodorus leaned over slightly towards me, with a broad grin on his face, and whispered in my ear: 'I'm warning you, Socrates; whichever way the lad answers he will be proved wrong.'

While he was saying this Cleinias replied, so I was unable to put him on his guard. He said it was the wise who were learners.

Then Euthydemus asked: 'And are there, or are there not, persons whom you call teachers?'

He agreed that there were.

'And the teachers of the learners are teachers in the same way as your lute-master and your writing-master, I imagine, were teachers of you and your fellow pupils?'

He assented.

'Now, of course, when you were learning, you did not as yet know the things you were learning?'

'No,' he replied.

'So you were wise while still ignorant of those things?'

'Certainly not,' he said.

'Then if not wise, foolish?'

'Exactly.'

'So when you were learning what you did not know, you learned while being foolish.'

The young man nodded agreement.

'In that case it is the foolish who learn, Cleinias—not the wise, as you fancy.'

When he finished speaking all those disciples of Dionysodorus and Euthydemus raised a cheer and burst out laughing, like a chorus at a sign from their director. Before the lad had fully recovered his breath Dionysodorus took over and said: 'Well now, Cleinias, whenever your writing-master dictated from memory, which of the pupils learned the piece recited, the wise or the foolish?'

'The wise,' said Cleinias.

'So it is the wise who learn, and not the foolish; therefore the answer you gave Euthydemus just now was incorrect.'

At this there was a great deal of laughter and deafening applause from the pair's adorers, who admired their cleverness. As for ourselves, we were crestfallen and held our peace. Then Euthydemus, noticing our dismay and intending to astonish us still further, would not leave the boy alone, but went on questioning him. Like a skilful dancer, he gave a double twist to his questions on a single point: 'Now do the learners', he asked, 'learn what they know, or what they do not?'

Dionysodorus whispered to me again softly: 'Here comes another, Socrates, just like the first.'

'Good God!' I retorted; 'surely the first question was enough for your purpose.'

'All our questions, Socrates,' he said, 'are like that; they leave no loophole.'

'That is the reason, presumably,' I remarked, 'for the great reputation you enjoy among your followers.'

Meanwhile Cleinias answered Euthydemus that learners learn what they do not know; so he had to face the same barrage of questions as before. 'Well then,' asked Euthydemus, 'do you not know your alphabet?'

'Yes,' he said.

'All of it?'

The answer was affirmative.

'Now when someone dictates a passage, isn't he dictating letters of the alphabet?'

The answer again was yes.

'And he dictates things of which you know something, since you know them all?'

Once more he agreed.

'Well now,' said Euthydemus, 'surely it's not *you* who learn whatever such a person dictates; isn't it rather he who does not know his letters that learns?'

'No,' he answered; 'I learn.'

'Then you learn what you already know, since you know all the letters of the alphabet.'

He agreed.

'So your answer was wrong,' said Euthydemus.

Euthydemus had hardly finished speaking when Dionysodorus caught the ball of argument, so to speak. Once again making the boy his target, he said: 'Euthydemus is leading you astray, Cleinias. Tell me, is not learning the reception of knowledge of that which one learns?'

Cleinias agreed.

'And what is knowing', he continued, 'but the possession of knowledge here and now?'

'Nothing but that,' assented Cleinias.

'Very well then: are those who receive something those who already possess it, or those who do not?'

'Those who do not.'

'And you have admitted that those who do not know belong also to the group of those who do not possess it?'

He nodded assent.

'And those who are learning are among the receivers, not among the possessors?'

He agreed.

'Very well then, it is those who do *not* know that learn, Cleinias, and not those who know.'

Euthydemus was about to throw the young man for a third time when I, perceiving that the lad was going to succumb, and wishing to give him a breathing space lest he should disgrace us by losing heart, encouraged him with these words: 'Don't be surprised, Cleinias, if you are baffled by this line of argument; probably you can't see what our two visitors are doing to you. They are acting just like the celebrants of Corybantic rites do when they enthrone a candidate for initiation. That ceremony, as you know, if you have been through it,

includes dancing and merry-making; so here these two are
dancing around you and playing the fool preparatory to your
initiation. So now you must imagine you are listening to the
first part of professorial mysteries. You have to begin, as
Prodicus says, by learning the correct use of words. This is the
very fact that our two visitors are making clear to you. You did
not realize that "learning" is the word used on the one hand
in the case of a man who, having originally no knowledge of a
particular subject, receives such knowledge in due course;
and that on the other hand the same word is employed when,
having the knowledge already, he uses it to investigate the
same subject whether occurring in action or in speech. True,
they tend in this last case to call it "understanding" rather
than "learning", but sometimes they call it "learning" too;
and this point, as our friends are now showing, has escaped
your notice—how the same word is applied to people who are
in the opposite situations of knowing and not knowing. A
similar point was at the back of their second question, when
they asked you whether people learn what they know or what
they don't know. Such things are the sport of the sciences; and
that is why I tell you these men are simply playing with you.
I call it sport because, although one were to learn many or
even all of such tricks, one would not be in the slightest degree
wiser as to the true state of the matters under discussion, but
only able to play the fool with others (owing to the difference
of verbal meanings) by tripping them up and sending them
head over heels—like people who quietly pull away a stool
when we are about to sit down, and laugh uproariously when
they see us on our backs. Up to this point, then, you must
regard these gentlemen's treatment of you as mere play; from
now onwards, I'm sure, they will let you see the real object
they have in mind. Meanwhile I shall keep them on the track
and make sure they carry out the promise they gave me. They
said they would demonstrate their skill in exhortation; but it
appears they saw fit to start by pulling your leg. Right. Now
then, Euthydemus and Dionysodorus, let's have no more of
your mirth; surely you've had enough of that. Your next task
is to give a demonstration of exhorting this young man as to
how he should devote himself to wisdom and virtue. First,
however, I shall explain to you how I look at the subject of our

discussion and the kind of treatment I want it to receive. If you think I'm handling it like a blundering ass, please don't load me with ridicule; I long so much for the fruits of your wisdom that I shall go blindly ahead even in your presence. So you and your disciples must control yourselves, and listen to me without laughing. Now then, son of Axiochus, answer this question:

'Do all we men desire prosperity? But perhaps that question is one of the absurdities I was frightened of just now; after all, I suppose the very question is ridiculous, since everyone must long to prosper.'

'Everyone, without exception,' said Cleinias.

'Well then,' I said, 'that leads us to the next question: How can we prosper? Will it depend on our possession of many goods? But I suppose this is an even more absurd question than my last; one can't expect any but an affirmative reply.'

He agreed.

'Right; then what sort of things do we look upon as being really good? Or do you regard the answer as easily discoverable, as offering no challenge to a really great mind? Won't anyone tell us that it is good to be rich?'

'Of course,' he said.

'Then the same holds good of being healthy and handsome, and of having many other physical endowments?'

He agreed.

'Once again, isn't it clear that noble birth, talents and honours conferred by one's country are good things?'

He assented.

'Then what other goods can we find?' I asked. 'How about being self-controlled, upright and brave? Tell me frankly, Cleinias: do you think we ought to rank these as goods, or exclude them? It's an open question; what is your view?'

'They are goods,' said Cleinias.

'Right then,' I continued; 'and whereabouts in the line shall we place wisdom? Among the goods, or where?'

'Among the goods.'

'Then take care we don't overlook any goods deserving of notice.'

'I don't think there are any that have escaped our notice,' said Cleinias.

Thereupon I remembered one and said: 'Lord, yes, we are nearly forgetting the greatest of all goods.'

'What is that?' he asked.

'Good fortune, Cleinias—something which all men, even the worst fools, recognize as the greatest of goods.'

'How right you are,' he said.

Once again I paused to think, and exclaimed: 'Son of Axiochus, you and I have come very near to making idiots of ourselves in the eyes of our visitors.'

'What's wrong now?' he asked.

'Why, having included good fortune in our earlier list, here we are discussing the same thing over again.'

'What are you getting at?'

'Surely it's absurd, when we've been looking at something all the time, to bring it up anew and cover the same ground twice.'

'To what are you referring?' he asked.

'Wisdom', I replied, 'is presumably good fortune; even a child could see that.'

Being young and simple-minded, Cleinias was rather puzzled. Noticing his perplexity, I went on: 'Surely you realize, Cleinias, that for success in flute-playing it is the flautists who have the best fortune.'

To that he agreed.

'Then in reading and writing letters it will be the schoolmasters.'

'Certainly.'

'Well now, as regards the perils of a voyage by sea, do you think any pilots, generally speaking, are more successful than those who are experts?'

'Of course not.'

'Suppose, too, that you were on active service: would you prefer to take your chance with a general who was experienced or otherwise?'

'With one who was experienced.'

'And supposing you were ill, to which sort of doctor would you choose to entrust yourself—a wise or an ignorant one?'

'To a wise one.'

'Your reason being', I said, 'that you would fare better in the hands of a wise than of an ignorant one?'

He assented.

'So in every field wisdom leads man to success. For surely she can never err, but is inevitably right in both operation and result, otherwise she would no longer be wisdom.'

Eventually we managed to reach agreement as follows: Generally speaking, no one with whom wisdom abides has need of success as well. And having arrived at this understanding, I began to question him again as to how we should view our previous conclusions. 'We agreed', I said, 'that if we were endowed with many goods we would be happy and prosperous.'

'Yes,' he said.

'In that case would the presence of goods make us happy if they conferred on us some benefit, or if they conferred none?'

'If they conferred some benefit,' he said.

'And would a thing benefit us if we merely possessed it and did not use it? For example, could we be said to derive benefit from a lot of food that we did not eat, or from a store of liquor that we did not drink?'

'Of course not,' he replied.

'Well then, if a craftsman had to hand all the requisites for his particular skill, but made no use of them, would he prosper by virtue of having acquired all that was necessary for the realization of his craft? For instance, if a carpenter were provided with all his tools and plenty of timber, but did no carpentry, could he possibly derive benefit from what he thus possessed?'

'Indeed, no,' said Cleinias.

'Good. Now suppose someone had acquired wealth and all those goods we mentioned a little while ago, but made no use of them: would the possession of such goods make him happy?'

'Surely not, Socrates.'

'It seems, therefore, that in order to be happy one must not only have acquired such goods, but must also *use* them; otherwise no benefit is derived from their possession.'

'True.'

'Very well, then, Cleinias, is the possession and use of those goods sufficient to make a man happy?'

'I think so.'

'Shall we say', I asked, 'if he uses them rightly, or equally so if he does not?'

'If rightly.'

'A very proper answer,' I said; 'for surely more mischief arises from the wrong use of a thing than from its non-use. In the former case evil results; in the latter, neither evil nor good. Isn't that right?'

He agreed.

'To proceed then: Is there in the handling of wood anything that has a bearing on its right use but a knowledge of carpentry?'

'Nothing at all,' he said.

'I presume likewise that in the business of making furniture it is knowledge that produces what is required.'

'Yes,' he said.

'So also', I continued, 'in the use of those goods we first mentioned—wealth, health and beauty—was it knowledge that guided man to the right use of such advantages and ordered their functions, or was it something else?'

'Knowledge,' he replied.

'Knowledge therefore, it would seem, supplies man not only with good fortune, but also with welfare, in respect of anything he either does or possesses.'

He agreed.

'I ask you then, can we derive any benefit from all other gifts without the wisdom that is understanding? Are we going to say that a man profits more by having much and doing much when he is devoid of sense than he will if he does and possesses little? Look at it this way: would he not err less if he did less, thus accomplishing less evil and therefore being less miserable?'

'Certainly,' he said.

'In which of the two cases will one be likely to do less—when one is poor or when one is rich?'

'When one is poor,' he said.

'And when one is weak, or when one is strong?'

'Weak.'

'And when one has high position, or has none?'

'None.'

'Will one do less as a coward, or when brave and self-controlled?'

'As a coward.'

'Likewise when idle rather than busy?'

He agreed.

'And when slow rather than quick, and dim in eyes and ears rather than sharp?'

We agreed with one another as to these and all such cases.

'To sum up then, Cleinias,' I continued, 'it seems that all those things which we originally described as goods need to be discussed, not so much from the point of view of how they are in themselves and by nature good, as from another standpoint —which is this: if they are guided by ignorance, they are greater evils than their opposites, according as they are more capable of subserving their evil guide; whereas if they are guided by understanding and wisdom, they are greater goods; but in themselves neither sort is of any value.'

'I think what you suggest is right,' he answered.

'Well, what is the upshot of our remarks? Surely just this: that wisdom is good, ignorance bad, and all the rest are neutral.'

He agreed.

'Let us then consider', I said, 'the further conclusion that lies before us. Since we all long to be happy, and since it has been admitted that we become so by using things *rightly* (knowledge being that which provides the rightness and good fortune), it seems that every man must use all available means to prepare himself with a view to becoming as wise as possible. Isn't that true?'

'Yes,' he said.

'A man may well think that he ought to obtain this endowment from his father much more than money, and also from his guardians and ordinary friends, and from those who style themselves his lovers—begging and imploring them to give him his share of wisdom. If that is so, Cleinias, there is no disgrace or lack of dignity in making it a pretext for attending upon and being a slave either to one's lover or to any man, and for being ready to perform any service that is honourable in one's eagerness to become wise. Don't you agree?' I asked.

'I think you are perfectly right,' he answered.

'Yes, Cleinias,' I said; 'if wisdom is teachable, and does not arise spontaneously in mankind—for this is a question that we have still to consider as not yet agreed on by you and me——'

'Personally, Socrates,' he said, 'I think it is teachable.'

At that I was glad, and said: 'Well spoken, my dear friend! How kind of you not to involve me in a long inquiry as to whether wisdom is teachable! Now that you think it is both teachable and the only thing in the world that makes man happy and fortunate, can you help saying that it is necessary to pursue wisdom, or intending to pursue it yourself?'

'Indeed, Socrates,' he replied, 'I do say so, with all my heart.'

Delighted at hearing this, I remarked: 'There, Dionyso-dorus and Euthydemus, you have my illustration of what I expect a hortatory argument to be—rough and ready, perhaps, and somewhat laboured. Now let either of you who wishes give us an example of an artist's handling of the same theme. If you prefer, let your demonstration begin where I left off, and show the lad whether he ought to acquire every kind of knowledge, or whether there is a single brand of it which one must obtain if one is to be both happy and a good man, and what it is. For as I was saying at the outset, it really is of paramount importance to us that this young fellow should become wise and good.'

Those were my words, Crito. I prepared to listen closely to what might follow, to note how they would deal with the question and how they would set about exhorting the youth to practise wisdom and virtue. Well, the elder of them, Dionyso-dorus, made a start; we all gazed upon him expecting to hear forthwith some wonderful arguments. And this result we certainly obtained. For wondrous, in a way, Crito, was the argument he proceeded to usher forth; it is worth your hearing as a notable incitement to virtue.

'Tell me, Socrates,' he said, 'and the rest of you who say you desire this lad to become wise, whether you say so in jest or really and earnestly desire it.'

At this I reflected that earlier on, when we asked them to talk with Cleinias, they must have thought we were joking, and therefore failed to take our request seriously. Anyway, this reflection made me insist all the more that we were utterly sincere.

Then Dionysodorus said: 'Be careful, Socrates, that you don't find yourself having to eat your words.'

'I know what I'm about,' I said; 'I know I shall never deny what I say now.'

'Well then,' he continued, 'you tell me you wish him to become wise.'

'Certainly.'

'And at present,' he asked, 'is Cleinias wise or not?'

'He says he is not yet so—he's no braggart.'

'And you', he went on, 'wish him to become wise and not remain ignorant?'

I agreed.

'So you wish him to become what he is not, and to be no longer what he now is.'

Hearing this I was staggered; and he, striking in on my confusion, said: 'Of course then, since you wish him *to be* no longer as he now is, you wish him, apparently, to be dead.[1] But what valuable friends and lovers they must be who would give anything to know their darling was dead and gone!'

Ctesippus, on hearing that, was angry on his favourite's account, and said: 'Stranger from Thurii, if it were not a rather rude thing to say, I would tell you exactly what I think of your behaviour in speaking so falsely of me and my friends as to make out—to me it's almost too outrageous to repeat— that I could wish this boy out of the world.'

'But, Ctesippus,' said Euthydemus, 'do you think it possible to lie?'

'Of course I do,' he answered: 'I should be mad if I didn't.'

'Do you mean, when one tells the thing about which one is telling, or when one does not?'

'When one tells it,' he said.

'Then if you tell it, you tell just that thing which you tell, and nothing else whatever?'

'Naturally,' said Ctesippus.

'Now the thing that you tell is a single one, distinct from all others?'

---

[1] The quibbling here and later is an intentional failure to distinguish two uses of *einai* ('to be'). One denotes existence, while the other serves merely as copula.

'Exactly.'

'Then the man who tells that thing tells that which *is*?'

'Yes.'

'But surely, he who tells what *is*, or things that *are*, tells the truth; in which case Dionysodorus, if he tells things that are, tells the truth and utters no lie about you.'

'Yes,' said Ctesippus; 'but anyone who speaks as he did, Euthydemus, is not saying things that are.'

Then Euthydemus asked him: 'And the things which *are not*, surely are not?'

'They are not.'

'Then the things that are not can be nowhere?'

'Nowhere.'

'Then is it possible for anyone to deal with these "things that are not" in such a way as to make them be when they are nowhere?'

'I presume not,' said Ctesippus.

'Well now, when orators address the Assembly, do they do nothing?'

'No, they do something,' he replied.

'Then if they do, they also perform, don't they?'

'Yes.'

'Now is speaking doing and performing?'

He agreed that it was.

'No one, presumably, speaks what is not—otherwise he would be performing something; and you have admitted that one cannot perform what is not—so according to you yourself no one speaks what is false; and if Dionysodorus speaks, he speaks what *is*—that is, what is true.'

'Quite, quite, Euthydemus,' said Ctesippus; 'but somehow or other he speaks what *is*, only not *as it is*.'

'How do you mean, Ctesippus?' asked Dionysodorus. 'Are there persons who tell things as they are?'

'Why surely,' he replied, 'there are gentlemen—people who speak the truth.'

'Well,' Dionysodorus went on, 'good things are in good case, bad in bad, are they not?'

He assented.

'And you admit that gentlemen tell things as they are?'

'I do.'

'In which case, Ctesippus, good people speak evil of evil things, if they speak of them as they are.'

'Upon my word yes, very much so, when for example they speak of evil men; among whom, if you take my advice, you will avoid being included, lest the good speak ill of you. For, I assure you, the good speak ill of the evil.'

'And they speak greatly of the great,' asked Euthydemus, 'and hotly of the hot?'

'Very likely,' said Ctesippus; 'at any rate they speak frigidly of the frigid and call their manner of arguing frigid.'

'You are becoming abusive, Ctesippus,' exclaimed Dionysodorus, 'really quite abusive.'

'Not I, by heaven, Dionysodorus, for I like you. I'm only giving you a friendly hint and trying to persuade you never to say anything so uncouth in my presence as that I wish these most esteemed friends of mine to be dead and gone.'

I felt that things were getting a little out of hand, so I began to poke fun at Ctesippus. 'Ctesippus,' I said, 'it is my belief that we should accept from our visitors what they so kindly offer us, and not quarrel over a word. If they know how to do away with people in such a manner as to change them from wicked and witless to honest and intelligent beings (whether they have discovered for themselves or learned from someone else this remarkable sort of destruction or undoing, which enables them to destroy a man in his wickedness and restore him in honesty); if, I say, they know how to do this—and obviously they do, for you remember they said their newly found art consisted in turning wicked men into good—let us recognize them as having this power. Let them destroy the lad for us and make him sensible, and all the rest of us likewise. If you young fellows are afraid, let the experiment be made on me as a worthless object; being well on in years, I am ready to take the risk and entrust myself to Dionysodorus, as if he were Medea of Colchis. Let him destroy me, and if he likes let him boil me down, or do to me whatever he pleases; only he must make me good.'

'I too, Socrates,' said Ctesippus, 'am ready to offer myself to be skinned by these foreigners even more thoroughly, if they choose, than they are doing now, provided my skin is not to finish up by being turned into a bottle, like that of Marsyas,

but into virtue. You know, Dionysodorus here thinks I'm
annoyed with him. I'm not annoyed at all; I only contradict
the remarks which I think he has so unhandsomely directed at
me. Come now, Dionysodorus, be fair and don't call contradiction abuse; abuse is something altogether different.'

Whereupon Dionysodorus retorted: 'As if there were any
such thing as contradiction! Is that your manner of argument,
Ctesippus?'

'Most assuredly it is,' he answered; 'do you, Dionysodorus,
maintain that there is not?'

'Well,' he said, 'you at all events can't prove that you've
ever heard anyone contradicting another.'

'Is that so?' he replied. 'Well, let us hear now whether I
can put my finger on a case—Ctesippus contradicting
Dionysodorus.'

'Will you make good that claim?'

'Certainly,' he said.

'Well then,' the other continued, 'am I right in saying that
every single thing that is has its own description?'

'Certainly.'

'Do you mean, according as it *is*, or according as it *is not*?'

'According as it is.'

'Exactly,' he said; 'for if you remember, Ctesippus, we
showed just now that no one speaks what is not.'

'Well, what of that?' asked Ctesippus. 'Are you and I
contradicting any the less?'

'Tell me,' he said, 'could we contradict if we both uttered
the description of the same thing? In such a case, would we
not surely be speaking identical words?'

Ctesippus agreed.

'Would we be contradicting if neither of us uttered the
description of the thing?' he asked. 'Or shall we say that in
such a case neither of us would have touched on the matter at
all?'

This also he admitted.

'Well now, suppose I utter the description of one thing,
while you give that of some other thing. Are we contradicting
then? Or am I describing the thing while you are not describing it at all? How can he who does not describe contradict him
who does?'

Ctesippus remained silent; but I, surprised at the argument, inquired: 'How do you mean, Dionysodorus? Frankly, although I have heard this argument put forward by many people on various occasions, it always astonishes me. The followers of Protagoras used it a good deal; so did others even before his time; but to me it always seems to have a curious way of overturning not only other views, but itself as well. I believe I shall learn the truth of it from you far better than from anyone else. Am I not right in taking the essence of your statement to be that there is no such thing as speaking falsehood? Either one speaks and speaks the truth, or one doesn't speak at all?'

He agreed.

'Then may we say that speaking falsehood "is not", but thinking falsehood "is"?'

'No,' he said, 'the same applies in the case of thinking.'

'Therefore', I said, 'there is no such thing as false opinion.'

'No,' he said.

'Nor ignorance, nor ignorant men; or must not ignorance be present, if it ever can be, when we put things falsely?'

'Certainly.'

'But there is no such thing as this,' I said.

'No.'

'Do you propound this theory, Dionysodorus, merely for its own sake—just to say something extraordinary—or is it your honest belief that there is no such thing as an ignorant man?'

'Go ahead and refute me,' he replied.

'Well, does your argument allow of such a thing as refutation, if no one can utter falsehood?'

'There is no such thing as refutation,' said Euthydemus.

'So Dionysodorus did not order me just now to refute him?'

'No; how can one order something that is not? Do you give orders for any such thing?'

'Well, Euthydemus,' I said, 'the fact is that I don't at all understand these clever devices, even when they are sound; I am a little dull-witted. Consequently I may perhaps be going to say something rather absurd; but do please forgive me. Here it is: if there is no such thing as speaking or thinking falsehood, or being stupid, surely there can be no possibility of making a mistake when one does something. For in doing it there is no mistaking the thing done. That represents your view, does it not?'

'Certainly,' he replied.

'My absurd question', I continued, 'is now before you. If we make no mistake either in doing or saying or intending, I ask you what in heaven's name, on that assumption, is the subject you two profess to teach? Didn't you say a while ago that your speciality was to put any man who wished in the way of learning virtue?'

'Come, come, Socrates,' interrupted Dionysodorus; 'are you such an old dotard as to recall what we said at the beginning of this discussion, and even what I may have said last year, and yet be powerless to deal with the arguments put forward here and now?'

'But, you see,' I replied, 'they are extremely formidable, and naturally so; for they proceed from the mouths of sages. And this is further revealed by the great difficulty of meeting the one you have just advanced. For what on earth do you mean, Dionysodorus, by saying I am powerless to deal with it? Or is it clear that you mean I am at a loss how to refute it? You must tell me what else can be intended by your phrase "powerless to deal with the arguments".'

'But it's not all that hard to deal with *your* phrase "can be intended". Just answer me.'

'What, before you've answered me, Dionysodorus?' I said.

'You refuse to answer?'

'Is it fair?'

'Quite fair,' he replied.

'On what principle,' I asked, 'unless on the principle that you come before us here claiming to be universally skilled in debate, and so can judge when an answer should be given, and when not? Accordingly you will not answer a word, because you can see you ought not to do it.'

'You talk a lot of rubbish', said he, 'instead of answering as you should. Come along, sir, do as I tell you and answer, since you admit I'm a wise man.'

'Ah well, I must obey,' I said, 'and of necessity, it seems; for you are the master. Ask away.'

'Then tell me, do things that "intend" have life when they intend, or do inanimate objects also do it?'

'Only those that have life.'

'Well, do you know of any phrase that has life?'

'Good heavens, no.'

'Why then did you ask just now what could be intended by my phrase?'

'My mistake,' I said; 'I'm so dim-witted. But perhaps, after all, it was not a mistake, and I was right in saying that phrases intend. Do you hold I was mistaken or not? If I was not mistaken, then all your skill will not avail to refute me, and you are powerless to deal with the argument; whereas if I *was* mistaken, you are wrong again, for you hold there is no such thing as making a mistake. Finally, what I say was not directed against what you said last year. However, Dionyso-dorus and Euthydemus,' I continued, 'our argument appears to be in the same condition as before: it still suffers from the old weakness of bowling others over and then tumbling down itself; and even your art has discovered no way of escaping from this weakness—in spite, too, of the marvellous show it makes of accurate reasoning.'

At this point Ctesippus exclaimed: 'Ay, your talk is quite remarkable, you men of Thurii or Chios, or wherever or how-ever it is you are pleased to get your names; for you do not hesitate to chatter like a couple of fools.'

I was afraid we might be in for some violent abuse, so I calmed Ctesippus once again, saying: 'Ctesippus, I repeat to you what I told Cleinias a while ago, that you don't realize how wonderfully skilled our visitors are. The only trouble is that they won't give us a demonstration of their ability in real earnest; they persist in treating us to jugglers' tricks after the manner of Proteus, that cunning Egyptian. Let us therefore take a tip from Menelaus, and hold on to these gentlemen until they give us a genuine display of their art. I believe they'll produce something of great value once they begin to be serious. Come, let us beg and implore them to manifest themselves in their true character. Personally, I would like to lead off once again by explaining what sort of men I pray they may turn out to be. Starting from where I left off earlier, I shall do my best to describe what follows on from my previous remarks, in the hope of rousing them to action and obliging them, out of sympathy for my earnest endeavour, to be earnest themselves.

'Will you, Cleinias,' I asked, 'be so good as to remind me of the point at which we broke off? If I remember rightly it was to the effect that one ought to pursue wisdom; wasn't that what we finally agreed?'

'Yes,' he said.

'And am I not right in saying that this pursuit—it is called philosophy—is an acquiring of knowledge?'

'Yes,' he said.

'Then what knowledge would we acquire if we acquired it rightly? Is it not perfectly clear that it must be such knowledge as will profit us?'

'Certainly,' he replied.

'And will we derive profit from being able to tell, as we travel around, where the largest seams of gold lie buried?'

'Perhaps,' he said.

'And yet', I went on, 'we have already refuted that proposition. Even if without any trouble or digging the ground we were to obtain all the gold in the world, we should gain nothing—no, not if we knew how to turn the very rocks into gold—unless we knew how to use that gold. We agreed upon that, don't you remember?' I asked.

'Indeed I do,' he said.

'Nor, it seems, do we derive any advantage from all other knowledge—money-making, medicine or any other crafts—without knowing how to use the end product. Isn't that so?'

He agreed.

'Again, if there were a branch of knowledge enabling one to render human beings immortal, we should be unlikely to benefit therefrom if we lacked the knowledge of how to use immortality. That too seems to follow from our earlier admissions.'

We agreed on all those points.

'Then, my dear boy,' said I, 'the sort of knowledge we require is that in which production and knowing how to use the product are happily united.'

'Apparently,' he said.

'We ought therefore, it seems, to aim at something quite

different from being lyre-makers or possessing knowledge of that kind. In this case the art that produces and the art that uses are quite distinct, dealing separately with the same thing; for there is a substantial difference between the art of making lyres and that of harping. Isn't that so?'

He agreed.

'Nor again, evidently, do we need an art of flute-making; for this is another of the same sort.'

He assented.

'Now truthfully', I said, 'we might perhaps learn the art of speech-making; but can that be the art we should acquire if we would be happy?'

'I for one think not,' said Cleinias, interrupting.

'Upon what evidence do you rely?'

'I see', he said, 'certain speech-writers who don't know how to make use of the particular arguments composed by themselves, like lyre-makers in regard to their lyres. In the former case, too, there are other persons able to use what the authors produce, though themselves incapable of composing the written speech. It is therefore obvious that in the realm of speech also there are two distinct arts, one of producing and one of using.'

'I think you have offered sufficient proof,' I said, 'that the speech-writer's art cannot be the one whose acquisition would make us happy. Nevertheless I had an idea that the knowledge we've been looking for all this while would make its appearance somewhere about here. For when I'm in the company of these speech-writers, Cleinias, not only do they strike me as clever beyond words, but their art itself seems lofty to the point of inspiration. However, this is not surprising; for it is part and parcel of the sorcerer's art, and only a little inferior to that. The sorcerer's art is the charming of snakes, tarantulas, scorpions and other beasts, and diseases, while the other is simply the charming and soothing of juries, assemblies, crowds and so forth. Or do you take a different view?' I asked.

'No,' he replied, 'I think what you say is true.'

'Which way, then,' I asked, 'shall we turn now? What kind of art shall we try?'

'I've no suggestions,' he answered.

'Why, I believe I've found it myself,' I said.

'What is it?' said Cleinias.

'Generalship', I replied, 'strikes me as the art whose acquisition above all others would make one happy.'

'I don't think so.'

'Why not?' I asked.

'In a sense, generalship is the art of hunting men.'

'So what?'

'No phase of actual hunting', he replied, 'is more important than the pursuit and catch. But the captors, having achieved what they set out to do, cannot make use of the quarry; huntsmen and fishermen turn it over to the caterers. So too with geometers, astronomers and calculators; these also, in their way, are hunters, since none of them is a mere maker of diagrams, but discovers abstract truths. Not knowing how to use their prey, but only how to hunt, they hand over their discoveries to competent dialecticians—if any are to be found who are not complete nitwits.'

'Splendid, Cleinias!' I said. 'You're no less ingenious than handsome. But is that really so?'

'Of course it is; and the same is true of generals. When they have captured a city or an army, they turn it over to the politicians (simply because they themselves don't know how to use what they've captured), just as quail-trappers, I imagine, hand over their birds to quail-keepers. Therefore,' he continued, 'if we are in search of that art which itself includes knowledge of how to use what it has acquired either by way of pursuing or producing, and if this is the kind that will give us bliss, we must reject generalship and look for something else.'

CRI. Good gracious, Socrates! Do you mean to say such a pronouncement was uttered by that youngster?

SOCR. You don't believe it came from him, Crito?

CRI. I most certainly don't. If he said that, I'm quite sure he needs no tutoring from Euthydemus or anyone else.

SOCR. Heavens above now! I wonder if it *was* Cleinias who said it? My memory fails me.

CRI. It sounds more like Ctesippus.

SOCR. Well, at all events I'm certain that the speaker was neither Euthydemus nor Dionysodorus. Tell me, Crito, do you think the words may have been uttered by some superior power which came expressly for that purpose? I'm absolutely sure I heard them.

CRI. Indeed yes, Socrates; I fancy it was some superior power —and very superior at that. Anyway, did you continue with your search for an appropriate art? Did you eventually catch up with your quarry, or not?

SOCR. Catch up with it, my dear fellow! We were in a most absurd situation; like children chasing crested larks, we kept on believing at every moment that we were about to seize this or that form of knowledge, while they as often slipped from our grasp. But I need not tell you the story at length. When we reached the kingly art, and were examining it to see whether we had here what provides and produces happiness, we became entangled as it were in a labyrinth; just as we imagined we had reached the end, we turned around again and found ourselves almost back at the beginning of our quest—as needy as when we set out.

CRI. How did that happen, Socrates?

SOCR. I'll tell you. We came to the conclusion that the statesman's and the monarch's art were one and the same.

CRI. Well, what then?

SOCR. To this art, we thought, generalship and the rest handed over management of their own products, because this one alone knew how to make use of them. It therefore seemed clear to us that this was the one we were seeking, and was the cause of right behaviour in the state. We shared Aeschylus's belief [1] that it sits alone at the helm of state, steering the whole, commanding the whole, and making the whole useful.

CRI. A very proper sentiment, Socrates, don't you think?

SOCR. You shall decide that, Crito, if you care to hear what befell us thereafter. For later on we reconsidered it more or less as follows: 'Come now, does the kingly art, that rules over all, produce any effect or not?' 'Why, of course it does,' we assured one another. Wouldn't you agree, Crito?

CRI. I would.

SOCR. Well, what would you say is its effect? For example, if I asked you whether medicine, in ruling all that comes within its scope, has any effect to show, wouldn't you say, 'Yes, health'?

[1] Cf. *Seven Against Thebes*, 2

CRI. I would.

SOCR. And how about your own art of agriculture? In ruling over all that comes within its scope, what effect does it produce? Wouldn't you say that it supplies us with food from the soil?

CRI. I would.

SOCR. And what of the kingly art? In ruling over all that lies within its jurisdiction, what does it produce? Perhaps you haven't a ready answer.

CRI. Indeed I haven't, Socrates.

SOCR. Nor had we, Crito; but you know at any rate that if this is truly the art we are seeking, it must be beneficial.

CRI. Of course.

SOCR. Then surely it must supply something good?

CRI. Inevitably, Socrates.

SOCR. And you know Cleinias and I agreed between ourselves that nothing except some sort of knowledge can be good.

CRI. Yes, so you told me.

SOCR. And it was found that the sum total of effects which can be ascribed to statesmanship—and the number must, presumably, be great if the citizens are to be rendered wealthy, free, and immune from sedition—was neither bad nor good, while the art required must impart knowledge and make us wise, if it really was to be the one that benefited us and made us happy.

CRI. True; such at least you said was your joint conclusion.

SOCR. Well, do you think that kingship makes men wise and good?

CRI. Why not, Socrates?

SOCR. But does it make all men good, and in all respects? Is this the art that confers every sort of knowledge—shoemaking, carpentry and so on?

CR. No, I think not, Socrates.

SOCR. Well, what knowledge does it impart? What use can one make of it? The art we are looking for must not produce effects that are neither bad nor good, and it must confer no knowledge other than itself. Shall we try to explain what kingship is, and how it is to be used? Do you mind, Crito, if we describe it as that whereby we shall make other men good?

CRI. I fully agree.

Socr. In what respect then are we going to have these men good,
and in what useful? Or may we rather say that they will make
others good, and these again others? There is absolutely
nothing to show that they can possibly be good, since we have
discredited the whole business commonly known as politics,
and it is simply a case of vain repetition. As I was saying, we
are equally or even further astray as regards discovering what
that knowledge can be which is to make us happy.

Cri. Upon my word, Socrates, you appear to have got yourselves
into a pretty fix there.

Socr. Well, Crito, finding myself thus adrift, I began to plead
at the top of my voice with the two foreigners as though I were
calling upon the Heavenly Twins to save the lad and myself
from the overwhelming wave of the argument. I begged them
to do everything in their power for us, and show us clearly
what that knowledge can be of which we must lay hold if we
are to spend the remainder of our lives as we ought.

Cri. And did Euthydemus condescend to enlighten you?

Socr. Oh, certainly. He began his discourse, my dear friend, in
this most lordly fashion: 'Would you rather, Socrates, that I
instructed you as regards this knowledge that has so long
eluded you, or proclaim that you have it?'

'Oh sir,' I exclaimed, 'is it in your power to do so?'

'Certainly it is,' he replied.

'Then for heaven's sake', I cried, 'declare that I possess it.
This will be much easier than learning for a man of my
age.'

'Come then, answer me this,' he said. 'Do you know
anything at all?'

'Yes indeed,' I replied; 'many things, though mere
trivialities.'

'Enough,' he said; 'now do you think it possible that anything that is should not be that which it actually is?'

'Good gracious, not I.'

'Well,' he said, 'you know something.'

'I do.'

'Then you are knowing, if you really know.'

'Certainly, in just that one respect.'

'That makes no difference; if you are knowing, it does not
mean that you necessarily know everything.'

'No, of course not,' I replied; 'for there are many other things which I do not know.'

'Then if there is something you do not know, you are not-knowing?'

'Not in respect of that thing, my good sir,' I replied.

'Are you on that account any the less not-knowing? Just now you said you were knowing; so here you are, actually the very man that you are, and again, not that man, in regard to the same matter and at the same time.'

'Granted, Euthydemus,' I said. 'As the saying goes, "Well said, whatever you say". How therefore do I know that knowledge for which we are seeking? For it is undoubtedly impossible for the same thing to be so and not be so—I could not at one and the same time be knowing and not-knowing; and as I know everything, I possess that knowledge into the bargain. Is that your line of argument? Is this your wisdom?'

'Yes; you see, Socrates, you are convicted out of your own mouth.'

'That's all very fine, Euthydemus,' I continued, 'but are you not in the same plight? I assure you, so long as I had you and dear Dionysodorus here to share my lot, however hard, I should have nothing of which to complain. Tell me, you both of course know some existent things, and others you do not?'

'By no means, Socrates,' said Dionysodorus.

'How do you mean?' I asked. 'Do you not then know anything?'

'Oh yes, we do,' he said.

'So you know everything,' I asked, 'by virtue of your knowing anything?'

'Everything,' he replied; 'yes, and you too know all if you know one thing.'

'God above,' I exclaimed, 'what an amazing statement! What a great blessing of which to boast! And do the rest of mankind know everything, or nothing?'

'Surely', he said, 'they cannot know some things and not others; that would involve their being at once knowing and not-knowing.'

'So what?' I asked.

'All men', he replied, 'know all things if they know one.'

'Goodness, Dionysodorus,' I said. 'Now I can see both of you are serious, whereas earlier I had difficulty in persuading you to be so. Do you yourselves really know *everything*? Carpentry, for instance, and shoemaking?'

'Certainly,' he said.

'And you are expert leather-stitchers?'

'Why, yes indeed, and expert cobblers too,' he said.

'And are you good also at such things as counting the stars and the sand?'

'Of course,' he said; 'you surely don't think we would not admit that as well?'

At this point Ctesippus interrupted. 'Dionysodorus,' he said, 'please be so kind as to lay before me some such evidence as will convince me that what you say is true.'

'What evidence shall I offer?'

'Do you know how many teeth Euthydemus has, and does he know how many you have?'

'Are you not satisfied', he retorted, 'with the assurance that we know everything?'

'Now, none of that,' he replied; 'just go one stage further, answer my question, and show us that you are speaking the truth. If you tell us how many teeth each of you has, we will proceed to count them; and then, if you are found to have known the right number, we shall believe you thereafter in everything else.'

Well, they imagined we were leg-pulling, and therefore declined; but when Ctesippus enumerated a whole host of subjects, one after another, and asked them if they knew the answers, they claimed that they did. Ctessipus, indeed, before he had done with them, questioned them on all sorts of matters, even the most unseemly, without the slightest reserve. But they, like boars driven against spears, boldly faced up to his questions, and claimed to have the knowledge in every case. Personally, Crito, I became quite incredulous, and was obliged to finish by asking if Dionysodorus knew also how to dance. To which he replied, 'Certainly.'

'I don't fancy', I said, 'that you have attained to such a degree of skill as to do sword-dancing, or to be whirled around on a wheel at your age.'

'There is nothing', he said, 'that I cannot do.'

'Then tell me,' I went on, 'do you know everything only here and now, or for ever?'

'For ever too,' he answered.

'And did you know even as new-born babes and children?'

'Everything,' they replied in unison.

To us the thing seemed incredible. Then Euthydemus spoke: 'Don't you believe it, Socrates?'

'All I can say', I replied, 'is that you must be extremely clever.'

'Why,' he said, 'if you will deign to answer me, I will prove that you too must admit to possessing these remarkable gifts.'

'I look forward very much', I replied, 'to being refuted in this matter. For if I am ignorant of my own cleverness, and you are going to show me that I know everything always, I cannot imagine a greater stroke of luck in the whole of my life.'

'Then answer me,' he said.

'Ask away; I'm ready to answer.'

'Well now, Socrates,' he inquired, 'have you knowledge of something, or not?'

'I have.'

'And tell me, do you know with that whereby you have knowledge, or with something else?'

'With that whereby I have knowledge; I take it you mean the soul, or is that not what you have in mind?'

'You should be ashamed of yourself, Socrates, asking a question while you are under examination.'

'Very well then,' I said; 'but how am I to proceed? I will do whatever you tell me. When I can't understand what you are asking, do you require me to answer all the same, without inquiry as to your question?'

'Why,' he replied, 'you surely attribute *some* meaning to what I say.'

'I do,' I replied.

'Answer then to the meaning you think my words convey.'

'Well,' I said, 'if you ask a question intending to convey something different from what I take its meaning to be, and I answer to the latter, do you not mind receiving an irrelevant answer?'

'Personally I don't mind at all; but it seems to me that you will not be satisfied.'

'Then by heaven I shall not answer,' I said, 'unless and until I am clear as to the question.'

'You refuse to answer', he said, 'to the meaning as you understand it in each case, because you will go on talking rubbish, you hopeless old dotard.'

I realized he was annoyed with me for distinguishing the phrases used, when he hoped to trap me in verbal snares. This reminded me of Connus; he too gets annoyed with me whenever I refuse to give in to him, with the result that he now takes less trouble over me as being stupid. So as I was anxious to receive instruction from this new teacher, I decided I had better yield, in case he took me for a dunce and barred me from his classes. Accordingly I said: 'Well, Euthydemus, if you see fit to proceed on those lines, we must do so; in any case I suppose you understand the art of debating better than I do, you being an expert and I a mere tyro. Resume your questions, please.'

'Answer me once again,' he said; 'is it, or is it not, by means of something that you know what you know?'

'It is', I replied, 'by means of my soul.'

'There he goes again', cried Euthydemus, 'answering more than he is asked! I'm not asking what the means is, but only whether you know by *some* means.'

'Yes, I was guilty there', I confessed, 'through lack of education; but forgive me, and I will now reply simply that it is by some means that I know what I know.'

'By one and the same means always,' he asked, 'or sometimes by one and sometimes by another?'

'Always, whenever I know,' I replied, 'it is by this means.'

'Again!' he cried. 'Please do stop qualifying your statements in this way.'

'But I'm so afraid this word "always" may trip us up.'

'Not *us*,' he retorted; '*you*, if anyone. Now answer: do you know by this means always?'

'Always,' I replied, 'since I have to cut out the "whenever".'

'Granted then that you always know by this means, do you

know some things by this means of knowing, and some things by another means, or do you know everything by this?'

'Everything by this,' I replied; 'everything, that is, that I know.'

'Again and yet again!' he cried. 'The same old qualification!'

'Well, I withdraw the words "that is, that I know".'

'No, don't withdraw a single word,' he said; 'I ask you for no concession. Only answer me this: could you know all things if you did not know everything?'

'It would be astonishing if I could.'

'You may therefore', he continued, 'now add whatever you please; for you admit that you know all things.'

'Apparently I do,' I replied, 'since my expression "that I know" is invalid, and I know everything.'

'You have likewise admitted that you know always by the means whereby you know, whenever you know—or however you care to express it. For you have granted that you *always* know, and that you know *everything* into the bargain. Hence it is obvious that you knew even as a child, yes, even at the time of your birth and, before that, of your conception. Nay, you knew all things before you yourself came into being or heaven and earth existed, since you *always* knew. Yes, and, by heaven,' he concluded, 'you yourself *will* always know all things, if it be my good pleasure.'

'Oh, let it be your good pleasure,' I replied, 'most honoured Euthydemus, if what you say is really true. Only I don't feel absolutely sure of your efficacy unless your brother here, Dionysodorus, shares your own good pleasure; if he does, you will probably succeed. Now tell me something,' I went on. 'You yourselves have said that I know everything; and I cannot hope in a general way to dispute that statement with persons so amazingly clever. But I want to know, Euthydemus, how I am to say that I know, for instance, that good men are unjust? Come, tell me, do I know this or not?'

'Of course you know it,' he said.

'Know what?' I said.

'That the good are not unjust.'

'Quite so,' I replied; 'I've known that for a long time, but

N ⁴¹⁸

it is not what I asked you. My question was, where did I learn that the good *are* unjust?'

'Nowhere,' said Dionysodorus.

'Then here', said I, 'is something I do not know.'

'You are destroying the argument,' said Euthydemus; then, addressing Dionysodorus: 'We shall discover that this fellow does not know, and is at once both knowing and unknowing.'

Dionysodorus flushed.

'But you,' I said, 'what do *you* mean, Euthydemus? Do you consider that your brother, who knows everything, has slipped up?'

'I a brother of Euthydemus?' quickly interposed Dionysodorus.

To that I replied: 'Hands off, sir, till Euthydemus has taught me that I know good men are unjust; don't begrudge me this instruction.'

'You are running away, Socrates,' said Dionysodorus; 'you decline to answer.'

'Naturally,' I said; 'for I am weaker than either of you, so I have every reason to run away from the two together. You see, I'm greatly inferior to Heracles, who was no match for the Hydra—that professorial lady who was so ingenious that she grew many heads of debate in place of each one that was cut off. Nor could he cope with another sort of professor, this time a crab from the sea—freshly come ashore, I believe. When the hero was outmanœuvred by its leftward barks and bites, he summoned his nephew Iolaus to the rescue, and thus obtained relief. But if any kinsman of mine came to my assistance, he would do more harm than good.' [1]

'Well, answer this,' said Dionysodorus, 'when you've done with that sententious talk: Was Iolaus more Heracles's nephew than yours?'

'I see I had best answer you, Dionysodorus,' I said; 'for you will go on putting questions—and I'm fairly sure I'm not mistaken here—in a spirit of envious obstructionism, in order to prevent Euthydemus from teaching me that clever trick.'

'Then answer,' he said.

'My answer', I replied, 'is that Iolaus was Heracles's nephew, but not mine in any way whatever, so far as I can

[1] i.e. by increasing the number of your victims.

see. For my brother Patrocles was not his father, though Heracles's brother Iphicles had a name somewhat similar to his.'

'And Patrocles', he said, 'is your brother?'

'Certainly—by the same mother, that is; not by the same father.'

'Then he is your brother and yet not your brother.'

'Not by the same father, sir,' I replied. 'His father was Chaeredemus, mine Sophroniscus.'

'So Sophroniscus and Chaeredemus', he said, 'were "father"?'

'Certainly—the former mine, the latter his.'

'Then surely', he resumed, 'Chaeredemus was other than "father"?'

'Other than mine, at any rate,' I said.

'Why then, he was father while being other than father. Or are you the same as that famous stone?' [1]

'I fear you may prove me so,' I said, 'though I don't feel like it.'

'Then are you other than the stone?'

'Other, I must say.'

'Then of course', he went on, 'if you are other than stone, you are not stone. And if you are other than gold you are not gold.'

'Agreed.'

'Therefore Chaeredemus,' he said, 'being other than father, cannot be "father".'

'Apparently', I said, 'he is not a father.'

Here Euthydemus interrupted: 'No, for I presume that if Chaeredemus is a father, Sophroniscus in his turn, being other than a father, is not a father; so you, Socrates, must be fatherless.'

Ctesippus then took him up, observing: 'And what about your own father? Isn't he in exactly the same position? Is he other than my father?'

'Far from it,' said Euthydemus.

'What,' asked Ctesippus, 'is he the same?'

'Indeed he is.'

[1] In *Gorgias*, 494 A, 'the life of a stone' is given as an example of a life devoid both of pleasure and of pain.

'I should hate to think so. But tell me, Euthydemus, is he my father only, or everybody else's too?'

'Everybody else's too,' he replied; 'or do you suppose that a given man, being a father, can be no father?'

'I did imagine so,' said Ctesippus.

'What,' said the other, 'and that a thing being gold could be not gold? Or being a man, not man?'

'I rather think, Euthydemus,' said Ctesippus, 'you are knotting flax with cotton,[1] as the saying is. You've reached a very strange conclusion if you maintain that your father is father of all.'

'He is, though,' came the reply.

'Of all men, do you mean?' asked Ctesippus. 'Or of horses too, and of all other animals?'

'Of all animals,' he said.

'And is your mother a mother likewise?'

'My mother too.'

'And is your mother the mother of sea-urchins?'

'Yes, and so is yours.'

'Then you must be a brother of the gudgeons and whelps and swine.'

'Yes, and so are you.'

'Then your father is a boar and a dog.'

'Yours is too,' he said.

'Yes,' remarked Dionysodorus, 'and if you will answer me, Ctesippus, it will not take you more than a moment to acknowledge all this. Just tell me, do you keep a dog?'

'Yes, a real rascal.'

'Has he got puppies?'

'Yes, rascals like himself.'

'Then is the dog their father?'

'Indeed yes; I myself saw him covering the bitch.'

'Well now, isn't the dog yours?'

'Certainly,' he replied.

'Thus he is a father, and yours; and accordingly the dog turns out to be your father, and you a brother of whelps.'

To prevent Ctesippus from getting in a word before him, Dionysodorus quickly followed up: 'Just one more small point: do you beat this dog?'

---

[1] i.e. treating two different things on an equal footing.

Ctesippus said with a laugh: 'Good heavens, yes, since I cannot beat you!'

'So you beat your own father?' he observed.

'I should be far more justified, though, in beating yours for being such a fool as to beget clever sons like you. Yet I doubt', Ctesippus went on, 'if your father, Euthydemus—the puppies' father—has profited much from this wisdom of yours.'

'Well, he has no need of much profit, Ctesippus; and nor have you.'

'And have you yourself, Euthydemus, no need either?' he asked.

'No, nor has any other man. Tell me, Ctesippus, whether you think it is good for a sick man to drink physic when he requires it, or whether you consider it not good; or for a man to go to the wars with arms rather than without.'

'The first alternative in each case, I think; nevertheless I believe you are going to utter one of your witticisms.'

'You'll soon find out,' he said; 'just answer me. Since you admit that physic is good for a man to drink when necessary, surely one ought to drink this good thing as much as possible; in which case it will be a good thing to pound and infuse into it a wagon-load of hellebore?'

To this Ctesippus replied: 'Ah, quite so, Euthydemus, at all events if the drinker is as large as that statue at Delphi.'

'Again,' continued Euthydemus, 'since we are agreed that in war it is good to possess arms, ought one not to have as many spears and shields as possible?'

'I suppose so,' said Ctesippus; 'and do you, Euthydemus, take the other view—that it should be one shield and one spear?'

'Yes, I do.'

'What?' he said. 'And would you arm Geryon and Briareus in that way? I thought you more of an expert than that, considering you and your companion here are men-at-arms.'

Euthydemus remained silent, and Dionysodorus proceeded to ask some questions on Ctesippus's previous answers. 'Is gold,' he said, 'in your opinion, a good thing to have?'

'Certainly, and—here I agree—plenty of it, too,' said Ctesippus.

'Well then, don't you think it right to have good things always and everywhere?'

'Assuredly,' he replied.

'Then do you admit that gold also is a good?'

'I've already admitted it,' he said.

'So we ought always to have it, and everywhere, especially in ourselves? One will be happiest if one has three talents of gold in one's belly, a talent in one's skull, and a golden stater in each eye?'

'Well, Euthydemus,' replied Ctesippus, 'they say that among the Scythians those are the best and happiest men who have a lot of gold in their own skulls—rather as you were saying just now that "dog" is "father"; and—still more wonderful—it is told how they gild and drink out of their skulls, gazing into them and holding their own headpiece in their hands.'

'Tell me,' said Euthydemus, 'do the Scythians and men in general see things possible of sight, or things impossible?'

'Possible, I assume.'

'And you do so too?'

'I too.'

'Then you see our cloaks?'

'Yes.'

'And have they power of sight?' [1]

'Remarkably so,' said Ctesippus.

'What do they see?' he asked.

'Nothing. You perhaps don't think they see—you're such an innocent. I'm inclined to think, Euthydemus, that you've fallen asleep with your eyes open, and, if it be possible to speak and simultaneously say nothing, that this is what you are doing.'

'But why should there not be', asked Dionysodorus, 'a speaking of the silent?' [2]

'Quite impossible,' replied Ctesippus.

'Or a silence of speaking?'

'Even more impossible.'

---

[1] There is play here with the twofold meaning of *dunata horan*: 'possible to see' and 'able to see'.

[2] Another play on a twofold meaning, this time of *sigōnta legein*: 'the speaking of a silent person' and 'speaking of silent things'.

'Now when you speak of stones, and pieces of wood or iron, are you not speaking of the silent?'

'Not if I'm walking past a forge. There, as they say, the iron speaks and cries aloud when touched; so here your cleverness has lured you into nonsense. But come along, you still have to prove your second point, that there may be a silence of speaking.'

(It occurred to me that Ctesippus was over-excited on account of his favourite's presence.)

'When you are silent', said Euthydemus, 'do you not maintain a silence of all things?'

'Yes,' he replied.

'Then it is a silence of speaking things also, if the speaking are among all things.'

'What,' exclaimed Ctesippus. 'Are not all things silent?'

'I rather think not,' said Euthydemus.

'But then, my dear sir, do all things speak?'

'Yes, at any rate all those that speak.'

'Oh, that's not what I'm asking,' he said. 'Are all things silent, or do they speak?'

'Neither and both,' said Dionysodorus abruptly. 'I'm sure that is an answer that will fox you.'

At this, Ctesippus in his usual way let out a loud guffaw. 'Ah, Euthydemus,' he cried, 'your brother has rendered the argument ambiguous with his "both"; he's thoroughly beaten.'

Cleinias was quite delighted and laughed, which made Ctesippus feel strong with the strength of ten. But I fancy that rogue Ctesippus had overheard those words from the men themselves, because such wisdom is nowhere else to be found among our contemporaries. So I asked: 'Why do you laugh, Cleinias, at such beautiful and impressive things?'

'Look, Socrates,' said Dionysodorus, 'have you ever seen a beautiful thing?'

'Yes, I have,' I replied, 'and many of them, Dionysodorus.'

'Did you find them different from the beautiful,' he said, 'or the same as the beautiful?'

This put me in a real quandary, and I felt I had got what I deserved for having interrupted. However, I answered that they were different from the beautiful itself, though an element of beauty was present in each.

'So if an ox is present to you,' he said, 'you are an ox, and since I am present to you now, you are Dionysodorus.'

'Oh, shut up!' I cried.

'But in what way can one thing, by having something else present with it, be itself different?'

'Are you at a loss there?' I asked. 'I was in the act of imitating the cleverness of you two men, so anxious was I to obtain it.'

'How should I not be at a loss, and every mortal man with me, in face of what cannot be?'

'What is that you say, Dionysodorus?' I asked. 'Isn't the beautiful beautiful, and the ugly ugly?'

'Yes, if I think so,' he answered.

'Then do you think so?'

'Certainly,' he said.

'In that case the same also is the same, and the different different? After all, surely the different cannot be the same; I would not have thought even a child could fail to recognize that the different is different. Yet you, Dionysodorus, have purposely ignored this point; though I feel that, on the whole, you two are handling your side of the debate in excellent style, like craftsmen each giving the final touches to his particular bit of work.'

'Well,' he asked, 'do you know what is each craftsman's particular bit of work? To begin with, whose business is it to forge brass? Can you tell me that?'

'I can—a brazier's.'

'Next, whose to make pots?'

'A potter's.'

'And whose to slaughter and skin, and, after cutting up the joints, to stew or roast?'

'A caterer's,' I said.

'Now if one exercises one's own special craft,' he asked, 'won't one do it properly?'

'Yes, of course.'

'And is it, as you say, the caterer's special craft to skin and cut up a carcass? Did you, or did you not, admit that?'

'I did so,' I replied; 'but please forgive me.'

'Evidently then', he continued, 'if someone slaughters the caterer and cuts him up, and then stews or roasts him, he will be exercising his special work; and if he hammers the brazier and moulds the potter, he will be doing his own business likewise.'

'Poseidon!' I exclaimed. 'There you give the finishing touch to your wisdom. I wonder if this skill could ever become present to me in such manner as to be my very own.'

'Socrates,' he asked, 'would you recognize it if it did become your own?'

'Yes indeed,' I answered, 'if only you will condescend.'

'But do you imagine', he went on, 'that you perceive what is yours?'

'Yes, if I understand you correctly. All my hopes originate from you, and end in Euthydemus here.'

'Then tell me,' he said, 'do you reckon as yours those things which you control and are free to use as you like? For example, an ox or a sheep—would you reckon them as yours if you were at liberty to sell or make a present of them, or sacrifice them to any god you chose? Conversely, do you count as *not* yours those things which you cannot treat in that way?'

Now I was sure, from the very trend of the questions, that some brilliant conclusion would leap into view. And since I was anxious to hear it as quickly as possible I answered: 'Just as you say; such things alone are mine.'

'Well,' he proceeded, 'do you call those things animals which have life?'

'Yes,' I said.

'And you admit that those animals alone are yours which you are free to dispose of in the various ways I mentioned just now?'

'I admit that.'

After a noticeably ironical pause, as though he were pondering some matter of prime importance, he asked: 'Tell me, Socrates, have you an ancestral Zeus?' [1]

Here I suspected the discussion was nearing the point at which in fact it ultimately terminated; so I tried desperately to wriggle out of the net in which I now felt myself entangled, and replied: 'I have not, Dionysodorus.'

[1] Zeus was the ancestral or tutelary god of the Dorian race.

'What a wretch you must be,' he said, 'and no Athenian at all, if you have neither gods, nor shrines, nor anything else that is the mark of a gentleman.'

'One moment, Dionysodorus; be careful what you say, and don't be so ready with your disapproval. I have altars and shrines, domestic and ancestral, and everything else of the kind that other Athenians possess.'

'Then haven't other Athenians their ancestral Zeus?' he asked.

'None of the Ionians', I replied, 'give him this title, neither ourselves here nor those who have settled as colonists abroad. They have an ancestral Apollo, because Apollo was father of Ion. Among us the word "ancestral" is not used of Zeus; he is known as "guardian" and "tribal", and we have a tribal Athena.'

'Good enough,' said Dionysodorus; 'you have, it seems, Apollo and Zeus and Athena.'

'Exactly.'

'Then they must be your gods,' he said.

'My ancestors', I said, 'and lords.'

'Well at all events you have them—unless you deny admitting they are yours.'

'I have admitted it,' I replied; 'now what is to be my fate?'

'Are not these gods animals? Remember, you have agreed that whatever has life is an animal. Or have these gods no life?'

'They have.'

'Then are they not animals?'

'Yes, animals,' I said.

'And you have recognized as yours', he continued, 'those animals which you are free to bestow, or sell, or sacrifice to any god you choose.'

'I have admitted it; there is no escape for me, Euthydemus.'

'Come then,' he said, 'don't beat about the bush. Granted that Zeus and those other gods are yours, tell me whether you are at liberty to sell or bestow them, or treat them just as you please, like other animals.'

Well, Crito, I was knocked out, as it were, and lay speechless. Then Ctesippus hurried to the rescue: 'Bravo, Heracles!' he cried. 'A splendid argument!'

And then Dionysodorus put this question: 'Do you mean that Heracles is a bravo, or that bravo is Heracles?'

'Poseidon!' exclaimed Ctesippus. 'What a frightful use of words! I surrender; these two fellows are invincible.'

Well, well, my dear Crito, all present wildly applauded the pair and their argument; they nearly died of laughing, clapping and cheering. Their earlier successes had been enthusiastically acclaimed, but only by the admirers of Euthydemus, whereas now the very pillars of the Lyceum might be said to be taking part in that joyous acclamation. For myself, I was quite disposed to admit that I'd never set eyes on such brilliant people, and I was so completely enthralled by their skill that I started praising and congratulating them: 'Oh, you blessed pair! What astounding genius, to attain such heights so quickly and in so short a time! Among the many fine characteristics of your achievement in debate, Euthydemus and Dionysodorus, one stands out with special lustre: you care nothing for the average man, not even for more important and distinguished types, but only for those of your own sort. But I am quite sure that there are but few like yourselves whom you would satisfy with these arguments; the rest of the world regard them as arguments with which, I assure you, they would feel it a greater disgrace to refute others than to be refuted themselves. At the same time there is a popular and kindly element in your talk. When you say there is nothing either beautiful, or good, or white, and so forth, and no difference whatever between things, you are in fact merely stitching up men's mouths, as you expressly claim to do; while as to your apparent power of stitching up your own mouths as well, it is a piece of politeness that prevents your words from giving offence. Most remarkable of all is the extraordinary nature and skilful contrivance of your faculty, which is such that anyone on earth can learn it of you in a very short time. This I realized after watching Ctesippus and observing how quickly he succeeded in imitating you while the debate was still in progress. Now, in so far as your accomplishment can be rapidly imparted, it is altogether satisfactory; but it is hardly appropriate to public discussion. If you take my advice, you will be chary of talking in presence of a large audience, lest they learn the whole thing straightway and give you no

credit for it. You had much better talk to each other in private;
failing that, if a third person is present, it should be someone
ready to pay you a substantial fee. And if you have common-
sense you will advise your own pupils likewise, never to
converse with anybody except you and each other. For it is the
rare, Euthydemus, that is precious; water, though best (as
Pindar says [1]), is also the cheapest drink. However,' I concluded, 'see if you can admit me and Cleinias here to your
lectures.'

Such, Crito, was our conversation, and after exchanging a
few more words we departed. Do please arrange to join us in
taking lessons from that pair; they say they can teach anyone
who is ready to pay, and that no sort of character or age will
prevent anyone from an easy acquisition of their wisdom. And
incidentally, I must assure you in particular that they guarantee that their art is no obstacle to moneymaking.

CRI. Indeed, Socrates, I love attending lectures, and would
gladly learn from them. On the other hand, I fear that, unlike
Euthydemus, I'm one of those people whom you described
just now as sure to prefer being refuted to refuting by means
of such arguments. Now look here, I feel ridiculous giving you
advice, but still I want to tell you something I heard just now.
I was taking a stroll when I was approached by someone who
had left your discussion, a man [2] who considers himself
extremely wise, one of those who are so clever at turning out
forensic orations. This is what he said: 'Aren't you taking
lessons from these wise men, Crito?'

'No indeed,' I replied; 'there was such a crowd that
although I stood quite close I couldn't catch a word.'

'Well, let me tell you,' he said, 'it was well worth hearing.'

'What was it?' I asked.

'You would have heard a disputation conducted by men
who are the most accomplished of our day in that kind of
address.'

To this I replied: 'Well, what did you get from them?'

'Merely the sort of stuff', he said, 'that you may hear such
people speaking at any time, making an absurd to-do about
matters of no consequence.' Those were his very words.

[1] *Ol.* 1.
[2] Probably Isocrates.

'Nevertheless,' I said, 'philosophy is a delightful pursuit.'

'Delightful is it, my poor innocent?' he exclaimed. 'Nay, downright trash I call it. Why, if you'd been in that company just now I think you would have been thoroughly ashamed of your great friend: he was so strangely willing to give his attention to men who don't care a straw what they say, but fasten on any random phrase that happens to occur. And these fellows, as I was saying, are today the leaders of their profession. The fact is, Crito,' he proceeded, 'the business itself and its devotees are worthless and ridiculous.'

Now in my opinion, Socrates, he was not right in decrying the pursuit of philosophy; he was wrong, and so is anyone else who belittles it. I confess, however, that I felt him right in denouncing the readiness to engage in discussion with such people before a large audience.

SOCR. Crito, these folk are most peculiar. But I don't yet know what answer to give you. That man who stopped you and denounced philosophy—was he an orator, one of those who shine in the courts, or one of those who equip orators for the fray by composing the speeches they deliver at the bar?

CRI. Nothing of an orator, I'll swear to that; nor do I believe he has ever appeared in court. On the other hand, he is said to be an expert in the business of writing first-rate speeches for others.

SOCR. Now I understand; he was one of those people to whom I myself was about to refer. They have been described by Prodicus as occupying the no-man's-land between philosopher and politician, yet they fancy themselves the wisest of all mankind, believing also that a great many others regard them as such; and accordingly they consider that none but devotees of philosophy bar the way to their universal renown. Hence they imagine that if they can bitterly discredit the latter, the prize of victory will by common consent be awarded to themselves, without dispute or delay, and their claim to wisdom will be firmly established. For they consider themselves to be in very truth the wisest, but discover that, when lured into private conversation, they are cut off short by Euthydemus and his set. This conceit of their wisdom is altogether natural, since they regard themselves as fairly well versed in philosophy and politics. In doing so they are not without warrant; for they have dabbled in both to the extent of their needs, and, evading all risk and endeavour, are content to harvest the fruits of wisdom.

CRI. Well, Socrates, do you think there is anything in what they say? It cannot be denied that these men have some pretext for their statement.

SOCR. Yes, Crito, that is so: pretext rather than truth. It is not easy to convince them that when persons or objects stand midway between two other things and have a share of both, then (a) if they are compounded of bad and good, they are found to be better than the one and worse than the other; but (b) if they are compounded of two good things which have not the same end, they are worse than either of their components in relation to the end to which each is adapted; while (c) if they stand between and are compounded of two bad things which have not the same end, this is the only case in which they are better than either of the two things whose natures they share. Now if philosophy and the activity of a statesman are both good, each of them having a different purpose, and if these people stand midway between them, sharing in both, their claims are invalid; for they are inferior to both. If one is good and the other bad, they are better than the one and worse than the other; whereas if both are bad there will be some truth in what they say—but not otherwise. Now I don't think they will admit either that both philosophy and statesmanship are bad, or that one is bad and the other good; the fact is that these people, having a share in both, are inferior to both in respect of the ends for which statesmanship and philosophy are important; and while they are really in the third place they expect to be accorded the first. However, we should take a lenient view of their ambition and not feel aggrieved, though still judging them to be what they really are. For we should be well disposed to anyone, whoever he may be, who says any-thing that has an element of good sense, and who labours with manly determination in its pursuit.

CRI. You know, Socrates, as I've so often told you, I'm worried about what to do with my boys. The younger is as yet quite a little fellow; but Critobulus is already grown up, and needs someone who will be of service to him. When I'm in your company I feel I'm just crazy to have done as much as I have

in all sorts of ways for the benefit of my children. My marriage
was intended to give them the very best blood on the distaff
side; I've made a pile of money so as to leave them as well off
as possible; but I have neglected the training of the boys
themselves. On the other hand, when I take a glance at those
who profess to educate their fellow men, I am simply horri-
fied; between ourselves, I feel convinced that not one of them
is properly qualified. So I can't see how I am to give my lad a
taste for philosophy.

SOCR. My dear Crito, surely you know that in every trade there
are many worthless blockheads, whereas good craftsmen are
worth any price. Why, don't you regard athletics, money-
making, rhetoric and generalship as fine things?

CRI. Of course I do.

SOCR. Well, don't you find that the majority of practitioners in
these respective arts make fools of themselves?

CRO. Yes, I know; what you say is perfectly true.

SOCR. Then will you yourself on that account eschew all those
pursuits and prevent your son from having anything to do with
them?

CRI. No, that would be quite unreasonable, Socrates.

SOCR. Then avoid at least what is wrong, Crito. Let those who
practise philosophy have their way, whether they are helpful
or mischievous. When you have made a thorough test of the
business, if you find it unworthy, turn everyone you can away
from it—your sons included; but if you find it to be such as I
think it is, you and yours, as the saying goes, may pursue and
ply it without fear.